Japanese
phrase book

Berlitz Publishing Company, Inc.

Princeton   Mexico City   Dublin   Eschborn   Singapore

Cover photo: David Austen/Tony Stone Images

ISBN 2-8315-6267-8
Fourth printing–April 1999
Printed in Spain.

Developed and produced for Berlitz Publishing Company by:
G&W Publishing Services, Oxfordshire, U.K.
Japanese edition: Kazumi Honda and Yukari Werrell

Contents

Pronunciation 6

Basic Expressions 10

Greetings/Apologies 10
Communication 11
  difficulties
Questions 12
  Where? 12
  When? 13
  What sort of ...? 14
  How much/many? 15

Why? 15
Who?/Which?/Whose? 16
How? 17
Is it .../Are there ...? 17
Can/May? 18
What do you want? 18
Other useful words 19
Exclamations 19

Accommodations 20

Reservations 21
Reception 22
Price/Decision 24
Requirements 26

Renting 28
Youth hostel 29
Camping 30
Checking out 32

Eating Out 33

Restaurants 33
Japanese cuisine 34
Finding a place to eat 35
Reserving a table 36
Ordering 37
Fast food/Café 40
Complaints 41
Paying 42
Course by course 43
  Breakfast/Appetizers 43

Soups/Egg dishes 44
Fish and seafood 45
Meat 46
Vegetables/Salad 47
Rice 48
Noodles/Tofu 48
Cheese 49
Dessert/Fruit 49
Drinks 50
Menu Reader 52

Travel 65

Safety	65	Hitchhiking	83
Arrival	66	Taxi [Cab]	84
Plane	68	Car/Automobile	85
Train	72	Car rental	86
Long-distance bus [Coach]	78	Gas [Petrol] Station	87
Bus/Streetcar [Tram]	78	Breakdown	88
Subway [Metro]	80	Accidents	92
Ferry	81	Legal matters	93
Bicycle/Motorbike	83	Asking directions	94

Sightseeing 97

Tourist information	97	Impressions	101
Excursions	98	Tourist glossary	102
Sights	99	Who/What/When?	104
Admission	100	In the countryside	106

Leisure 108

Events	108	Nightlife	112
Movies [Cinema]	110	Children	113
Theater	110	Sports	114
Opera/Ballet/Dance	111	At the beach	116
Music/Concerts	111	Skiing	117

Making Friends 118

Introductions	118	Enjoying your trip?	123
Where are you from?	119	Invitations	124
Who are you with?	120	Encounters	126
What do you do?	121	Telephoning	127

Stores & Services 129

Opening hours	132	Jeweler	149
Service	133	Newsstand [News-	
Paying	136	agent]/Tobacconist	150
Complaints	137	Photography	151
Repairs/Cleaning	137	Police	152
Bank/Changing money	138	Lost property/Theft	153
Pharmacy	140	Post office	154
Clothing	143	Souvenirs/Gifts	156
Health and beauty	147	Antiques	157
Household articles	148	Supermarket/Minimart	158

Health 161

Doctor/General	161	Gynecologist	167
Accident and injury	162	Hospital	167
Symptoms	163	Optician	167
Doctor's inquiries	164	Dentist	168
Parts of the body	166	Payment and insurance	168

English–Japanese dictionary & index 169
Japanese–English glossary 208

Reference 216

Numbers	217	Time	221
Days	218	Map	223
Months/Dates/Seasons	219	Quick reference	224
Public holidays	220	Emergency	224

Pronunciation

This section is designed to familiarize you with the sounds of Japanese using our simplified phonetic transcription. The pronunciation of the Japanese sounds is explained below, together with their "imitated" equivalents. This system is used throughout the phrase book. When you see a word spelled phonetically, simply read the pronunciation as if it were English, noting any special rules.

The Japanese language

Japanese is a unique language. Apart from a similarity of script (the Japanese adopted Chinese ideograms) it bears no resemblance to Chinese or other Asian languages, except for Korean. Where Japanese comes from is still a matter of conjecture. Japan, its people, customs, and language were almost totally isolated until the late nineteenth century.

Today there are many foreign "loan" words that have been adopted into Japanese. From *pan* (from the Portuguese for *bread*) to *sportsman*, you will come across many foreign words, the majority of which are from English. At first hearing you may not recognize such words because of the change in pronunciation and, conversely, you may not be understood when using a "loan" word until you give it a Japanese pronunciation.

Written Japanese

Japanese is composed of three different "scripts" or ways of writing: **kanji** (Chinese characters or ideograms), **hiragana** (an alphabet or, more properly, a syllabary in which each symbol represents a spoken syllable), and **katakana** (another distinct syllabary). These three systems are used in combination to write modern Japanese.

Hiragana is used to link **kanji** ideograms together. **Katakana** is used to write foreign "loan" words, of which there are many, most English in origin. Therefore if you learn to read the **katakana** symbols you will be able to read some Japanese and may recognize the original English word from which it was derived. You will find both the **hiragana** and **katakana** syllabaries listed on page 9.

In addition to these three "scripts" you will find **romaji**, the Roman alphabet used to write Japanese. In Japan important signs and names are often given in **romaji**, for example the names of subway [underground] stations.

Traditionally Japanese is written from the top to the bottom of the page starting in the upper right-hand corner. Today it is also commonly written horizontally and from left to right. The Japanese phrases you will see given in this book will incorporate a mixture of **kanji**, **hiragana** and **katakana** ➤ 9.

Japanese sounds

Japanese is composed less of vowels and consonants than of syllables, consisting of a consonant and a vowel. All syllables are pronounced with equal force – there is no stress – except for emphasis.

Consonants

Letter	Approximate pronunciation	Symbol	Example	Pronunciation
b, d, g, h, j, k, m, p, s, t, ch	approximately as in English			
f	different from the English **f**, pronounce with lips flattened and without putting lower teeth against lower lip	f	お風呂	o furo
n	1. before vowels like *n* in now	n	長い	nagai
	2. at the end of a word, said without letting your tongue touch the roof of your mouth		さん	san
r	different from the English **r**, put the tip of the tongue against the gum behind the upper front teeth	r	りんご	ringo
w (semi-vowel)	the lips are not rounded but left slack	w	分かる	wakaru
z	1. at the beginning of words, like *ds* in be*ds*	y	ゼロ	zero
	2. in the middle of words, like z in zoo		水	mizu

Double consonants should be pronounced "long", i.e. hold the sound for a moment. The doubling of a consonant is important as it can change the meaning of a word.

Vowels

Letter	Approximate pronunciation	Symbol	Example	Pronunciation
a	like the *a* in c*a*t, pronouced forward in the mouth	*a*	魚	*sakana*
e	like *e* in g*e*t	*e*	テレビ	*terebi*
i	like *i* in s*i*t	*i*	イギリス	*igirisu*
o	like *o* in n*o*t	*o*	男	*otoko*
u	like *u* in p*u*t, but without rounding the lips	*u*	冬	*fuyu*

Long vowels: (**aa, ee, ii, oo, uu**) should have the sound sustained for twice the amount of time. This is important in Japanese and can change the meaning of words, e.g. **oba(san)** means *aunt* while **obaa(san)** means *grandmother*.

Vowel clusters: when two vowels occur together (**ie, ai, ue, ao**) they should be pronounced separately with each vowel keeping its normal sound.

Consonant/double vowels clusters: (e.g. **kya, kyu, kyo**) these are two sounds said quickly so that they become one: **kya** is **ki** and **ya** run together.

Whispered vowels: sometimes **i** and **u** are devoiced, that is whispered or even omitted. This happens when **i** and **u** occur between voiceless consonants: **ch, f, h, k, p, s, sh, t,** and **ts**. These are represented in the phrase book by the symbols *(i)* and *(u)*.

Sentence pitch

As has been mentioned Japanese words and phrases are pronounced very evenly, and stress is used only to emphasize meaning. However, pitch does vary. A normal sentence will begin on a high note and finish on a low one.

As in English, questions normally have an interrogative rise at the end of the sentence.

Kanji

Kanji are ideograms: Each simple character represents a word. These are then combined to form other words or part words. The table shows a few simple **kanji**.

山	川	水	火
mountain	river	water	fire
太陽	月	星	大地
sun	moon	star	earth

Hiragana

Hiragana characters are used for words of Japanese, rather than Chinese, origin. They are also used for endings of words written in **kanji**. Below are the basic **hiragana** symbols. Further sounds are formed by adding diacritical marks (" and º) to the **hiragana** symbols, e.g. か (**ka**) becomes が (**ga**) and は (**ha**) becomes ば (**ba**) or ぱ (**pa**) with the addition of the diacritical marks.

あ a	か ka	さ sa	た ta	な na	は ha	ま ma	や ya	ら ra	わ wa
い i	き ki	し shi	ち chi	に ni	ひ hi	み mi		り ri	
う u	く ku	す su	つ tsu	ぬ nu	ふ fu	む mu	ゆ yu	る ru	
え e	け ke	せ se	て te	ね ne	へ he	め me		れ re	
お o	こ ko	そ so	と to	の no	ほ ho	も mo	よ yo	ろ ro	を (w)o
				ん n					

Katakana

Katakana is used for writing words that have come from other languages. Here are the basic **katakana** symbols. Further sounds are formed by adding diacritical marks (" and º) to the **hiragana** symbols, e.g. カ (**ka**) becomes ガ (**ga**) and ハ (**ha**) becomes バ (**ba**) or パ (**pa**) with the addition of the diacritical marks.

ア a	カ ka	サ sa	タ ta	ナ na	ハ ha	マ ma	ヤ ya	ラ ra	ワ wa
イ i	キ ki	シ shi	チ chi	ニ ni	ヒ hi	ミ mi		リ ri	
ウ u	ク ku	ス su	ツ tsu	ヌ nu	フ fu	ム mu	ユ yu	ル ru	
エ e	ケ ke	セ se	テ te	ネ ne	ヘ he	メ me		レ re	
オ o	コ ko	ソ so	ト to	ノ no	ホ ho	モ mo	ヨ yo	ロ ro	ヲ (w)o
				ン n					

Basic Expressions

Greetings/		Why?	15	
Apologies	10	Who?/Which?	16	
Communication		Whose?	16	
difficulties	11	How?	17	
Questions	12	Is it …/Are there …?	17	
Where?	12	Can/May?	18	
When?	13	What do you want?	18	
What sort of …?	14	Other useful words	19	
How much/many?	15	Exclamations	19	

ESSENTIAL

Yes./No.	はい。/いいえ。 hai/iie
Okay.	オーケー。 ookee
Please. (asking for a favor)	お願いします。 onegai shimas(u)
Please. (offering a favor)	どうぞ。 doozo
Thank you (very much).	(どうも)ありがとう。 (doomo) arigatoo

Greetings/Apologies あいさつとおわび

Hello./Hi!	こんにちは。 kon-nichi-wa
Good morning./Good afternoon.	おはようございます。/こんにちは。 ohayoo gozaimas(u)/kon-nichi-wa
Good evening.	こんばんは。 konban wa
Good night.	おやすみなさい。 oyasumi nasai
Good-bye.	さようなら。 sayoonara
Excuse me! (getting attention)	すみません。 sumimasen
Excuse me. (May I get past?)	失礼します。 shitsuree shimas(u)
Excuse me!/Sorry!	すみません。/ごめんなさい。 sumimasen/gomen nasai
Don't mention it.	気にしないでください。 ki ni shinai de kudasai
Never mind.	大丈夫です。 daijoobu des(u)

Communication difficulties
コミュニケーション

Do you speak English?
英語ができますか。
eego ga dekimas(u) ka

Does anyone here speak English?
英語ができる人はいますか。
eego ga dekiru hito wa imas(u) ka

I don't speak (much) Japanese.
日本語は（あまり）話せません。
nihongo wa (amari) hanase masen

Could you speak more slowly?
ゆっくり言ってください。
yukkuri itte kudasai

Could you repeat that?
もう一度、言ってください。
moo ichido itte kudasai

Excuse me? [Pardon?]
すみません。*sumimasen*

What was that?
何ですか。*nan des(u) ka*

Please write it down.
書いてください。
kaite kudasai

Can you translate this for me?
訳してください。
yakush(i)te kudasai

What does this/that mean?
これ/それは、何という意味ですか。
kore/sore wa nan to yuu imi des(u) ka

Please point to the phrase in the book.
この本の言葉を指してください。
kono hon no kotoba o sash(i)te kudasai

I understand.
分かりました。
wakari mash(i)ta

I don't understand.
分かりません。
wakari masen

Do you understand?
分かりますか。
wakari mas(u) ka

– *sen sanbyaku gojuu en des(u).*
– wakarimasen.
– *sen sanbyaku gojuu en des(u).*
– kaite kudasai … aah, "350 yen" … doozo.

Questions 質問

Where? どこ？

Where is it?	どこですか。	*doko des(u) ka*
Where are you going?	どこへ行くんですか。	*doko e ikun des(u) ka*
at the meeting place [point]	待ち合わせ場所で	*machiawase basho de*
downstairs	下	*sh(i)ta*
from the U.S.	アメリカから	*amerika kara*
here (to here)	ここ（ここへ）	*koko (koko e)*
in the car	車の中	*kuruma no naka*
in Japan	日本に	*nihon ni*
inside (inside ...)	中（...の中）	*naka (... no naka)*
near the bank	銀行の近く	*ginkoo no chikaku*
next to the building	ビルのとなり	*biru no tonari*
opposite the school	学校の向かい	*gakkoo no mukai*
on the left/right	左/右に	*hidari/migi ni*
there (to there)	そこ（そこへ）	*soko (soko e)*
to the hotel	ホテルへ	*hoteru e*
towards Yokohama	横浜の方へ	*yokohama no hoo e*
outside the café	喫茶店の外	*kissaten no soto*
up to the traffic lights	信号まで	*shingoo made*
upstairs	上	*ue*

When? いつ？

When does the museum open?	博物館は、いつ開きますか。 *hakubutsukan wa itsu akimas(u) ka*
When does the train arrive?	列車は、いつ来ますか。 *ressha wa itsu kimas(u) ka*
10 minutes ago (It came 10 minutes ago.)	10分前 (10分前に来ました。) *juppun mae (juppun mae ni kimash(i)ta)*
after lunch (It opens after lunch.)	お昼の後 (お昼の後、開きます。) *ohiru no ato (ohiru no ato akimas(u))*
always	いつも *itsumo*
around midnight/around 8 o'clock	夜中の12時ごろ/8時ごろ *yonaka no juuni-ji goro/hachi-ji goro*
at 7 o'clock	7時に *shichi-ji ni*
before Friday	金曜日前に *kin-yoobi mae ni*
by tomorrow	明日までに *ash(i)ta made ni*
early	早く *hayaku*
every week	毎週 *maishuu*
for 2 hours	2時間 *ni jikan*
from 9 a.m. to 6 p.m.	午前9時から午後6時まで *gozen ku-ji kara gogo roku-ji made*
immediately	今すぐ *ima sugu*
in 20 minutes	20分以内に *ni-juppun inai ni*
not yet	まだ *mada*
now	今 *ima*
often	ひんぱんに *hinpan ni*
on March 8	3月8日に *san gatsu yooka ni*
on weekdays	ウイークデーに *uiikudee ni*
sometimes	時々 *tokidoki*
soon	もうすぐ *moosugu*
then	その時 *sono toki*
within 2 days	2日以内 *futs(u)ka inai*

What sort of ...? どんな...?

	I'd like something ...	...ものをください。 ... mono o kudasai
	It's ...	...です。... desu
	beautiful/ugly	美しい/みにくい utsukushii/minikui
better/worse		もっと良い/もっと悪い motto ii/motto warui
big/small		大きい/小さい ookii/chiisai
cheap/expensive		安い/高い yasui/takai
clean/dirty		きれい/汚い kiree/kitanai
dark/light		暗い/明るい kurai/akarui
delicious/revolting		おいしい/まずい oishii/mazui
easy/difficult		かんたん/難しい kantan/muzukashii
good/bad		良い/悪い ii/warui
heavy/light		重い/軽い omoi/karui
hot, warm/cold		熱い、暖かい/冷たい atsui, atatakai/tsumetai
long/short		長い/短い nagai/mijikai
modern/old-fashioned		新しい/古い atarashii/furui
narrow/wide		せまい/広い semai/hiroi
old/new		古い/新しい furui/atarashii
tall/short		高い/低い takai/hikui
quick/slow		速い/遅い hayai/osoi
right/wrong		正しい/違う tadashii/chigau
That's right/wrong.		そうです/違います。 soo des(u)/chigai mas(u)
It's empty/full.		空/いっぱいです。kara/ippai des(u)
It's open/shut.		開いて/閉まっています。 aite/shimatte imas(u)
It's pleasant, nice/unpleasant.		気持ち良い、すてき/気持ち悪いです。 kimochi ii, s(u)teki/kimochi warui des(u)
It's quiet/noisy.		静か/うるさいです。shizuka/urusai des(u)
It's vacant/occupied.		空いて/塞がっています。 aite/fusagatte imas(u)
He's/she's young/old.		若い/年寄りです。wakai/toshiyori des(u)

Japanese nouns have no articles (a, an, the) and, with the exception of very few nouns, no plural forms. Whether the noun is singular or plural is judged from the context, or by a number modifying the noun.

Yokohama made kippu o kudasai.   I'd like a ticket to Yokohama.

Yokohama made (kippu o) sanmai kudasai.   I'd like three tickets to Yokohama.

For information on Japanese numbers ➤ 216.

How much/many? いくら/いくつ?

How much is that?	いくらですか。 ikura des(u) ka
How many are there?	いくつありますか。 ik(u)tsu arimas(u) ka
1/2/3	一/二/三 ichi/ni/san
4/5	四/五 shi (or yon)/go
none: There is none.	一つもありません。 hitotsu mo arimasen
about 100 yen	百円くらい hyaku-en kurai
a little	少し s(u)koshi
a lot of milk	牛乳をたくさん gyuunyuu o tak(u)san
enough	十分 juubun
few: a few of them	それを少し sore o s(u)koshi
more than that	もっと motto
less than that (quantity)	それより少し sore yori s(u)koshi
much more	もっとたくさん motto tak(u)san
nothing else: There is nothing else.	他には、何もありません。 hoka niwa nani mo arimasen
It's too much. (quantity)	多すぎます。 oo sugimas(u)

Why? なぜ?

Why is that?	なぜですか。 naze des(u) ka
because of the weather	天気のため tenki no tame
because I'm in a hurry	急いでいるから isoide irukara
I don't know.	分かりません。 wakarimasen

Who?/Which? 誰？/どちら？

Who's there?	誰ですか。	*dare des(u) ka*
It's me!	私です。	*watashi des(u)*
It's us!	私たちです。	*watashi-tachi des(u)*
someone	誰か	*dareka*
no one: There is no one.	誰もいません。	*daremo imasen*
Which one do you want?	どちらがいいですか。	*dochira ga ii des(u) ka*
this one/that one	これ/それ	*kore/sore*
one like that	それみたいなもの	*sore mitaina mono*
not that one: It's not that one.	それではありません。	*sore dewa arimasen*
something	何か	*nanika*
nothing: There is nothing.	何もありません。	*nani mo arimasen*
none: There is none.	一つもありません。	*hitotsu mo arimasen*

Whose? 誰の

Whose is that?	誰のですか。	*dareno des(u) ka*
It's ...	...です。	*... des(u)*
mine/ours/yours	私の/私たちの/あなたの	*watashi no/watashi-tachi no/anata no*
his/hers/theirs	彼の/彼女の/彼らの	*kare no/kanojo no/karera no*
It's ... turn.	...番です。	*... ban des(u)*
my/our/your	私の/私たちの/あなたの	*watashi no/watashi-tachi no/anata no*
his/her/their	彼の/彼女の/彼らの	*kare no/kanojo no/karera no*

GRAMMAR

Personal pronouns are used sparingly in Japanese. Use the person's name + **san** instead of a pronoun, or omit the pronoun completely if it is clear who is being addressed or referred to. Personal pronouns are:

watashi	I	**anata*** (singular)	you
watashi tachi	we	**anatagata*** (plural)	you

*Avoid using these pronouns as they are very familiar and appropriate only between husband and wife, boyfriend and girlfriend.

How? 何で？

How would you like to pay?	何でお支払いになりますか。 *nani de o-shiharai ni narimas(u) ka*
by credit card	(クレジット)カードで *(kurejitto) kaado de*
cash	現金で *genkin de*
How are you getting here?	何で来られますか。 *nani de korare mas(u) ka*
by car/by bus/by train	車で/バスで/電車で *kuruma de/basu de/densha de*
on foot	歩いて *aruite*
quickly	速く *hayaku*
slowly	ゆっくり *yukkuri*
too fast: It's too fast	速すぎます。 *haya sugi mas(u)*
very	とても *totemo*
with a friend	友人と *yuujin to*
without a passport	パスポート無しで *pas(u)pooto nash(i) de*

Is it .../Are there ...? ...ですか。/...ありますか。

Is it ...?	...ですか。 *des(u) ka*
Is it free of charge?	無料ですか。 *muryoo des(u) ka*
It isn't ready.	まだです。 *mada des(u)*
Is/Are there ...?	...はありますか。 *... wa arimas(u) ka*
Is there a shower in the room?	部屋にシャワーはありますか。 *heya ni shawaa wa arimas(u) ka*
Are there buses into town?	町へ行くバスはありますか。 *machi e iku basu wa arimas(u) ka*
There is a good restaurant near here.	この近くに、おいしいレストランがあります。 *kono chikaku ni oishii resutoran ga arimas(u)*
There aren't any towels in my room.	部屋にタオルがありません。 *heya ni taoru ga arimasen*
Here it is/they are.	こちらです。 *kochira des(u)*
There it is/they are.	そちらです。 *sochira des(u)*

Can/May? お願い

Can I/we have ...?	...をお願いします。 ... *o onegai shimas(u)*
May I speak to ...?	...をお願いします。 ... *o onegai shimas(u)*
Can you tell me ...?	...を教えてください。 ... *o oshiete kudasai*
Can you help me?	手伝ってください。 *tetsudatte kudasai*
Can you direct me to ...?	...への行き方を教えてください。 ... *eno ikikata o oshiete kudasai*
I can't.	できません。*dekimasen*

What do you want? 何がよろしいですか。

I'd like ...	...をください。 ... *o kudasai*
Could I have ...?	...をお願いします。 ... *o onegai shimas(u)*
We'd like ...	...をください。 ... *o kudasai*
Give me ...	...をください。 ... *o kudasai*
I'm looking for ...	...を探しています。 ... *o sagash(i)te imas(u)*
I need ...	...が要るんですが。 ... *ga irun des(u) ga*
I'd like to go to ...	...へ行きたいんですが。 ... *e ikitain des(u) ga*
I'd like to find ...	...を探しているんですが。 ... *o sagash(i)te irun des(u) ga*
I'd like to see ...	...を見たいんですが。 ... *o mitain des(u) ga*
I'd like to speak to ...	...をお願いします。 ... *o onegai shimas(u)*

– sumimasen.
– *hai.*
– nitta-san o onegai shimas(u).
– *shoo shoo omachi kudasai.*

18

Other useful words
知っておくと便利な言葉

fortunately	幸い *saiwai*
of course	もちろん *mochiron*
perhaps/possibly	もしかしたら *mosh(i)ka sh(i)tara*
probably	多分 *tabun*

Exclamations 感嘆

At last!	やっと。 *yatto*
Go on.	続けて。 *tsuzukete*
I don't mind.	何でも結構です。 *nan demo kekkoo des(u)*
No way!	いけません。 *ikemasen*
Really?	本当ですか。 *hontoo des(u) ka*
Nonsense.	くだらない。 *kudaranai*
That's enough.	もう十分です。 *moo juubun des(u)*
That's true.	もっともです。 *mottomo des(u)*
How are things?	いかがですか。 *ikaga des(u) ka*
Fine, thank you.	おかげさまで。 *okage samade*
It's ...	...です。 *... des(u)*
great/terrific	たいへん結構 *taihen kekkoo*
very good	たいへん結構 *taihen kekkoo*
fine	結構 *kekkoo*
okay	オーケー *oo kee*
terrible	ひどい *hidoi*
It's not good.	あまり、よくありません。 *amari yoku arimasen*
It's not bad.	あまり、悪くありません。 *amari waruku arimasen*

GRAMMAR

To make possessive pronouns use the grammar marker **no** following the person's name or the personal pronoun as suitable.

Honda-san no hon	Mr./Mrs. Honda's book
Watashi no hon	my book

Accommodations

Reservations	21	Requirements	26
Reception	22	Renting	28
Price	24	Youth hostel	29
Decision	24	Camping	30
Problems	25	Checking out	32

Welcome Inn Reservation Center offers a free reservation service for **minshuku** and **ryokan**. Reservation request forms are available at Japan National Tourist Organization (JNTO) overseas offices. Most major hotels belong to the Japan Hotel Association: 2-2-1 Otemachi, Chiyoda-ku, Tokyo ☎ (03)3279.2706.

ホテル *hoteru*
Western-style hotels. These are comparable to hotels in Europe and the U.S. They offer Western-style facilities and cuisine, as well as Japanese food.

ビジネスホテル *bijinesu hoteru*
Business hotels. The rooms are small, often with no room service. They are clean and comfortable and are usually located near train stations.

ラブホテル *rabu hoteru*
Love hotels. In the cramped housing conditions so common in Japan, love hotels offer private space. The architectural style of the hotels is often bizarre. Rooms are usually rented in two-hour blocks, but overnight stays are possible, Check-in times are late (11 p.m.) with check-out by 8 a.m.

旅館 *ryokan*
Japanese-style inns. For a taste of the Japanese way of life, a stay at a **ryokan** is recommended. Many are situated in beautiful settings with access to hot springs. Room prices include breakfast, dinner, and service charge. The majority offer only traditional style bathrooms, meals, and sleeping arrangements.

民宿 *minshuku*
Guest houses. Like **ryokan**, **minshuku** are a good way of sampling Japan. They are often family run and have an informal, friendly atmosphere. The overnight charge includes dinner and breakfast.

宿防 *shuk(u)boo*
Temple accommodation. For those with a particular interest in Buddhism, a stay at a temple will allow you to join in the monks' daily life.

ユースホステル *yuusu hos(u)teru*
Youth hostels. There are over 500 youth hostels in every part of Japan, and they provide the cheapest accommodation available.

<u>Reservations</u> 予約

<u>In advance</u> 前もって

Can you recommend a hotel in ...?	...で良いホテルを教えてください。 ... de ii hoteru o oshiete kudasai
Is it in the town center?	中心地ですか。 chuushin-chi des(u) ka
How much is it per night?	一泊、いくらですか。 ippaku ikura des(u) ka
Do you have a cheaper room?	もっと安い部屋はありますか。 motto yasui heya wa arimas(u) ka
Could you reserve [book] a room for me there, please?	一部屋、予約してください。 hito-heya yoyaku sh(i)te kudasai
How do I get there?	どうやって行くんですか。 dooyatte ikun des(u) ka

<u>At the hotel</u> ホテルで

Do you have a room?	部屋はありますか。 heya wa arimas(u) ka
Is there another hotel nearby?	近くに他のホテルはありますか。 chikaku ni hoka no hoteru wa arimas(u) ka
I'd like a single/double room.	シングル/ダブルルームをお願いします。 shinguru/daburu ruumu o onegai shimas(u)
Can I see the room, please?	部屋を見せてください。 heya o misete kudasai
I'd like a room with ...	...付の部屋をお願いします。 ... tsuki no heya o onegai shimas(u)
twin beds	ツインベット tsuin beddo
a double bed	ダブルベッド daburu beddo
a bath/shower	バス/シャワー basu/shawa

– heya wa arimas(u) ka?
daburu ruumu o onegai shimas(u).
– *mooshiwake gozaimasen ga, manshitsu des(u).*
– chikaku ni hoka no hoteru wa arimas(u) ka?
– *hai. tookyoo hoteru ga sugu soko ni arimas(u).*

Reception 受付

I have a reservation.	予約してあります。 *yoyaku sh(i)te arimas(u)*
My name is ...	(私の名前は)...です。 *(watashi no namae wa) ... des(u)*
We've reserved a double and a single room.	ダブルルーム一部屋とシングルルーム一部屋、予約してあります。*daburu ruumu hito-heya to shinguru ruumu hito-heya yoyaku sh(i)te arimas(u)*
I confirmed my reservation by mail.	手紙で予約を確認しました。 *tegami de yoyaku o kakunin shimash(i)ta*
Could we have adjoining rooms?	続きの部屋をお願いします。 *tsuzuki no heya o onegai shimas(u)*

Amenities and facilities 設備

Is there (a/an) ... in the room?	部屋に...はありますか。 *heya ni ... wa arimas(u) ka*
air conditioning	エアコン *eakon*
TV/telephone	テレビ/電話 *terebi/denwa*
Does the hotel have a(n)...?	ホテルに...はありますか。 *hoteru ni ... wa arimas(u) ka*
cable TV/satellite TV	有線テレビ/衛星放送付テレビ *yuusen terebi/eesee hoosoo tsuki terebi*
laundry service	洗濯サービス *sentaku saabisu*
swimming pool	プール *puuru*
Could you put ... in the room?	部屋に...を入れてください。 *heya ni ... o irete kudasai*
an extra bed	ベッドをもう一つ *beddo o moo hitotsu*
a crib [a child's cot]	ベビーベッド *bebii beddo*
Do you have facilities for children/the disabled?	子供/身体障害者用の設備はありますか。*kodomo/shintai-shoogai-sha yoo no setsubi wa arimas(u) ka*

How long ...? どのくらい

We'll be staying ...	...泊まります。
	... tomari mas(u)
one night only	一泊だけ *ippaku dake*
a few days	二、三日 *ni san nichi*
a week (at least)	(最低) 一週間 *(saitee) isshuu-kan*
I don't know yet.	まだ分かりません。*mada wakarimasen*
I'd like to stay an extra night.	もう一泊させてください。
	moo ippaku sasete kudasai
What does this mean?	これは、どういう意味ですか。
	kore wa dooyuu imi des(u) ka

- *kon-nichi-wa. jon nyuuton des(u)*
- *irasshaimase.*
- *ni-haku sasete kudasai.*
- *kashikomari mash(i)ta. kono toorok(u) kaado ni go-kinyuu kudasai.*

パスポートをお見せください。	May I see your passport, please?
この用紙にご記入ください。	Please fill in this form.
お車のナンバーを	What is your car
お教えください。	registration number?

素泊まり…円	room only ... yen
朝食込み	breakfast included
お食事あり	meals available
姓/名	last name/first name
現住所	home address
国籍/職業	nationality/profession
生年月日/出生地	date/place of birth
パスポート番号	passport number
車のナンバー	car registration number
場所/日付	place/date
署名/サイン	signature

Price 値段

How much is it ...?	...いくらですか。 ... ikura des(u) ka
per night/week	一泊/一週間 ippaku/isshuukan
for bed and breakfast	朝食込みで chooshok(u) komi de
excluding meals	食事抜きで shokuji nuki de
for full board (American Plan [A.P.])	3食込みで san-shok(u) komi de
for half board (Modified American Plan [M.A.P.])	2食込みで ni-shok(u) komi de
Does the price include ...?	この値段は...込みですか。 kono nedan wa ... komi des(u) ka
breakfast	朝食 chooshoku
sales tax [VAT]	消費税 shoohi zee
Do I have to pay a deposit?	前金は要りますか。 maekin wa irimas(u) ka
Is there a reduction for children?	子供の割引はありますか。 kodomo no waribiki wa arimas(u) ka

Decision 部屋を決める

May I see the room?	部屋を見せてください。 heya o misete kudasai
That's fine. I'll take it.	結構です。泊まります。 kekkoo des(u). tomari mas(u)
It's too ...	...すぎます。 ... sugimas(u)
dark/small	暗/小さ kura/chiisa
noisy	うるさ urusa
Do you have anything ...?	...部屋はありますか。 ... heya wa arimas(u) ka
bigger/cheaper	もっと大きい/安い motto ookii/yasui
quieter/lighter	もっと静かな/明るい motto shizukana/akarui
No, I won't take it.	すみません。やめておきます。 sumimasen. yamete okimas(u)

Problems 困った時

The ... doesn't work.	…が壊れています。
	... ga kowarete imas(u)
air conditioning	エアコン eakon
fan	扇風機 senpuuki
heating	暖房 danboo
light	電気 denki
I can't turn the heat [heating] on/off.	暖房が付けられ/消せません danboo ga tsukerare/kese masen
There is no hot water/ toilet paper.	お湯/トイレットペーパーがありません oyu/toiretto-peepaa ga arimasen
The faucet [tap] is dripping.	蛇口から水が漏れています。 jaguchi kara mizu ga morete imas(u)
The sink/toilet is blocked.	流し/トイレがつまっています。 nagushi/toire ga tsumatte imas(u)
The window/door is jammed.	窓/ドアが開きません。 mado/doa ga akimasen
My room has not been made up.	部屋がかたずいていません。 heya ga katazuite imasen
The is broken.	…が壊れています。 ... ga kowarete imas(u)
blinds/lamp	ブラインド/ランプ buraindo/ranpu
lock/switch	鍵/スイッチ kagi/suitchi
There are insects in our room.	部屋に虫がいます。 heya ni mushi ga imas(u)

Action 処置

Could you have that seen to?	どうにかしてください。 doonika sh(i)te kudasai
Could you bring it, please?	持ってきてください。 motte kite kudasai
I'd like to move to another room.	部屋を替えてください。 heya o kaete kudasai
I'd like to speak to the manager.	支配人を呼んでください。 shihainin o yonde kudasai

Requirements 一般注意事項

At **ryokan** and **minshuku** there may only be a communal bath with separate facilities for men and women, or separate bathing times. Sometimes you will find mixed-sex baths, and may be required to wear a bathing costume. In Japan bathing is a form of relaxation, and the serious washing is done before getting into the bath. Use the basins and taps provided to wash and rinse yourself down. When you are clean, step into the steaming bath and relax. Don't pull the plug out when you leave! Note: It is usual for bathing to be done in the evening. You will almost certainly find that there is no hot water in the morning, and the communal bath will be empty.

About the hotel ホテルについて

Where's the ...?	…はどこですか。 ... wa doko des(u) ka
communal bath	お風呂 ofuro
dining room/bar	食堂/バー shokudoo/baa
elevator [lift]	エレベーター erebeetaa
parking lot [car park]	駐車場 chuusha-joo
shower/sauna	シャワー/サウナ shawaa/sauna
swimming pool	プール puuru
tour operator's bulletin board	ツアーオペレーターの掲示板 tsuaa opereetaa no keeji-ban
Where is the bathroom [toilet]?	トイレはどこですか。 toire wa doko des(u) ka
What time is the front door locked?	正面玄関は、何時に閉まりますか。 shoomen genkan wa nan-ji ni shimari mas(u) ka
What time is breakfast served?	朝食は何時ですか。 chooshoku wa nan-ji des(u) ka
Is there room service?	ルームサービスはありますか。 ruumu saabisu wa arimas(u) ka

外線は…番を お回しください。	dial ... for an outside line
起こさないでください	do not disturb
耐火扉	fire door
非常口	emergency exit
シェーバー専用	razors [shavers] only

Personal needs 身の回り

Japanese-style toilets are floor level and lack seats – you squat, facing the flushing handle. In **ryokan** and **minshuku** plastic toilet slippers are provided at the entrance, and you should put these on in place of your house slippers, which you leave at the entrance. Public toilets are scarce, although most train stations have them (Japanese style). In many modern restaurants, big hotels, and department stores the toilets are generally Western style. The door locks, but it is customary to knock twice to see if it's occupied; you rap back twice. Carry tissues with you when using public toilets.

The key to room ..., please.	...号室の鍵をください。 *... goo-shitsu no kagi o kudasai*
I've lost my key.	鍵をなくしました。 *kagi o nakushi mash(i)ta*
I've locked myself out of my room.	鍵を部屋に置いてきてしまいました。 *kagi o heya ni oite kite shimai mash(i)ta*
Could you wake me at ...?	...時に起こしてください。 *... ji ni okosh(i)te kudasai*
I'd like breakfast in my room.	朝食は部屋でとります。 *chooshoku wa heya de tori mas(u)*
Can I leave this in the safe?	これを金庫に預けたいんですが。 *kore o kinko ni azuketain des(u) ga*
Could I have my things from the safe?	私のものを金庫から出してください。 *watashi no mono o kinko kara dash(i)te kudasai*
Where is our tour guide?	ツアーコンダクターはどこですか。 *tsuaa kondak(u)taa wa doko des(u) ka*
May I have an extra ...?	...をもう一つください。 *... o moo hitotsu kudasai*
bath towel/blanket	バスタオル/毛布 *basu taoru/moofu*
hanger/pillow	ハンガー/枕 *hangaa/makura*
soap	石鹸 *sekken*
Is there any mail for me?	手紙は来ていますか。 *tegami wa kite imas(u) ka*
Are there any messages for me?	メッセージはありますか。 *messeeji wa arimas(u) ka*

BREAKFAST ➤ 43; CHANGING MONEY ➤ 138

Renting 借家

We've reserved an apartment/cottage in the name of ...	...の名前でマンション/家を予約してあります。 *... no namae de manshon/ie o yoyaku sh(i)te arimas(u)*
Where do we pick up the keys?	鍵はどこで受け取れますか。 *kagi wa doko de uketore mas(u) ka*
Where is the ...?	...はどこですか。 *... wa doko des(u) ka*
electricity meter	電気のメーター *denki no meetaa*
fuse box	ヒューズボックス *hyuuzu bokkusu*
valve [stopcock]	ストップコック *s(u)toppu kokku*
water heater	湯沸かし *yuwakashi*
Are there any spare ...?	...の予備はありますか。 *... no yobi wa arimas(u) ka*
fuses	ヒューズ *hyuuzu*
gas bottles	ガスタンク *gas(u) tanku*
sheets	シーツ *shiitsu*
Which day does the maid come?	クリーナーは何曜日に来ますか。 *kuriinaa wa nan-yoobi ni kimas(u) ka*
Where/When do I put out the trash [rubbish]?	ゴミはどこへ/いつ出すんですか。 *gomi wa doko e/itsu dasun des(u) ka*

Problems 困った時

Where can I contact you?	どうやって連絡したら、いいですか。 *dooyatte renraku sh(i)tara iides(u) ka*
How does the stove [cooker]/water heater work?	コンロ/湯沸かしはどうやって使うんですか。 *konro/yuwakashi wa dooyatte tsukaun des(u) ka*
The ... is/are dirty.	...が汚れています。 *... ga yogorete imas(u)*
The ... has broken down.	...が壊れました。 *... ga koware mash(i)ta*
We have accidentally broken/lost ...	間違って...を壊して/なくしてしまいました。 *machigatte ... o kowash(i)te/nakush(i)te shimai mash(i)ta*
That was already damaged when we arrived.	それは初めから壊れていました。 *sore wa hajime kara kowarete imash(i)ta*

Useful terms 知っておくと便利な言葉

boiler	ボイラー	*boiraa*
crockery and cutlery	食器	*shokki*
refrigerator/freezer	冷蔵庫/冷凍庫	*reezooko/reetooko*
frying pan	フライパン	*furaipan*
kettle	やかん	*yakan*
lamp	ランプ	*ranpu*
saucepan	鍋	*nabe*
stove [cooker]	コンロ	*konro*
toilet paper	トイレットペーパー	*toiretto peepaa*
washing machine	洗濯機	*sentakki*

Rooms 部屋

In Japanese houses, **ryokan**, **minshuku**, and some public buildings and community centers you must remove your outdoor shoes at the entrance (**genkan**) and put on the house slippers provided. Keep them on while in the building, unless you enter the toilet where another shoe change must be made in plastic slippers. Do not forget to exchange the toilet slippers for the house slippers on leaving the toilet! To do so is a real faux pas!

balcony	ベランダ	*beranda*
bathroom	風呂場	*furoba*
bedroom	寝室	*shinshitsu*
dining room	ダイニングルーム	*dainingu ruumu*
kitchen	キッチン	*kitchin*
living room	リビングルーム	*ribingu ruumu*
toilet	トイレ	*toire*

Youth hostel ユースホステル

Do you have any places left for tonight?	今晩、泊まれますか。	*konban tomare mas(u) ka*
Do you rent [hire] out bedding?	シーツは借りれますか。	*shiitsu wa karire mas(u) ka*
What time are the doors locked?	門限は何時ですか。	*mongen wa nan-ji des(u) ka*
I have an International Student Card.	国際学生証を持っています。	*kok(u)sai-gak(u)see-shoo o motte imas(u)*

REQUIREMENTS ➤ 26; CAMPING ➤ 30

Camping キャンプ

Camping is not very popular in Japan, though there are some campsites to be found. The government sponsored **kokumin shuk(u)sha** (public lodges) provide cheap basic accommodation which includes two meals. The same applies to **kokumin kyuka mura** (vacation villages with recreational facilities). Reservations should be made through the Japan Travel Bureau.

Reservations 予約

Is there a campsite near here?	この近くに、キャンプ場はありますか。 *kono chikaku ni kyanpu-joo wa arimas(u) ka*
Do you have space for a tent/trailer [caravan]?	テント/キャンピングカー用の場所はありますか。*tento/kyanpingu-kaa yoo no basho wa arimas(u) ka*
What is the charge ...?	…の料金はいくらですか。 *... no ryookin wa ikura des(u) ka*
per day/week	一日/一週間 *ichi-nichi/isshuukan*
for a tent/a car	テント/自動車 *tento/jidoosha*
for a trailer [caravan]	キャンピングカー *kyanpingu-kaa*

Facilities 設備

Are there cooking facilities on site?	炊事場はありますか。 *suiji-ba wa arimas(u) ka*
Are there any electric outlets [power points]?	電源はありますか。 *dengen wa arimas(u) ka*
Where is/are the ...?	…はどこですか。 *... wa doko des(u) ka*
drinking water	飲料水 *inryoosui*
trash cans [dustbins]	ゴミ箱 *gomi-bako*
laundry facilities	洗濯場 *sentaku-ba*
showers	シャワー *shawaa*
Where can I get some butane gas?	ブタンガスは、どこで買えますか。 *butan-gasu wa doko de kaemas(u) ka*

飲料水	drinking water
キャンプ禁止	no camping
焚火/バーベキュー禁止	no fires/barbeques

Complaints 苦情

It's too sunny here.	ここは日当たりがよすぎます。 koko wa hiatari ga yo sugimas(u)
It's too shady/crowded here.	ここは日陰/込み合いすぎます。 koko wa hikage/komiai sugimas(u)
The ground's too hard/uneven.	地面が硬い/でこぼこすぎます。 jimen ga kata/dekoboko sugimas(u)
Do you have a more level spot?	もっと平らな場所はありますか。 motto tairana basho wa arimas(u) ka
You can't camp here.	ここではキャンプできません。 koko dewa kyanpu deki masen

Camping equipment キャンプ用品

butane gas	ブタンガス butan-gasu
campbed	キャンプベッド kyanpu beddo
charcoal	炭 sumi
flashlight [torch]	懐中電灯 kaichuu-dentoo
groundcloth [groundsheet]	グランドシート gurando-shiito
guy rope	ガイロープ gai-roopu
hammer	ハンマー hanmaa
kerosene [primus] stove	小型コンロ kogata konro
knapsack	ナップザック nappuzakku
mallet	木槌 kizuchi
matches	マッチ matchi
(air) mattress	（エア）マットレス (ea) mattoresu
paraffin	パラフィン parafin
penknife	ペンナイフ pen-naifu
sleeping bag	寝袋/スリーピングバッグ nebukuro/suriipingu-baggu
tent	テント tento
tent pegs	ペッグ peggu
tent pole	ポール pooru

Checking out チェックアウト

What time do we have to checkout by?	チェックアウトは何時までですか。 *chekkuauto wa nan-ji made des(u) ka*
Could we leave our baggage [luggage] here until ... p.m.?	午後…時まで、荷物を預かってください。 *gogo ... ji made nimotsu o azukatte kudasai*
I'm leaving now.	今、出発します。 *ima shuppats(u) shimas(u)*
Could you order me a taxi, please?	タクシーを呼んでください。 *tak(u)shii o yonde kudasai*
It's been a very enjoyable stay.	とても快適でした。 *totemo kaiteki desh(i)ta*

Paying 支払い

A note of warning: Although the use of credit cards is spreading, do not rely on paying by credit card, especially at older hotels and **ryokan**, etc. You will not be able to use foreign credit cards to obtain cash from ATM machines, except from Citibank (the only foreign bank operating in Japan at present). In rural areas the banks will often not have currency exchange facilities. The safest solution is to have cash with you at all times.

Tipping isn't customary and is officially discouraged. Porters at airports and train stations charge a set fee. Hotels, **ryokan**, and restaurants add a 10–15% service charge to the bill.

May I have my bill, please?	会計をお願いします。 *kaikee o onegai shimas(u)*
I think there's a mistake in this bill.	この請求書は、ちょっと違います。 *kono seekyuusho wa chotto chigai mas(u)*
I've made ... telephone calls.	電話は…回かけました。 *denwa wa ... kai kake mash(i)ta*
I've taken ... from the mini-bar.	ミニバーから…を出しました。 *mini-baa kara ... o dashi mash(i)ta*
Can I have an itemized bill?	明細書をお願いします。 *meesaisho o onegai shimas(u)*
Could I have a receipt, please?	レシートをお願いします。 *reshiito o onegai shimas(u)*

Eating Out

Restaurants	33	Fish and		
Japanese cuisine	34	seafood	45	
Finding a place to eat	35	Meat		46
Reserving a table	36	Vegetables/Salad		47
Ordering	37	Rice		48
Fast food/Café	40	Noodles/Tofu		48
Complaints	41	Dessert/Fruit		49
Paying	42	Drinks		50
Course by course	43	Sake		50
Breakfast	43	Spirits and liqueurs		50
Appetizers/Starters	43	Beer/Wine		51
Soups	44	Tea		51
Egg dishes	44	Menu Reader		52

Restaurants レストラン

Japan offers an enormous variety of places to eat. The Japanese like to eat out and to entertain in restaurants. As a result there is a huge variety of dining choices – you will find you can satisfy virtually every craving. In cities you will also find foreign restaurants: French, Italian, Indian, etc.

Many restaurants have very realistic plastic replicas of the dishes they serve displayed in the window. These are very helpful to the tourist, you can always point to what you want!

料理屋 ryoori-ya/料亭 ryootee

These restaurants specialize in Japanese-style food only. The former specialize in traditional Japanese food as do the latter, but the latter are very exclusive and expensive and may not always welcome foreigners.

レストラン街 res(u)toran-gai

These are found in most department stores, usually on upper floors, and are open until about 10 p.m. They can be accessed after store closing time by express elevators. You'll find restaurants catering to most tastes, from Western – Italian, French, and 'family restaurant' – to Chinese and a variety of Japanese. Typical Japanese restaurants found on these floors include **sushi-ya**, **tonkatsu-ya**, and **soba-ya**, but regional restaurants can sometimes be found. Recommended if you're looking for somewhere to eat in a strange place.

小料理屋 *koryoori-ya*
Small restaurants serving traditional Japanese food of high quality.

炉端焼屋 *robatayaki-ya*
Country-style restaurants serving meat, fish, and vegetables grilled over a hearth (**ro**) in front of guests. Some are designed so that guests themselves sit around the brazier and grill their own food.

バー *baa*
These bars serve drinks and snacks. Most bars have hostesses and karaoke singing.

喫茶店 *kissaten*
These coffee shops are very common throughout Japan and serve coffee and snacks. Some are very up-market with marvelous coffee-making apparatus, delicate bone china cups and plates, and delicious cakes.

飲み屋 *nomiya*
These are sake bars specializing in **nihonshu** (Japanese rice wine), they also serve beer and other alcoholic drinks and a variety of snacks. Many stay open until late.

スナックバー *sunakku baa*
These snack bars offer a good choice of drinks. A few are open all night and many stay open late.

屋台 *yatai*
These are street stalls (pushcarts), serving roasted sweet potatoes, octopus balls, noodles, stews and barbecued food. Very popular, they open in the evening and stay open until late at night.

Japanese cuisine 日本料理

Many eating places are named after their speciality: **shushi-ya**, **yakitori-ya**, **okonomiyaki-ya**, etc. The name of the restaurant is the same as the food with **-ya** (屋) added. So when choosing a restaurant first decide what you feel like eating.

Some of the food, raw or cooked, may be strange to the Western palate, but it is eminently edible and nourishing and, once your taste buds have acclimatized, absolutely delicious. As a general rule, food is served warm rather than hot – the Japanese do not feel it loses its flavor if you let it go cold while sampling something else, since many dishes are served simultaneously. At the start of each meal you'll be presented with an **oshibori** – a hot (or cold) towel for your hands and face.

A table for ..., please.	...お願いします。
	... onegai shimas(u)
1/2/3/4	1人/2人/3人/4人
	hitori/futari/san-nin/yo-nin
Thank you.	ごちそうさまでした。
	goch(i)soo sama desh(i)ta
I'd like to pay.	お勘定、お願いします。
	o-kanjoo onegai shimas(u)

Finding a place to eat
レストランを探す

Can you recommend a good restaurant?	おいしいレストランを教えてください。 *oishii res(u)toran o oshiete kudasai*
Is there a ... near here?	この近くに...はありますか。 *kono chikaku ni ... wa arimas(u) ka*
traditional local restaurant	伝統的な郷土料理の店 *dentooteki na kyoodo ryoori no mise*
Chinese restaurant	中華料理の店 *chuuka ryoori no mise*
fish restaurant	魚料理の店 *sakana ryoori no mise*
Italian restaurant	イタリア料理の店 *itaria ryoori no mise*
Are there any inexpensive restaurants around here?	この近くに安いレストランはありますか。 *kono chikaku ni yasui res(u)toran wa arimas(u) ka*
vegetarian restaurant	ベジタリアンの店 *bejitarian no mise*
Where can I find a(n) ...?	...はどこにありますか。 *... wa doko ni arimas(u) ka*
burger stand	ハンバーガーの店 *hanbaagaa no mise*
café/restaurant	喫茶店/レストラン *kissaten/res(u)toran*
fast food restaurant	ファストフードの店 *faas(u)to fuudo no mise*
ice-cream parlor	アイスクリーム・パーラー *ais(u)kuriimu paaraa*
pizzeria	ピザ・レストラン *piza res(u)toran*
steak house	ステーキハウス *s(u)teeki hausu*
Japanese noodle restaurant	そば屋 *soba ya*
sushi restaurant	寿司屋 *sushi ya*

DIRECTIONS ➤ 94

Reserving a table テーブルの予約

I'd like to reserve a table for two.	2人分のテーブルを予約したいんですが。 *futari bun no teeburu o yoyaku sh(i)tain des(u) ga*
For this evening/ tomorrow at …	今晩/明日…時に *konban/ash(i)ta … ji ni*
We'll come at 8:00.	8時に行きます。 *hachi-ji ni ikimas(u)*
A table for two, please.	2人、お願いします。 *futari onegai shimas(u)*
We have a reservation.	予約してあります。 *yoyaku sh(i)te arimas(u)*

お名前は？	What's the name, please?
申し訳ございませんが、ただいま込み合っております/満席です。	I'm sorry. We're very busy/full up.
…分ほどでテーブルが空きます。	We'll have a free table in … minutes.
…分後に、お戻りください。	You'll have to come back in … minutes.

Where to sit 席を選ぶ

Is this seat free?	この席、空いていますか。 *kono seki aite imas(u) ka*
Could we sit …?	…に座れますか。 *… ni suware mas(u) ka*
over there	そこ *soko*
outside	外 *soto*
in a non-smoking area	禁煙席 *kin-en-seki*
by the window	窓際 *madogiwa*
Smoking or non-smoking?	喫煙席と禁煙席のどちらがよろしいですか。 *kitsuen-seki to kin-en-seki no dochira ga yoroshii des(u) ka*

– konban, teeburu o yoyaku sh(i)tain des(u) ga.
– *nan mei sama des(u) ka?*
– yon mee des(u).
– *nan ji goro okoshini narimas(u) ka?*
– hachi-ji ni ikimas(u).
– *onamae wa?*
– sumisu des(u).
– *kash(i)komari mash(i)ta. omachi sh(i)te orimas(u).*

Ordering 注文

Excuse me!/Please!	すみません。/お願いします。 *sumimasen/onegai shimas(u)*
May I see the wine list, please?	ワインリストをお願いします。 *wain ris(u)to o onegai shimas(u)*
Do you have a set menu?	セットメニュー/定食はありますか。 *setto menyuu/teeshoku wa arimas(u) ka*
Can you recommend some typical local dishes?	この地方でおいしい料理は何ですか。 *kono chihoo de oishii ryoori wa nan des(u) ka*
Could you tell me what … is?	…は何ですか。 *… wa nan des(u) ka*
What's in it?	何が入っていますか。 *nani ga haitte imas(u) ka*
What kind of … do you have?	どんな…がありますか。 *don-na … ga arimas(u) ka*
I'd like …	…をください。 *… o kudasai*
I'll have …	…にします。 *… ni shimas(u)*
a bottle/glass of…	…を一本/一杯ください。 *… o ippon/ippai kudasai*

ご注文はお決まりですか。	Are you ready to order?
何がよろしいですか。	What would you like?
お飲物を先にご注文なさいますか。	Would you like to order drinks first?
…がお薦めです。	I recommend …
…はございません。	We don't have …
…分、かかりますが。	That will take … minutes.

– go-chuumon wa okimari des(u) ka?
– kono chihoo de oishii ryoori wa nan des(u) ka?
– …ga o-susume des(u).
– dewa, sore ni shimas(u).
– kash(i)komari mash(i)ta. o-nomimono wa nan ni nasai mas(u) ka?
– biiru o ippai onegai shimas(u).
– kash(i)komari mash(i)ta.

DRINKS ➤ 50; MENU READER ➤ 52

Side dishes / Accompaniments
付け合わせ

Could I have … without the …?

…に…を付けないでください。
… ni … o tsuke nai de kudasai

Can I have a side order of …, please?

付け合わせに…をお願いします。
tsuke awase ni … o onegai shimas(u)

Does the meal come with rice/bread?

ご飯/パンは付いていますか。
gohan/pan wa tsuite imas(u) ka

Do you have any …?

…はありますか。
… wa arimas(u) ka

Worcestershire/soy sauce

ソース/醤油
soosu/shooyu

ketchup

ケチャップ *kechappu*

Would you like … with that?

それに…をお付けになりますか。
sore ni … o otsuke ni narimas(u) ka

salad

サラダ *sarada*

mashed potatoes

マッシュポテト *masshu poteto*

jacket potatoes

ジャケットポテト *jaketto poteto*

fries

ポテトフライ *poteto furai*

rice

ご飯/ライス *gohan/raisu*

ice

アイス/氷 *aisu/koori*

May I have some …?

…をお願いします。
… o onegai shimas(u)

bread

パン *pan*

butter

バター *bataa*

lemon

レモン *remon*

mustard

マスタード/からし
mas(u)taado/karashi

pepper

コショウ *koshoo*

salt

塩 *shio*

sugar

砂糖 *satoo*

artificial sweetener

ダイエットシュガー *daietto shugaa*

vinaigrette [French dressing]

フレンチドレッシング
furenchi doresshingu

General questions 一般的な質問

Could I/we have a(n) clean …, please?	きれいな…をください。 *kiree na … o kudasai*
ashtray	灰皿 *haizara*
cup/glass	カップ/グラス/コップ *kappu/gurasu/koppu*
fork/knife/chopsticks	フォーク/ナイフ/箸 *fooku/naifu/hashi*
serviette [napkin]	ナプキン *nap(u)kin*
plate/spoon	お皿/スプーン *o-sara/s(u)puun*
I'd like some more …, please.	…をもっとください。 *… o motto kudasai*
Nothing more, thanks.	もう結構です。 *moo kekkoo des(u)*
Where are the bathrooms [toilets]?	トイレはどこですか。 *toire wa doko des(u) ka*

Special requirements 特別な注文

I can't eat food containing …	…が入っているものは食べられません。 *… ga haitte iru mono wa taberare masen*
flour/fat	小麦粉/脂肪 *komugiko/shiboo*
salt/sugar	塩/砂糖 *shio/satoo*
Do you have meals/drinks for diabetics?	糖尿病の人のための食事/飲物はありますか。 *toonyoo-byoo no hito no tame no shokuji/nomimono wa arimas(u) ka*
Do you have vegetarian meals?	ベジタリアンの食事はありますか。 *bejitarian no shokuji wa arimas(u) ka*

For the children 子供用

Do you have a children's menu?	子供用のメニューはありますか。 *kodomo yoo no menyuu wa arimas(u) ka*
Could we have a child's seat, please?	子供用のイスをお願いします。 *kodomo yoo no isu o onegai shimas(u)*
Where can I change the baby?	おむつはどこで替えられますか。 *omutsu wa doko de kaerare mas(u) ka*
Where can I feed the baby?	おっぱい/ミルクは、どこであげられますか。 *oppai (breast milk)/miruku (formula) wa doko de agerare mas(u) ka*

CHILDREN ➤ 113

Fast food/Café
ファストフード/喫茶店

Something to drink 飲物

I'd like a cup of ...	...を一杯ください。 ... o ippai kudasai
tea/coffee	紅茶/コーヒー koocha/koohii
black/with cream	ブラック/クリーム burakku/kuriimu
I'd like a glass/bottle of ...	...を一杯/一本ください。 ... o ippai/ippon kudasai
red/white wine	赤/白ワイン aka/shiro wain
Do you have beer?	ビールはありますか。 biiru wa arimas(u) ka
bottled/draft [draught]	瓶入り/生 bin-iri/nama

And to eat ... 食べ物

..., please.	...をください。 ... o kudasai
I'd like two of those.	それを2つください。 sore o futatsu kudasai
burger	ハンバーガー hanbaagaa
cheeseburger	チーズバーガー chiizu baagaa
teriyaki burger	照焼バーガー teriyaki baagaa
fries/omelet	ポテトフライ/オムレツ poteto furai/omuretsu
..., please.	...お願いします。 ... onegai shimas(u)
small/medium/large	S/M/L es(u)/emu/eru
pizza	ピザ piza
ham/green pepper/salami/ onion	ハム/ピーマン/サラミ/玉ねぎ hamu/piiman/sarami/tamanegi
sandwich/cake	サンドイッチ/ケーキ sandoitchi/keeki
icecream	アイスクリーム ais(u) kuriimu
vanilla/chocolate/strawberry	バニラ/チョコレート/ストロベリー banira/chokoreeto/s(u)toroberii
It's to go [take away].	テークアウトです。 teeku auto des(u)
That's all, thanks.	それで結構です。 sorede kekkoo des(u)

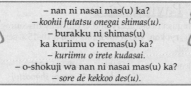

– nan ni nasai mas(u) ka?
– koohii futatsu onegai shimas(u).
– burakku ni shimas(u)
ka kuriimu o iremas(u) ka?
– kuriimu o irete kudasai.
– o-shokuji wa nan ni nasai mas(u) ka?
– sore de kekkoo des(u).

Complaints　苦情

I have no …	…がありません。 *… ga arimasen*
knife/fork/spoon/chopsticks	ナイフ/フォーク/スプーン/箸 *naifu/fooku/s(u)puun/hashi*
There must be some mistake.	間違いじゃないですか。 *machigai ja naides(u) ka*
That's not what I ordered.	注文したのと違います。 *chuumon sh(i)tano to chigai mas(u)*
I asked for …	…を注文しました。 *… o chuumon shimash(i)ta*
I can't eat this.	これは、食べられません。 *kore wa taberare masen*
The meat is …	この肉は… *kono niku wa …*
overdone	焼きすぎです *yaki sugi des(u)*
underdone	生焼けです *nama yake des(u)*
too tough	固すぎます *kata sugimas(u)*
This is too …	…すぎます *… sugimas(u)*
bitter/sour	苦/酸っぱ *niga/suppa*
The food is cold.	冷めています。 *samete imas(u)*
This isn't fresh/clean.	新鮮/きれいではありません。 *shinsen/kiree dewa arimasen*
How much longer will our food be?	後、どのくらいかかりますか。 *ato dono kurai kakari mas(u) ka*
We can't wait any longer. We're leaving.	もう待てません。帰ります。 *moo mate masen. kaeri mas(u)*
I'd like to speak to the manager.	支配人を呼んでください。 *shihainin o yonde kudasai*

Paying 会計

Tipping isn't customary and is officially discouraged.
Hotels, **ryokan**, and restaurants add a 10–15% service charge
to the bill.

The bill, please.	お勘定、お願いします。 *o-kanjoo* onegai shimas(u)*
We'd like to pay separately.	別々に、お願いします。 *betsubetsu ni onegai shimas(u)*
It's all together, please.	一緒にお願いします。 *issho ni onegai shimas(u)*
I think there's a mistake in this bill.	この会計は違っているようですが。 *kono kaikee wa chigatte iru yoo des(u) ga*
What is this amount for?	これは何の金額ですか。 *kore wa nan no kingaku des(u) ka*
Is service included?	サービス料込みですか。 *saabisu-ryoo komi des(u) ka*
I didn't have that. I had …	それは取りませんでした。注文したのは…です。 *sore wa torimasen desh(i)ta. chuumon sh(i)ta nowa … des(u)*
Can I pay with this credit card?	クレジットカードを使えますか。 *kurejitto kaado o tsukae mas(u) ka*
I've forgotten my wallet.	財布を忘れました。 *saifu o wasure mash(i)ta*
I don't have enough money.	お金が足りません。 *o-kane ga tari masen*
Could I have a receipt, please?	レシート、お願いします。 *reshiito onegai shimas(u)*
That was a very good meal.	おいしかった。ごちそうさまでした。 *oishikatta. goch(i)soo sama desh(i)ta*

** The initial **o** is an honorific, a prefix traditionally added to certain words to give them elegance and politeness.*

– sumimasen. o-kanjoo* onegai shimas(u).
 – *kash(i)komari mash(i)ta. doozo.*
– saabisu ryoo komi des(u) ka?
 – *hai.*
– kurejitto kaado o tsukae mas(u) ka?
 – *hai otsukai ni nare mas(u).*
– oishikatta. goch(i)soo sama desh(i)ta.

Course by course 各種料理

In large Western-style hotels you will have your choice of breakfast: Japanese, English/American, or Continental. However, in **ryokan** and **minshuku** you will be offered only a Japanese-style breakfast. This usually consists of grilled, smoked fish (e.g. salmon), rice, soup (**misoshiru**), and pickles served with tea. While you are out and about, coffee shops provide various dishes for breakfast, including very thick slices of buttered toast. Most Japanese seem to scoop out the middle and leave the rest.

Breakfast 朝食

I'd like …	…をください。 … o kudasai
bread/butter	パン/バター pan/bataa
a boiled egg	ゆで卵 yude tamago
fried eggs/scrambled eggs	目玉焼き/スクランブルエッグ medama yaki/sukuranburu eggu
fruit juice	フルーツジュース furuutsu juusu
orange/grapefruit	オレンジ/グレープフルーツ orenji/gureepufuruutsu
honey/jam	蜂蜜 (ハニー) /ジャム hachimitsu (hanii)/jamu
milk	牛乳/ミルク gyuunyuu/miruku
rolls	ロールパン rooru pan
toast	トースト toos(u)to

Appetizers/Starters 前菜/オードブル

O-tsumami are snacks that accompany drinks. You will find such things as salted rice crackers, nuts, and dried cuttlefish.

I'd like an appetiizer.	前菜をください。 zensai o kudasai
What do you recommend?	何がおいしいですか。 nani ga oishii des(u) ka
assorted appetizers	オードブルの盛り合わせ oodoburu no moriawase
salad	サラダ sarada
olives	オリーブ oriibu
ham/salami	ハム/サラミ hamu/sarami
oysters	牡蛎 kaki
Japanese snacks	おつまみ o-tsumami
Japanese pickled vegetables	漬物 tsukemono

Soups スープ

Japanese clear soup	すまし汁（お吸物） *sumashi jiru (o-suimono)*
miso soup	みそ汁 *miso-shiru*
vegetable soup	野菜スープ *yasai suupu*
creamed soup	ポタージュスープ *potaaju suupu*
sweetcorn soup	コーンスープ *koon suupu*
clear soup	コンソメ *kosome*

Always part of a traditional meal, there are two kinds of Japanese soup: **miso-shiru**, a light delicious soup often with a few finely chopped pieces of vegetable and/or bean curd, the distinctive flavor of which comes from the fermented bean curd paste (**miso**); and **sumashi jiru** or **suimono**, a tasty clear soup, again with a few additions.

In a Japanese meal the soup is not served as a first course, but simultaneously with the main course or boiled rice and other items.

寄せ鍋 *yosenabe*
This is a thick soup of chicken, shellfish, prawns, bean curd, and vegetables. A cosy meal, you sit round the **nabe** (pot) in the middle of the table and help yourself.

ラーメン *raamen*
These are Chinese noodles served in a broth with a variety of additions, such as meat, fish, seafood, and vegetables, or mixtures of these. **Raamen** makes a tasty, inexpensive meal.

Egg dishes 卵料理

卵焼き *tamago yaki*
A thick sweet omelet, sometimes used as a sushi ingredient.

目玉焼き *medama yaki*
Fried eggs.

オムレツ *omuretsu*
Omelet.

オムライス *omuraisu*
Omelet stuffed with fried ketchuped rice.

茶碗蒸 *chawan mushi*
A savory egg custard with vegetables, fish, and chicken.

Fish and seafood 海鮮料理

In Japanese cuisine fish and seafood play a major role. This is reflected in the variety and quality.

鰹（カツオ）	*katsuo*	bonito (mackerel family)
鱈（タラ）	*tara*	cod
たらこ	*tarako*	cod roe
ロブスター	*robus(u)taa*	lobster
鯖（サバ）	*saba*	mackerel
ムール貝	*muuru gai*	mussels
蛸（タコ）	*tako*	octopus
牡蠣（カキ）	*kaki*	oysters
鮭（サケ）	*sake*	salmon
いくら	*ikura*	salmon roe
帆立貝	*hotate gai*	scallop
いか	*ika*	squid
海老（エビ）	*ebi*	shrimp [prawns]
鱒（マス）	*masu*	trout
鮪（マグロ）	*maguro*	tuna
白子（シラス）	*shirasu*	whitebait

刺身 *sashimi*
Raw fish sliced into small bite-sized pieces, served with soy sauce and horseradish (**wasabi**). Dip your sashimi into the soy sauce and **wasabi** mixture. Sashimi is usually served as part of a larger meal. It is not cheap, and sashimi restaurants are expensive.

寿司 *sushi*
Slightly vinegared rice balls topped with green horseradish (**wasabi**) and various varieties of raw fish and seafood. Dip in soy sauce when eating.

焼き魚 *yaki zakana*
Grilled fish.

天ぷら *tenpura*
Various kinds of fresh fish, seafood, and vegetables coated in a very light batter and quickly deep-fried.

煮魚 *ni zakana*
Fish cooked in various sauces.

Meat 肉料理

ベーコン	*beekon*	bacon
牛肉	*gyuu niku*	beef
鶏肉/チキン	*tori niku/chikin*	chicken
鴨	*kamo*	duck
ハム	*hamu*	ham
ラム肉	*ramu niku*	lamb
レバー	*rebaa*	liver
豚肉	*buta niku*	pork
ソーセージ	*sooseeji*	sausages
ステーキ	*s(u)teeki*	steak

Meat cuts 肉の切り身

fillet steak	ひれステーキ *hire s(u)teeki*
sirloin steak	サーロインステーキ *saaroin s(u)teeki*
thin slices	薄切り *usugiri*

すき焼 *sukiyaki*

Thin slices of tender beef, leeks and other vegetables, bean curd, thin noodles, and burdock simmered in an aromatic mixture of soy sauce, mirin (sweet sake) or sake, water, and a little sugar. This dish is cooked in an iron pan over a gas or charcoal fire in front of you. Traditionally served with a whisked raw egg for dipping.

しゃぶしゃぶ *shabu shabu*

Thinly sliced beef cooked with vegetables in a broth. It is often a do-it-yourself meal – the waitress will show you what to do.

焼肉 *yaki niku*

Korean dish of marinated meat and vegetables grilled on a hot plate at the table and dipped in various sauces.

とんかつ *ton katsu*

Breaded pork cutlet deep fried and served with shredded cabbage and rice. You can specify which cut of meat you prefer: **roosu**, the standard, or **hire,** the more expensive pork fillet.

カツ丼 *katsu don*

Deep fried breaded pork on bed of rice cooked with egg, onions, and peas.

Vegetables　野菜料理

ご飯	*gohan*	boiled rice
キャベツ	*kyabetsu*	cabbage
にんじん	*ninjin*	carrots
白菜	*hak(u)sai*	Chinese leaves
きゅうり	*kyuuri*	cucumber
なす	*nasu*	eggplant [aubergine]
ぎんなん	*gin-nan*	gingko nuts
さやいんげん	*saya ingen*	green beans
ねぎ	*negi*	leeks
レタス	*retasu*	lettuce
マッシュルーム	*masshuruumu*	mushrooms
玉ねぎ	*tamanegi*	onions
グリンピース	*gurinpiisu*	peas
ポテト/じゃがいも	*poteto/jagaimo*	potatoes
かぼちゃ	*kabocha*	pumpkin
トマト	*tomato*	tomatoes
大根	*daikon*	white radish
椎茸（しいたけ）	*shiitake*	shitake mushrooms
なめたけ	*nametake*	type of fungi*

*You will find many different types of fungi used in Japanese cookery.

野菜炒め **yasai itame**
Fried vegetables.

野菜の煮物 **yasai no nimono**
Stewed vegetables.

漬物 **tsukemono**
Japanese pickled vegetables.

おひたし **ohitashi**
Boiled green vegetables served with soy sauce.

Salad　サラダ

Salad isn't part of traditional Japanese cuisine. Pickled vegetables are a more authentic equivalent. However, many Western-style restaurants and bars offer a variety of salads and dressings.

Rice ご飯

In a Japanese meal rice (**gohan**) is served separately in an individual bowl. It is short grained and slightly sticky.

Although plain, rice is perhaps the most important part of the meal. The Japanese consider it a heresy to mix other food items or sauces into the rice. When eating it is usual to raise the bowl to the lips and push the rice into your mouth with your chopsticks. On a Western-style menu rice is usually called **raisu**.

Noodles 麺類

Noodle dishes are very popular. They make delicious and filling simple meals. It's all right to make slurping noises while eating them – the extra oxygen is supposed to improve the taste.

そば／うどん soba/udon

Noodles served with a sprinkling of shredded pork, beef, chicken, or egg with vegetables in a bowl of stock. **Soba** are buckwheat noodles, and **udon**, which are thicker, are made of wheat flour. They may also be served cold with soy sauce, freshly-chopped onions, ginger, and horseradish.

ラーメン raamen

Chinese noodles in a broth served hot or cold.

そうめん soomen

Very thin wheat-flour noodles, usually served chilled with diced cucumber and a soy sauce, ginger, and onion dip.

Tofu 豆腐

Tofu is a pale soybean curd with a very delicate flavor and a firm, creamy texture. It is normally eaten on its own with soy sauce or included in other dishes and soups.

揚出し豆腐 age dashi doofu

Lightly fried plain **tofu**.

田楽豆腐 dengaku doofu

Slices of **tofu** on bamboo skewers, grilled over charcoal and served with **miso** (fermented soybean paste).

湯豆腐 yudoofu

Cubes of **tofu** cooked with fish and vegetables, served with a soy sauce dip, finely chopped green onions, grated ginger, and dried bonito flakes.

Cheese チーズ

Cheese is not a traditional Japanese food item. In supermarkets you will only find processed cheese. For a variety of imported cheese, you will need to look in the more cosmopolitan food halls of central Tokyo and other large cities.

Dessert デザート

Dessert is not a typical part of a Japanese meal. Called **dezaato**, it was introduced from the West. Today you will find a variety of Western-style desserts along with a number of desserts made from more typically Japanese ingredients.

チョコレートケーキ	*chokoreeto keeki*	chocolate cake
チョコレートサンデー	*chokoreeto sandee*	chocolate sundae
バナナフリッター	*banana furittaa*	banana fritters
ピーチメルバ	*piichi meruba*	peach Melba
フルーツカクテル	*furuutsu kakuteru*	fruit cocktail
お汁粉	*oshiruko*	sweet red bean paste soup

Fruit フルーツ（果物）

りんご	*ringo*	apples
バナナ	*banana*	bananas
さくらんぼ	*sakuranbo*	cherries
グレープフルーツ	*gureepufuruutsu*	grapefruit
ぶどう	*budoo*	grapes
メロン	*meron*	melon
オレンジ	*orenji*	oranges
桃	*momo*	peaches
梨	*nashi*	pears
柿	*kaki*	persimmons
苺（いちご）	*ichigo*	strawberries
蜜柑（みかん）	*mikan*	tangerines
西瓜（すいか）	*suika*	watermelon

Drinks 飲物

Sake 酒

This is the general name for any drink, traditional or imported, but is usually used to refer to rice wine, more properly known as **nihonshu.** The special tidbits served with **sake** are known as **otsumami.** These include seafood and meat served on skewers, sweet-salty dried cuttlefish, sashimi, and many more.

This drink is served at table in small china carafes (**tokkuri**) and is drunk from little thimble-sized cups (**ochoko**) or wooden boxes. You can ask for your **nihonshu** to be served at different temperatures depending on your preference.

sake/nihonshu	お酒/日本酒 *o-sake/nihonshu*
cold	冷 *hiya*
luke warm	人肌 *hitohada*
hot	熱燗 *ats(u)kan*

Spirits and liqueurs その他の酒類

Shoochuu is a distilled liquor (up to 90% proof) made from either sweet potatoes or rice. This drink is not commonly known to visitors to Japan and is held in rather low esteem by the Japanese themselves. The best **shoochuu** is, however, excellent and is comparable to tequila, vodka, and other such spirits. Whisky is now a very popular drink in Japan and there are a number of good Japanese brands. The best known is probably **Suntory.**

whisky	ウイスキー *uis(u)kii*
straight [neat]/on the rocks	ストレート/オンザロック *s(u)toreeto/onzarokku*
with water	水割り *mizuwari*
with soda water	ウイスキーソーダ *uis(u)kii sooda*
brandy	ブランデー *burandee*
gin	ジン *jin*
gin and tonic	ジントニック *jin tonikku*
plum wine	梅酒 *umeshu*
rum	ラム酒 *ramu shu*
sherry/vermouth	シェリー/ベルモット *sherii/berumotto*
shoochuu	焼酎 *shoochuu*
vodka	ウォッカ *wokka*
single/double	シングル/ダブル *shinguru/daburu*
a glass/a bottle	グラス1杯/瓶1本 *gurasu ippai/bin ippon*

Beer ビール

The Japanese produce a number of different beers which are very drinkable and similar to English and German lager beers. Three well known brands are **Asahi**, **Kirin** and **Sapporo**. In most bars you can choose between bottled and draft.

bottled	瓶入り *bin-iri*
draft [draught]	生 *nama*
dark beer	黒ビール *kuro biiru*

Wine ワイン

Wine isn't an authentic Japanese drink and until recently was not produced in Japan. You will not find wine widely available outside of Western-style restaurants, big hotels, and department stores. Even here you may find the choice limited to sweeter-type white wines, although this is changing.

red wine	赤ワイン *aka wain*
white wine	白ワイン *shiro wain*
blush [rosé] wine	ロゼ *roze*
dry/sweet/sparkling	ドライ/スイート/スパークリング *dorai/suiito/supaakuringu*
chilled/at room temperature	冷えた/室温の *hieta/shitsuon no*

Tea お茶

Japanese green tea is often served in restaurants free of charge. It is drunk without any additions.

milk tea	ミルクティー *miruku tii*
lemon tea	レモンティー *remon tii*
iced tea	アイスティー *ais(u) tii*
green tea	お茶 *ocha*

Tea ceremony 茶会

A special tea (**matcha**) is used for this ceremony. It was first used by Buddhist monks to help them stay awake while meditating. Its spiritual roots are still apparent today in the highly ritualized format of a tea ceremony. The tea should not only refresh you physically, but also give you time to appreciate the beauty of the objects used in the ceremony and the surroundings, all leading to meditative reflection. You may find tea-ceremony rooms in museums and gardens, where you'll be able to try a little **matcha** for a small fee.

Menu Reader

This Menu Reader gives listings under main food headings. You will see that the Japanese characters are shown in large type. This is to help you to identify, from a menu that has no English, at least the basic ingredients making up a dish.

Meat, fish and poultry

肉	niku	meat (general)
牛	gyuu	beef
豚	buta	pork
猪	inoshishi	wild boar
ラム	ramu	lamb
鶏	tori	chicken
鴨	kamo	duck
魚	sakana	fish (general)
魚介類 or 海鮮料理	gyokai rui or kaisen ryoori	seafood (general)
海老	ebi	shrimp [prawns]
蟹	kani	crab
鰻	unagi	eel
卵	tamago	eggs (general)

Vegetables

野菜	*yasai*	vegetable(s) (general)
豆	*mame*	beans
ほうれん草	*hoorensoo*	spinach
ポテト	*poteto*	potatoes – name for potato when in Western-style dishes
馬鈴薯 or	*bareesho* or	– indigenous names for potatoes used when in
じゃがいも	*jagaimo*	Japanese dishes
ねぎ/葱	*negi*	leeks
にんじん/人参	*ninjin*	carrots
トマト	*tomato*	tomatoes
レタス	*retasu*	lettuce
きゅうり/胡瓜	*kyuuri*	cucumber
白菜	*hak(u)sai*	Chinese leaves
海苔 or	*nori*	types of seaweed – seaweed dried in flat sheets
わかめ or	*wakame*	– thin, fresh seaweed used in soups and salads
昆布	*konbu*	– thick piece of fresh seaweed
サラダ	*sarada*	salad (general)

Fruit

フルーツ or 果物	*furuutsu* or *kudamono*	fruit (general)
りんご	*ringo*	apple
オレンジ	*orenji*	orange
バナナ	*banana*	banana
メロン	*meron*	melon
梨	*nashi*	pear *Japanese pears are quite different from the European variety; they are round and hard like apples*
いちご/苺	*ichigo*	strawberries
キウィ	*kiui*	kiwi fruit
パイナップル	*painappuru*	pineapple
柿	*kaki*	persimmon *also known as Sharon fruit*
すいか/西瓜	*suika*	watermelon
みかん/蜜柑	*mikan*	tangerine
ぶどう/葡萄	*budoo*	grapes

Staples: bread, rice, pasta, etc.

パン	*pan*	bread
ご飯	*gohan*	rice *plain boiled rice*
うどん	*udon*	udon *wheat noodles*
そば	*soba*	soba *buckwheat noodles*
ラーメン	*raamen*	ramen *Chinese noodles in soup*
豆	*mame*	beans
パスタ	*pas(u)ta*	pasta
スパゲッティ	*s(u)pagetti*	spaghetti *term commonly used for all pasta*

Basics

塩	*shio*	salt
コショウ/胡椒	*koshoo*	pepper
味噌	*miso*	*paste made from fermented soybeans*
醤油	*shooyu*	soy (sauce)
味の素	*aji no moto*	MSG *monosodium glutamate*

天ぷら	tenpura	battered, deep-fried food
刺身	sashimi	raw (usually fish, but also meat)
焼き	yaki	fried or grilled
寿司	sushi	vinegared rice served with raw fish, and seafood
鍋	nabe	a stew or casserole
蒸し	mushi	steamed or poached
カレー	karee	curried
炉端焼き	robatayaki	barbequed
炒め	itame	stir-fried
揚げ	age	deep-fried
煮	ni	cooked in a sauce
酢	su	vinegared
茹で	yude	boiled
炒り	iri	dry-roast

すき焼	sukiyaki	thin slices of beef and vegetables cooked in sauce
しゃぶしゃぶ	shabu-shabu	thin slices of beef and vegetables cooked in broth
刺身(盛り合わせ)	sashimi (moriawuse)	(assorted) sashimi *raw fish*
ちり鍋	chirinabe	fish and vegetables cooked in broth
五目そば	gomoku soba	Chinese noodles in soup with assorted toppings
定食	teeshoku	set menu *usually rice, soup, fish or meat, and pickles*
天ぷらうどん	tenpura udon	tempura with udon *battered fish and vegetables served in a broth with noodles*
お好み焼き	okonomiyaki	savory pancakes
炒飯	chaahan	fried rice with pork, egg, peas and shrimp
焼鳥	yakitori	barbequed chicken pieces marinated in sweet soy sauce
カレーライス	karee raisu	Japanese-style curry on rice

水	mizu	water
ミルク	miruku	milk *use this word when ordering milk or milk-based drinks*
紅茶	koocha	tea
お茶	o-cha	green tea
アイスティー	ais(u) tii	ice tea
コーヒー	koohii	coffee
アイスコーヒー	ais(u) koohii	ice coffee
日本酒	nihonshu	sake *rice wine*
焼酎	shoochuu	grain wine
ウイスキー	uis(u)kii	whisky
ジン	jin	gin
ビール	biiru	beer
生ビール	nama biiru	draft [draught] beer
ワイン	wain	wine

ジュース	*juusu*	juice
オレンジ ジュース	*orenji juusu*	orange juice
アップル ジュース	*appuru juusu*	apple juice
ココア	*kokoa*	hot chocolate
レモネード	*remoneedo*	lemonade
コカコーラ	*koka koora*	Coca-Cola
セブンアップ	*sebun appu*	Seven-Up
ファンタ	*fanta*	Fanta
ソーダ	*sooda*	soda water
トニック	*tonikku*	tonic water
ミルクセーキ	*mirukuseeki*	milkshake
ミネラル ウォーター	*mineraru wootaa*	mineral water

ポテトフライ	*poteto furai*	fries [chips]
ハンバーガー	*hanbaagaa*	hamburger
クッキー	*kukkii*	cookies [biscuits]
サンドイッチ	*sandoitchi*	sandwich
ポテトチップス	*poteto chippusu*	chips [crisps]
ピーナッツ	*piinattsu*	peanuts
するめ	*surume*	dried squid
煎餅	*senbee*	rice crackers
蒲鉾	*kamaboko*	fish cakes
えんどう豆	*endoo mame*	boiled, salted green soy-bean pods
おにぎり	*onigiri*	rice parcel with savory filling
手巻き寿司	*temaki zushi*	sushi rice rolls in seaweed with various fillings
焼きとうもろこし	*yaki toomorokoshi*	barbequed corn on the cob
肉まん	*nikuman*	steamed meat-filled dumplings
餃子	*gyooza*	Chinese meat dumplings

Soups/soup-based dishes

みそ汁	*miso-shiru*	miso soup *fermented bean paste soup*
吸物 or すまし汁	*suimono* or *sumashi jiru*	clear soup made from fish bouillon or seaweed, soy sauce, sake, and salt
あんかけうどん	*ankake udon*	wheat noodles in a thick fish bouillon/ soy sauce soup with fish cake slices and vegetables
タンメン	*tanmen*	Chinese noodles in salt-flavored soup topped with fried vegetables
冷麦	*hiyamugi*	a summer dish of cold, thinly cut wheat noodles served with cold soup
ざるそば	*zaru soba*	cold buckwheat noodles served with cold soup
冷やし中華	*hiyashi chuuka*	cold Chinese noodles served with a cold sweet/ sour sauce, and sliced ham, fish cake, and cucumber
おでん	*oden*	a winter soup of vegetables, fish cakes, and eggs

チーズ	*chiizu*	cheese
ヨーグルト	*yooguruto*	yogurt
生クリーム	*nama kuriimu*	fresh cream
バター	*bataa*	butter
ミルク	*miruku*	milk *this word is used when ordering milk in a café/restaurant, also for baby formula*
牛乳	*gyuunyuu*	milk *this word is used when buying milk in a store and is written on the carton*
ヨーグルト ドリンク	*yooguruto dorinku*	yogurt drink
フレッシュ チーズ	*furesshu chiizu*	fromage frais
豆腐	*toofu*	tofu *soybean curd*
焼き豆腐	*yaki doofu*	grilled tofu
炒り豆腐	*iri doofu*	scrambled toofu

Desserts

餅	*mochi*	rice cake, traditionally eaten at New Year
あんみつ	*anmitsu*	white gelatin cubes with sweet bean paste and mixed fruit
氷あずき	*koori azuki*	sweet bean paste covered with shaved ice topped with sweet syrup
あべかわ餅	*abekawa mochi*	rice cakes covered with slightly sweet bean powder
フルーツみつ豆	*furuutsu mitsumame*	gelatin cubes and whole, sweet mitsumame beans topped with pieces of fruit served with syrup
磯巻き	*iso maki*	rice cakes seasoned with soy sauce and wrapped in dried seaweed
クリームあんみつ	*kuriimu anmitsu*	vanilla ice cream with gelatin cubes served with sweet bean paste and fruit pieces
クリームみつ豆	*kuriimu mitsumame*	gelatin cubes and whole, sweet mitsumame beans topped with ice cream and fruit

プリン	*purin*	crème caramel
アイスクリーム	*ais(u) kuriimu*	ice cream
あんまん	*anman*	hot steamed dumpling-like bun with sweet azuki bean paste
チョコレートパフェ	*chokoreeto pafe*	chocolate parfait
かき氷	*kaki goori*	shaved ice with various sweet syrup
葛餅	*kuzu mochi*	arrowroot cake with molasses syrup
ホットケーキ	*hotto keeki*	sweet pancake served with butter and maple syrup
フルーツサラダ	*furuutsu sarada*	fruit salad
おはぎ	*ohagi*	softly cooked rice balls covered with red bean paste
お汁粉	*oshiruko*	sweet red bean paste soup

Travel

Safety	65	Hitchhiking	83	
Arrival	66	Taxi [Cab]	84	
Plane	68	Car/Automobile	85	
Train	72	Car rental	86	
Tickets	74	Gas [Petrol] station	87	
Long-distance bus		Breakdown	88	
[Coach]	78	Car parts	90	
Bus/Streetcar [Tram]	78	Accidents	92	
Subway [Metro]	80	Legal matters	93	
Ferry	81	Asking directions	94	
Bicycle/Motorbike	83	Road signs	96	

ESSENTIAL

1/2/3 ticket(s) to …	… 行きの切符を１/２/３枚 … iki no kippu o ichi/ni/san mai
To …, please.	… までお願いします。 … made onegai shimas(u)
one way [single]	片道 katamichi
round-trip [return]	往復 oofuku
How much …?	… いくらですか。… ikura des(u) ka

When traveling in Japan it is best to use the public transportation system which is remarkably good. Avoid driving if possible. Your car journey may prove stressful and expensive.

Safety 安全

Would you accompany me to …?	… まで連れていってください。 … made tsurete itte kudasai
the bus stop	バス停 bas(u) tee
my hotel	ホテル hoteru
I don't want to … on my own.	一人で…ありません。 hitori de … arimasen
stay here	ここにいたく kokoni itaku
walk home	歩いて戻りたく aruite modoritaku

EMERGENCY, POLICE ➤ 152; EMERGENCY PHONE NUMBERS ➤ 224

Arrival 到着

To enter Japan you will need a valid passport, and you will have to fill in an embarkation/disembarkation card.

Visas. UK and Eire: no visa required for a stay of 180 days or less; America, Canada, New Zealand: no visa required for a stay of 90 days or less; Australia: obtain a free visa from a Japanese consulate or embassy before leaving home; South Africa: obtain a visa before leaving home.

Customs. There are two customs clearance exits at the airport: 免税 *Duty Free* (nothing to declare) and 課税 *Dutiable* (something to declare). There is no limit to the amount of currency you can bring in. You can take out up to one million yen. Fresh fruits and vegetables cannot be brought into the country. Also certain stimulants found in Western medicines are prohibited.

Duty free into:	Cigarettes	Cigars	Tobacco	Spirits	Wine
Japan	400 or	100 or	500g	3 bottles of $^3/4$ L each	
Canada	200 and	50 or	900g	1.1L or	1.1L
UK	200 or	50 or	250g	1L and	2 L
USA	200 and	100 and	*	1L or	1 L

* a reasonable quantity

Passport control 入国管理

We have a joint passport.	ジョイントパスポートを持っています。 *jointo pas(u)pooto o motte imas(u)*
The children are on this passport.	子供は、このパスポートに 載っています。 *kodomo wa kono pasupooto ni notte imas(u)*
I'm here on vacation [holiday]/ business.	観光/仕事で来ました。 *kankoo/shigoto de kimash(i)ta*
I'm just passing through.	立ち寄るだけです。 *tachiyoru dake des(u)*
I'm going to …	…へ行きます。 *… e ikimas(u)*
I'm …	…です。 *… des(u)*
on my own	ひとり *hitori*
with my family	家族と一緒 *kazoku to issho*
I'm with a group.	グループで来ました。 *guruupu de kimash(i)ta*

WHO ARE YOU WITH? ➤ 120

Customs 税関

I have only the normal
allowances.
免税の範囲内しかあり
ません。 *menzee no han-i
nai shika arimasen*

It's a gift.
贈物です。 *okurimono des(u)*

It's for my personal use
私が使います。 *watashi ga tsukai mas(u)*

申告するものはありますか。 Do you have anything to declare?
これには関税がかかります。 You must pay duty on this.
どこで買いましたか。 Where did you buy this?
このバッグを開けてください。 Please open this bag.
他に荷物はありますか。 Do you have any more luggage?

I would like to declare ...
...を申告します。 *... o shinkoku shimasu*

I don't understand.
分かりません。 *wakari masen*

Does anyone here speak
English?
英語ができる人はいますか。
eego ga dekiru hito wa imas(u) ka

入国手続き	passport control
税関検査	customs
免税	nothing to declare
課税	goods to declare
居住者	resident
非居住者	non-resident
免税品	duty-free goods

Duty-free shopping 免税店

What currency is this in?
どの通貨ですか。
dono tsuuka des(u) ka

Can I pay in ...
...で払えますか。
... de harae mas(u) ka

dollars
ドル *doru*

pounds
ポンド *pondo*

yen
円 *en*

Plane 飛行機

Tokyo is the principal port of entry with most international flights landing at New Tokyo International Airport (Narita). However, there are many other airports serving major cities that deal with international flights. All international airports have modern facilities, including duty-free shops, and good airport-bus connections to city centers and major hotels.

Tickets and reservations 航空券と予約

When is the … flight to Kyoto?	京都行きの…の便はいつですか。 *kyooto iki no … no bin wa itsu des(u) ka*
first/next/last	最初/次/最後 *saisho/tsugi/saigo*
I'd like two … tickets to Kyoto.	京都行きのチケットを…で2枚ください。 *kyooto iki no chiketto o … de ni-mai kudasai*
one-way [single]	片道 *katamichi*
round-trip [return]	往復 *oofuku*
first class	ファーストクラス *faas(u)to kurasu*
business class	ビジネスクラス *bijinesu kurasu*
economy class	エコノミー *ekonomii*
How much is a flight to …?	…まではいくらですか。 *… made wa ikura des(u) ka*
Are there any supplements/reductions?	割増/割引料金はありますか。 *warimashi/waribiki ryookin wa arimas(u) ka*
I'd like to … my reservation for flight number 301.	３０１便の予約を…してください。 *san rei ichi bin no yoyaku o … sh(i)te kudasai*
cancel/change/confirm	キャンセル/変更/確認 *kyanseru/henkoo/kakunin*

Inquiries about the flight フライトの問合わせ

What time does the plane leave?	この飛行機は、何時に出発しますか。 *kono hikooki wa, nan-ji ni shuppats(u) shimas(u) ka*
What time will we arrive?	何時に到着しますか。 *nanji ni toochaku shimas(u) ka*
What time do I have to check in?	チェックインは何時ですか。 *chekku-in wa nan-ji des(u) ka*

Checking in チェックイン

Where is the check-in desk for flight …?	…便のチェックイン・デスクはどこですか。 …bin no chekku-in des(u)ku wa doko des(u) ka
I have …	…あります。 … arimas(u)
three cases to check in	スーツケースが3個 suutsukeesu ga san ko
two pieces of hand luggage	手荷物が2個 tenimotsu ga ni ko

チケット/パスポートをお見せください。	Your ticket/passport, please.
お席は窓際がよろしいですか、通路側がよろしいですか。	Would you like a window or an aisle seat?
喫煙席がよろしいですか、禁煙席がよろしいですか。	Smoking or non-smoking?
出発ロビーまでお出でください。	Please go through to the departure lounge.
お荷物は何個ありますか。	How many pieces of baggage do you have?
重量超過です。	You have excess baggage.
割増料金を…円お支払いください。	You'll have to pay a supplement of … yen.
それは手荷物には重すぎます/大きすぎます。	That's too heavy/large for hand baggage.
お荷物は、ご自分で詰められましたか。	Did you pack these bags yourself?
刃物や電気製品は入っていますか。	Do they contain any sharp or electronic items?

到着	arrivals
出発	departures
セキュリティチェック	security check

BAGGAGE ➤ 71

Information 案内

Is there any delay on flight …?	…便は遅れていますか。 *… bin wa okurete imas(u) ka*
How late will it be?	どのくらい遅れますか。 *dono kurai okure mas(u) ka*
Has the flight from … landed?	…からの便は到着しましたか。 *… kara no bin wa toochaku shimash(i)ta ka*
Which gate does flight … leave from?	…便のゲートは何番ですか。 *… bin no geeto wa nanban des(u) ka*

Boarding/In-flight 搭乗/機内

Your boarding card, please.	搭乗券をお見せください。 *toojooken o o-mise kudasai*
Could I have a drink/ something to eat, please?	何か飲物/食べ物をお願いします。 *nanika nomimono/tabemono o onegai shimas(u)*
Please wake me for the meal.	食事の時は、起こしてください。 *shokuji no toki wa, okosh(i)te kudasai*
What time will we arrive?	何時に到着しますか。 *nanji ni toochaku shimas(u) ka*
An air sickness bag, please.	ごみ袋をください。 *gomi bukuro o kudasai*

Arrival 到着

Where is/are …?	…はどこですか。 *… wa doko des(u) ka*
currency exchange	両替所 *ryoogae-jo*
buses	バス *basu*
car rental [hire]	レンタカー *renta kaa*
exit	出口 *deguchi*
taxis	タクシー *tak(u)shii*
Is there a bus into town?	市街までのバスはありますか。 *shigai made no basu wa arimas(u) ka*
How do I get to the … hotel?	…ホテルには、どうやって行けますか。 *… hoteru niwa doo yatte ikemas(u) ka*

Baggage 荷物

Tipping. Porters at airports/train stations charge a set fee.

Porter! Excuse me!	すみません。 sumimasen
Could you take my luggage to …	この荷物を…まで運んでください。 kono nimotsu o … made hakonde kudasai
a taxi/bus	タクシー/バス tak(u)sii/basu
Where is/are …?	…はどこですか。 … wa doko des(u) ka
luggage carts [trolleys]	カート kaato
luggage lockers	コインロッカー koin rokkaa
baggage check [left-luggage office]	手荷物一時預り所 tenimotsu ichiji azukari jo
Where is the baggage from flight …?	…便の荷物はどこですか。 … bin no nimotsu wa doko des(u) ka

Loss, damage, and theft 紛失、破損、盗難

I've lost my baggage.	荷物がなくなりました。 nimotsu ga nakunari mash(i)ta
My baggage has been stolen.	荷物が盗まれました。 nimotsu ga nusumare mash(i)ta
My suitcase was damaged.	スーツケースが壊れています。 suutsukeesu ga kowarete imas(u)
Our baggage has not arrived.	荷物が届いていません。 nimotsu ga todoite imasen
Do you have claim forms?	紛失届用紙はありますか。 funshitsu todoke yooshi wa arimas(u) ka

どんなお荷物ですか。	What does your baggage look like?
お荷物引換証はお持ちですか。	Do you have the claim check [reclaim tag]?
お荷物は…	Your baggage …
…へ送られた可能性があります。	may have been sent to …
後ほど到着するかもしれません。	may arrive later today
明日、もう一度お越しください。	Please come back tomorrow.
この番号に電話して、お荷物が到着したかどうかをお問い合わせください。	Call this number to check if your baggage has arrived.

POLICE ➤ 152; COLORS ➤ 143

Train 列車

The rail network covers the whole country. There are many different rail operators, but the service is clean, safe, and punctual. First-class cars are called **guriin sha** (green cars) and are marked with a green four-leaf sign. To travel first class you need a special ticket in addition to the normal ticket. Second-class cars are often crowded.

All station names and important signs are given in English. In stations you will find designated smoking areas. On trains, even long-distance ones, smoking compartments are becoming rarer.

Many trains have dining or buffet cars where you can get snacks and drinks. There may also be a trolley service. On the train and at stations all over Japan you can buy a lunch box (**ekiben,** also **o-bentoo**). These contain traditional Japanese food: rice, fish, and vegetables.

Facilities for the disabled. Many provincial main stations now have elevators and other facilities for disabled travelers. However, smaller stations in Tokyo generally lack such facilities.

新幹線 *shinkansen*
The bullet train. This is the fastest rail service. There are lines in Honshu (main island), Kyushu (south island), and Hokkaido (north island). JR rail passes are not valid on this service.

特急 *tokkyuu*
Limited express. This service is for long-distance travel.

急行 *kyuuko*
Ordinary. This service is the ordinary medium-distance express.

快速 *kaisoku*
Rapid train. This commuter service has no surcharge above the basic fare.

普通 *futsuu*
Local train. This commuter service has no surcharge above the basic fare.

Tourists can obtain special passes which allow unlimited travel on the rail system, as well as on buses and ferries, throughout Japan. Passess run for different lengths of time according to your requirements. These passes must be bought outside Japan, from offices of Japan Air Lines, from travel agents, or from Japan Travel Bureau offices.

There are a number of other special travel discounts for travel along certain lines within designated areas over a set period, for example **Shuuyuuken** (周遊券), **Free kippu** (フリーきっぷ), and **Parent-Child Super Pass** (親子スーパーパス). Enquire about these tickets at station travel shops.

To the station　駅へ

How do I get to the train station?	駅には、どうやって行けますか。 *eki niwa doo yatte ikemas(u) ka*
Do trains to Kyoto leave from … station?	京都行きの列車は…駅から出ていますか。*kyooto iki no ressha wa … eki kara dete imas(u) ka*
How far is it?	距離はどのくらいですか。*kyori wa dono kurai des(u) ka*
Can I leave my car there?	そこに駐車できますか。*soko ni chuusha dekimas(u) ka*

At the station　駅で

Where is/are …?	…はどこですか。*… wa doko des(u) ka*
information desk	案内係 *an-nai gakari*
baggage check [left-luggage office]	手荷物一時預り所 *tenimotsu ichiji azukari-jo*
lost-and-found [lost property office]	お忘れ物承り所 *o-wasure mono uketamawari-jo*
luggage lockers	コインロッカー *koin rokkaa*
platforms	ホーム *hoomu*
snack bar	スナックバー *sunakku baa*
ticket office	きっぷうりば *kippu uriba*
waiting room	待合室 *machiai shitsu*

入口	entrance
出口	exit
案内	information
予約	reservations
到着	arrivals
出発	departures
改札口	ticket gate
きっぷうりば	ticket office
券売機	ticket vending machines

DIRECTIONS ➤ *94*

Tickets 切符

Most tickets are bought from vending machines. Locate your destination on the diagram found above the machines, insert money (change is given), and press the button for the appropriate amount. You can specify the number of tickets you want before putting money in by pressing another button (e.g. single, two, and three adults, etc.). The station names on the diagram are usually in Japanese only, so it is important to know the characters of the station you are going to. Most ticket barriers are automatic. There are special vending machines for Shinkansen tickets (non-reservation only), but it is probably best to use the station travel shop for these tickets.

I'd like a … ticket to Kyoto.	京都行きの切符を…で 1 枚ください。 *kyooto iki no kippu o … de ichi-mai kudasai*
one-way [single]	片道 *katamichi*
round-trip [return]	往復 *oofuku*
green car (first class)/ ordinary car (second class)	グリーン車/普通車 *guriin-sha/futsuu-sha*
concessionary	割引 *waribiki*
I'd like to reserve a seat.	座席を予約したいんですが。 *zaseki o yoyaku sh(i)tain des(u) ga*
aisle seat	通路側の席 *tsuuro gawa no seki*
window seat	窓際の席 *mado giwa no seki*
Is there a sleeping car [sleeper]?	寝台車はありますか。 *shindai-sha wa arimas(u) ka*
I'd like a … berth.	…の寝台をお願いします。 *… no shindai o onegai shimas(u)*
upper/lower	上段/下段 *joodan/gedan*

Price 運賃

How much is that?	いくらですか。 *ikura des(u) ka*
Is there a discount for …?	…割引はありますか。 *… waribiki wa arimas(u) ka*
children/families	子供の/家族の *kodomo no/kazoku no*
senior citizens/students	高齢者/学生 *kooreesha/gak(u)see*
Do you offer a cheap same-day round-trip [return] fare?	日帰り往復券の割引はありますか。 *higaeri oofuku-ken no waribiki wa arimas(u) ka*

Queries 問合せ

A Travel Help Line is run by the Japan National Tourist Organization (JNTO). An English-speaking travel expert is available daily from 9 a.m. to 5 p.m. Tokyo area: 03.3503.4400 Kyoto area: 075.371.5649

Do I have to change trains?	乗り換えはありますか。 *norikae wa arimas(u) ka*
Is it a direct train?	直通列車ですか。 *chok(u)tsuu ressha des(u) ka*
You have to change at …	…で乗り換えてください。 *… de norikaete kudasai*
How long is this ticket valid for?	この切符はいつまで有効ですか。 *kono kippu wa itsumade yuukoo des(u) ka*
Can I take my bicycle on to the train?	車内に自転車を持ち込めますか。 *shanai ni jitensha o mochikome mas(u) ka*
Can I return on the same ticket?	帰りも同じ切符が使えますか。 *kaeri mo onaji kippu ga tsukae mas(u) ka*
In which car [coach] is my seat?	私の席は、どの車両ですか。 *watashi no seki wa dono sharyoo des(u) ka*
Is there a dining car on the train?	食堂車はありますか。 *shokudoo-sha wa arimas(u) ka*

> – kyooto made onegai shimas(u).
> – katamichi des(u) ka, oofuku des(u) ka?
> – oofuku des(u).
> – san-man en ni narimas(u).
> – norikae wa arimas(u) ka?
> – yokohama de norikaete kudasai.
> – hai, doomo.

Train times 列車の時刻

Could I have a timetable, please?	時刻表をください。 *jikoku-hyoo o kudasai*
When is the … train to Kyoto?	京都行きの…の列車はいつですか。 *kyooto iki no … no ressha wa itsu des(u) ka*
first/next/last	最初/次/最後　*saisho/tsugi/saigo*

How frequent are the trains to …?	…行きの列車はたくさんありますか。 … iki no ressha wa tak(u)san arimas(u) ka
There is a train/ There are trains …	…あります。 … arimas(u)
once/twice a day	一日1本／2本 ichi-nichi ippon/ni-hon
five times a day	一日5本 ichi-nichi go-hon
every hour	1時間に1本 ichi-jikan ni ippon
What time do they leave?	何時に出ますか。 nan-ji ni demas(u) ka
They leave …	…出ます。 … demas(u)
on the hour	毎時ちょうどに mai-ji choodo ni
20 minutes past the hour	毎時20分過ぎに mai-ji ni-juppun sugi ni
What time does the train stop at …?	…には何時に停車しますか。 … niwa nan-ji ni teesha shimas(u) ka
What time does the train arrive in …?	…には何時に着きますか。 … niwa nan-ji ni tsuki mas(u) ka
How long is the trip [journey]?	どのくらいかかりますか。 dono kurai kakari mas(u) ka
Is the train on time?	列車は時間通りですか。 ressha wa jikan doori des(u) ka

Departures 発車

Which platform does the train to … leave from?	…行きの列車は何番ホームですか。 … iki no ressha wa nan-ban hoomu des(u) ka
Where is platform 4?	4番線のホームはどこですか。 yon-ban sen no hoomu wa doko des(u) ka
It's over there.	あちらです。 achira des(u)
It's on the right/left.	右/左です。 migi/hidari des(u)
Where do I change for …?	…行きはどこで乗り換えですか。 … iki wa doko de norikae des(u) ka
How long will I have to wait for a connection?	連絡の列車まで何分待ますか。 renraku no ressha made nan-pun machi mas(u) ka

TIME ➤ 221; DIRECTIONS ➤ 94

Boarding 乗車

Is this the right platform for …?	…行きのホームはここですか。 … iki no hoomu wa koko des(u) ka
Is this the train to …?	これは…行きの列車ですか。 kore wa … iki no ressha des(u) ka
Is this seat taken?	この席、空いていますか。 kono seki aite imas(u) ka
That's my seat.	そこは、私の席です。 soko wa watashi no seki des(u)
Here's my reservation.	これが私の指定券です。 kore ga watashi no sh(i)tee-ken des(u)
Are there any seats/berths available?	座席/寝台は空いていますか。 zaseki/shindai wa aite imas(u) ka
Do you mind if …?	…いいですか。 … ii des(u) ka
I sit here	ここに座って koko ni suwatte
I open the window	窓を開けて mado o akete

On the journey 旅行中

How long are we stopping here for?	ここに何分、止まりますか。 koko ni nan-pun tomari mas(u) ka
When do we get to …?	には、いつ着きますか。 … niwa itsu tsukimas(u) ka
Have we passed …?	…は過ぎましたか。 wa sugimash(i)ta ka
Where is the dining/sleeping car?	食堂車/寝台車はどこですか。 shokudoo-sha/shindai-sha wa doko des(u) ka
Where is my berth?	私の寝台はどこですか。 watashi no shindai wa doko des(u) ka
I've lost my ticket.	切符をなくしました。 kippu o nakushi mash(i)ta

非常ブレーキ/緊急停止用ブレーキ	emergency brake
警報	alarm
自動ドア	automatic doors

Long-distance bus [Coach]
長距離バス

Where is the bus [coach] station?	長距離バスのターミナルはどこですか。 *chookyori basu no taaminaru wa doko des(u) ka*
When's the next bus [coach] to …?	次の…行きのバスは、何時ですか。 *tsugi no … iki no basu wa nan-ji des(u) ka*
Where does it leave from?	どこから出ますか。 *doko kara demas(u) ka*
Where are the bus stops [coach bays]?	バス停はどこですか。 *bas(u) tee wa doko des(u) ka*
Does the bus [coach] stop at …?	…に止まりますか。 *… ni tomari mas(u) ka*
How long does the trip [journey] take?	時間はどのくらい、かかりますか。 *jikan wa dono kurai kakari mas(u) ka*
Are there … on board?	車内に…はありますか。 *shanai ni … wa arimas(u) ka*
refreshments/toilets	軽食/トイレ *keeshoku/toire*

Bus/Streetcar [Tram] バス/市電

There are extensive city and rural bus services. Some towns, such as Hakone, Nagasaki, and Kumamoto, have streetcars [trams]. When you board a bus take a numbered ticket and pay at the end. You can save money by buying multiple tickets (回数券/**kaisuuken**).

Where is the terminal [bus station]?	バスターミナルはどこですか。 *bas(u) taaminaru wa doko des(u) ka*
Where can I get a bus/ streetcar [tram] to …?	…行きのバス/市電は、どこで乗れますか。 *… iki no basu/shiden wa doko de nore mas(u) ka*
What time is the … bus to Narita?	成田行きの…のバスは何時ですか。 *narita iki no … no basu wa nan-ji des(u) ka*

あそこの停留所です。	You need that stop over there.
…番のバスに乗ってください。	You need bus number …
…でバスを乗り換えてください。	You must change buses at …

バス停留所/バス停	bus stop
禁煙	no smoking
出口/非常口	exit/emergency exit

Buying tickets 切符を買う

Where can I buy tickets?	切符はどこで買えますか。 *kippu wa doko de kaemas(u) ka*
A … ticket to Omiya, please.	大宮行きの切符を…で1枚ください。 *oomiya iki no kippu o … de ichi-mai kudasai*
one-way [single]	片道 *katamichi*
round-trip [return]	往復 *oofuku*
A booklet of tickets, please.	回数券をください。 *kaisuu ken o kudasai*
How much is it to …?	…までは、いくらですか。 *… made wa ikura des(u) ka*

Traveling 旅行

Buses and streetcars [trams] play prerecorded announcements telling passengers the name of the coming stop (and perhaps places nearby, e.g. a department store). These are very useful once your ear has adapted enough to recognize the name of the stop you want.

Is this the right bus/streetcar [tram] to …?	…行きのバス/市電はこれですか。 *… iki no basu/shiden wa kore des(u) ka*
Could you tell me when to get off?	下りる場所が来たら、教えてください。 *oriru basho ga kitara oshiete kudasai*
Do I have to change buses?	乗り換えはありますか。 *norikae wa arimas(u) ka*
How many stops are there to …?	…まで、後、いくつ止まりますか。 *… made ato ik(u)tsu tomari mas(u) ka*
Next stop, please!	次で下ります。 *tsugi de orimas(u)*

きっぷうりば	ticket office
券売機	ticket vending machines

– sumimasen. hakubutsukan iki basu wa kore des(u) ka?
– soo des(u). hachi-ban des(u).
– hakubutsukan made ichi-mai kudasai.
– hyaku-gojuu en des(u).
– oriru basho ga kitara oshiete kudasai.
– koko kara yottsu-me no teeryuujo des(u).

NUMBERS ➤ 217; DIRECTIONS ➤ 94

Subway [Metro] 地下鉄

Tokyo, Osaka, Nagoya, and other big cities have very efficient subway [metro] systems. A map showing the various lines and stations is displayed outside **chikatetsu** (subway [metro]) stations. Trains are frequent and run until around midnight. Station platform signs are in Japanese and English. The smaller print at the bottom of the sign indicates the previous and following stations. Avoid rush hours (7–9 a.m. and 5–7 p.m.), unless you like the 'sardine' experience!

General Inquiries 一般的質問

Where's the nearest subway [metro] station?	地下鉄の駅はどこですか。 *chikatetsu no eki wa doko des(u) ka*
Where can I buy a ticket?	切符はどこで買えますか。 *kippu wa doko de kaemas(u) ka*
Could I have a map of the subway [metro], please?	地下鉄の路線図をください。 *chikatetsu no rosenzu o kudasai*

Traveling 旅行中

Which line should I take for …?	…は、何線ですか。 *… wa nani-sen des(u) ka*
Is this the right train for …?	この電車は…へ行きますか。 *kono densha wa … e ikimas(u) ka*
Which stop is it for …?	…は、どの駅ですか。 *… wa dono eki des(u) ka*
How many stops is it to …?	…は、いくつ目ですか。 *… wa ik(u)tsu me des(u) ka*
Is the next stop …?	次は…ですか。 *tsugi wa … des(u) ka*
Where are we?	ここは、どこですか。 *koko wa doko des(u) ka*
Where do I change for …?	…へ行くには、どこで乗り換えますか。 *… e iku niwa doko de norikae mas(u) ka*
What time is the last train to …?	…行きの終電は何時ですか。 *… iki no shuuden wa nan-ji des(u) ka*

連絡会社線	to other lines/ transfer

NUMBERS ➤ 217; *BUYING TICKETS* ➤ 74, 79

Ferry フェリー

Ferry services run from Honshu (main island) to the other islands. Details about ports and sailings may be obtained from the Tourist Information Center (TIC). To sample the charms of the Inland Sea travel by ferry or hydrofoil is recommended.

When is the … car ferry to Okinawa?	沖縄行き…のカーフェリーは、何時ですか。 *okinawa iki no … no kaa ferii wa nan-ji des(u) ka*
first/next/last	最初/次/最後 *saisho/tsugi/saigo*
hovercraft/ship	ホーバークラフト/船 *hoobaakurafuto/fune*
A round-trip [return] ticket for …	…行きの往復切符を1枚 *… iki no oofuku kippu o ichi-mai*
one car and one trailer [caravan]	車1台とキャンピングカー1台 *kuruma ichi-dai to kyanpingukaa ichi-dai*
two adults and three children	大人2人と子供3人 *otona futari to kodomo san-nin*
I want to reserve a … cabin.	…のキャビンを予約したいんですが。 *… no kyabin o yoyaku sh(i)tain des(u) ga*
single/double	シングル/ダブル *shinguru/daburu*

救命ベルト	life preserver [life belt]
救命ボート	lifeboat
立入禁止	no access

Boat trips 船旅

Tokyo. Various cruises are available in the Tokyo bay area many departing from Hinode Pier (日の出桟橋/**hinode sanbashi**). Kobe. 50-minute port cruises departing from Naka Pier. Yokohama. 50-minute tours of the harbor leaving from near the retired cruise liner, *Hikawa Maru*.

Is there a …?	…はありますか。 *… wa arimas(u) ka*
boat trip/river cruise	遊覧船 *yuuransen*
What time does it leave?	何時に出発しますか。 *nan-ji ni shuppats(u) shimas(u) ka*
What time does it return?	何時に戻りますか。 *nan-ji ni modori mas(u) ka*
Where can we buy tickets?	切符はどこで買えますか。 *kippu wa doko de kaemas(u) ka*

TIME ➤ 221; BUYING TICKETS ➤ 74, 79

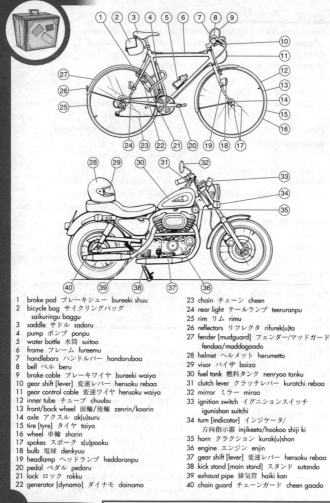

1 brake pad ブレーキシュー bureeki shuu
2 bicycle bag サイクリングバッグ
  saikuringu baggu
3 saddle サドル sadoru
4 pump ポンプ ponpu
5 water bottle 水筒 suitoo
6 frame フレーム fureemu
7 handlebars ハンドルバー handorubaa
8 bell ベル beru
9 brake cable ブレーキワイヤ bureeki waiya
10 gear shift [lever] 変速レバー hensoku rebaa
11 gear control cable 変速ワイヤ hensoku waiya
12 inner tube チューブ chuubu
13 front/back wheel 前輪/後輪 zenrin/koorin
14 axle アクスル ak(u)suru
15 tire [tyre] タイヤ taiya
16 wheel 車輪 sharin
17 spokes スポーク s(u)pooku
18 bulb 電球 denkyuu
19 headlamp ヘッドランプ heddoranpu
20 pedal ペダル pedaru
21 lock ロック rokku
22 generator [dynamo] ダイナモ dainamo

23 chain チェーン cheen
24 rear light テールランプ teeruranpu
25 rim リム rimu
26 reflectors リフレクタ rifurek(u)ta
27 fender [mudguard] フェンダー/マッドガード
   fendaa/maddogaado
28 helmet ヘルメット herumetto
29 visor バイザ baiza
30 fuel tank 燃料タンク nenryoo tanku
31 clutch lever クラッチレバー kuratchi rebaa
32 mirror ミラー miraa
33 ignition switch イグニションスイッチ
   igunishon suitchi
34 turn [indicator] インジケータ/
   方向指示器 injikeeta/hookoo shiji ki
35 horn クラクション kurak(u)shon
36 engine エンジン enjin
37 gear shift [lever] 変速レバー hensoku rebaa
38 kick stand [main stand] スタンド sutando
39 exhaust pipe 排気管 haiki kan
40 chain guard チェーンガード cheen gaado

REPAIRS ➤ 89

Bicycle/Motorbike 自転車/オートバイ

Bicycles can be hired in tourist resorts. Ask at the tourist
office where you can rent one.

I'd like to rent [hire] a …	…を借りたいんですが。 … o karitain des(u) ga
3-/10-speed bicycle	3速/10速の自転車 san-soku/jussoku no jitensha
scooter/motorbike	スクーター/オートバイ s(u)kuutaa/ootobai
How much does it cost per day/week?	1日/1週間、いくらですか。 ichi-nichi/isshuukan ikura des(u) ka
Do you require a deposit?	前金は要りますか。maekin wa irimas(u) ka
The brakes don't work.	ブレーキが壊れています。 bureeki ga kowarete imas(u)
There is/are no lights.	ライトが付きません。raito ga tsukimasen
The front/rear tire [tyre] has a flat [puncture].	前/後ろのタイヤがパンクしています。 mae/ushiro no taiya ga panku sh(i)te imas(u)

Hitchhiking ヒッチハイク

Although the Japanese rarely hitchhike themselves, hitchhiking is quite
easy and many tales are told of the great kindness shown to hitchhikers.
If you plan to hitch, have a sign in Japanese characters showing your
destination. Many drivers will not understand the meaning of an
outstretched thumb.

Where are you heading?	どこへ行くんですか。 doko e ikun des(u) ka
I'm heading for …	…へ行きます。… e ikimas(u)
Is that on the way to …?	そこは…の途中ですか。 sokowa … no tochuu des(u) ka
Could you drop me off …?	…で降ろしてください。 … de orosh(i)te kudasai
here/at …	ここ/…で koko/… de
at the … exit	…の出口で … no deguchi de
downtown	中心で chuushin de
Thanks for giving me a lift.	ありがとうございました。 arigatoo gozaimash(i)ta

DIRECTIONS ➤ 94; NUMBERS ➤ 217

<u>Taxi [Cab]</u> タクシー

Taxis are yellow or green. If the light in the bottom right-hand corner of the windshield [windscreen] is red, the taxi is free; if it's green, it's occupied. The rear doors are remote controlled – watch out you don't get knocked over by them! Few taxi drivers speak English, so have your destination written down on paper. Taxi drivers do not expect to be tipped.

Where can I get a taxi?	タクシーはどこで乗れますか。 *tak(u)shii wa doko de nore mas(u) ka*
Do you have the number for a taxi?	タクシー会社の電話番号はありますか。 *tak(u)shii gaisha no denwa bangoo wa arimas(u) ka*
I'd like a taxi ...	...タクシーお願いします。 *... tak(u)shii onegai shimas(u)*
now	今 *ima*
in an hour	1時間後に *ichi-jikan go ni*
for tomorrow at 9:00	明日9時に *ash(i)ta ku-ji ni*
The address is ..., I'm going to ...	住所は...です。...まで行きます。 *juusho wa ... des(u). ... made ikimas(u).*

空車	for hire

Please take me to (the) ...	...までお願いします。 *... made onegai shimas(u)*
airport	空港 *kuukoo*
train station	駅 *eki*
this address	この住所 *kono juusho*
How much will it cost?	いくらになりますか。 *ikura ni narimas(u) ka*
How much is that?	いくらですか。 *ikura des(u) ka*
Keep the change.	お釣りは結構です。 *otsuri wa kekkoo des(u)*

– eki made onegai shimas(u).
– *kash(i)komari mash(i)ta.*
– ikura des(u) ka?
– *500 Yen des(u). ... tsuki mash(i)ta.*
– doomo. otsuri wa kekkoo des(u).

Car/Automobile 自動車

Driving in Japan presents several problems – and if you are
not obliged to do so, then use the other easily available
means of transportion.

The Japanese drive on the left, so this will be familiar to British
drivers. However, traffic congestion can be very heavy, and parking is very
difficult and can be expensive. Using the highways [motorways] over any
distance can also prove expensive due to toll charges.

Finding your way is a major problem – very few streets have names and
most traffic signs are written in Japanese characters. It is therefore very easy
to get completely lost.

It is possible to rent a car with an English-speaking chauffeur, either
through your hotel or a travel agent.

A road map of Japan published in English by Buyodo Co. can be found in
main bookshops.

Conversion Chart

km	1	10	20	30	40	50	60	70	80	90	100	110	120	130
miles	0.62	6	12	19	25	31	37	44	50	56	62	68	74	81

Speed Limits

Speed limits kmph (mph)	Residential/Built-up areas	General	Highway [Motorway]
Cars	variable (check road signs)	60 (37)	100 (62)*
Motorbikes (250cc +)	variable (check road signs)	60 (37)	100 (62)*
Cars towing	variable (check road signs)	50 (31)	80 (50)*

* Minimum speed limit is 50 (31).

Cars are fitted with an alarm bell that rings automatically if you exceed the
top speed limit of 100 kmph. Under recent legislation it is now permissible
for individuals/companies to disconnect this alarm system if they wish.

Fuel 燃料

You will find that there are still many gas stations in Japan that are not
self-service. The staff are very helpful and will check oil, water, and tire
pressure for you if you want.

Gasoline [petrol]	Premium [super]/Regular	Diesel
ガソリン	スーパー/レギュラー	ディーゼル
gasorin	suupaa/regyuraa	diizeru

Car rental　レンタカー

There are places to rent cars in all major cities, and car rental offices run by JR can be found at most major rail stations. Except for holders of U.S. and Canadian driver's licenses, an International Driving Permit is necessary. Rental charges normally include third party and property liability, passenger liability, and fire and theft coverage.

Where can I rent a car?	レンタカーはどこで借りられますか。 *rentakaa wa doko de karirare mas(u) ka*
I'd like to rent a(n) …	…を借りたいんですが。 *… o karitain des(u) ga*
2-/4-door car	2/4ドア車 *tsuu/foo doa sha*
automatic	オートマチック　*ootomachikku*
car with 4-wheel drive	4輪駆動車 *yon rin kudoo sha*
car with air conditioning	エアコン付の車 *eakon tsuki no kuruma*
I'd like it for a day/week.	1日/1週間お願いします。 *ichi-nichi/isshuukan onegai shimas(u)*
How much does it cost per day/week?	1日/1週間いくらですか。 *ichi-nichi/isshuukan ikura des(u) ka*
Is insurance included?	保険料込みですか。 *hokenryoo komi des(u) ka*
Are there special weekend rates?	週末料金はありますか。 *shuumatsu ryookin wa arimas(u) ka*
Can I return the car at …?	車は…で返せますか。 *kuruma wa … de kaese mas(u) ka*
What sort of fuel does it take?	どのガソリンを使いますか。 *dono gasorin o tsukai mas(u) ka*
Where is the high [full]/ low [dipped] beam?	ハイ/ロービームのスイッチはどこ ですか。*hai/roo biimu no suitchi wa doko des(u) ka*
Could I have full insurance?	総合保険をお願いします。 *soogoo hoken o onegai shimas(u)*

Gas [Petrol] station ガソリンスタンド

In Japan all gas [petrol] is unleaded. It is illegal for cars and motorbikes to use leaded fuel.

Where's the gas [petrol] station, please?	ガソリンスタンドはどこですか。 gasorin s(u)tando wa doko des(u) ka
Is it self-service?	セルフサービスですか。 serufu saabisu des(u) ka
Fill it up, please.	満タンにしてください。 mantan ni sh(i)te kudasai
… liters, please.	…リットルお願いします。 … rittoru onegai shimas(u)
premium [super]/regular	スーパー/レギュラー suupaa/regyuraa
diesel	ディーセル dıızeru
Where is the air pump/water?	エアポンプ/水はありますか。 eaponpu/mizu wa arimas(u) ka

価格	price
リットル	liter

Parking 駐車

Street parking is limited, and it is common to have your car towed away, or booted [clamped]. It is an expensive and time consuming process to get it back. Your hotel may have parking facilities. Otherwise the best solution is to find and use designated parking lots [car parks].

Is there a parking lot [car park] nearby?	この近くに駐車場はありますか。 kono chikaku ni chuushajoo wa arimas(u) ka
What's the charge per hour/day?	1時間/1日いくらですか。 ichi-jikan/ichi-nichi ikura des(u) ka
Do you have some change for the parking meter?	料金メーター用の小銭はありますか。 ryookin meetaa yoo no kozeni wa arimas(u) ka
My car has been booted [clamped]. Who do I call?	車輪にクランプをはめられました。 どこに連絡すればいいですか。 sharin ni kuranpu o hamerare mash(i)ta. doko ni renraku sureba iides(u) ka

NUMBERS ➤ 217; DIRECTIONS ➤ 94

Breakdown 故障

Check when renting a car about what to do when the car breaks down. Conditions may vary, but generally do not get any repairs done before contacting the rental company. If the car breaks down on a highway, use the emergency telephones located along the hard shoulder to get assistance.

Where is the nearest garage?	いちばん近い修理工場はどこですか。 *ichiban chikai shuuri koojoo wa doko des(u) ka*
My car broke down.	車が壊れました。 *kuruma ga koware mash(i)ta*
Can you send a mechanic/ tow [breakdown] truck?	修理工/牽引車を手配してください。 *shuurikoo/ken-in-sha o tehai sh(i)te kudasai*
I'm a member of …	…に加入しています。 *… ni kanyuu sh(i)te imas(u)*
My registration number is …	ナンバーは…です。 *nanbaa wa … des(u)*
The car is …	車は… *kuruma wa …*
on the highway [motorway]	高速道路です。 *koosoku dooro des(u)*
2 km from …	…から2キロの距離です。 *… kara ni-kiro no kyori des(u)*
How long will you be?	どのくらい、かかりますか。 *dono kurai kakari mas(u) ka*

What is wrong? どうしましたか。

My car won't start.	スタートしません。*s(u)taato shimasen*
The battery is dead.	バッテリーが上がっています。 *batterii ga agatte imas(u)*
I've run out of gas [petrol].	燃料切れです。*nenryoo gire des(u)*
I have a flat [puncture].	パンクです。*panku des(u)*
There is something wrong with …	…がおかしいんですが。 *… ga okashiin des(u) ga*
I've locked the keys in the car.	鍵を中に置いたままロックしてしまいました。*kagi o naka ni oita mama rokku sh(i)te shimai mash(i)ta*

Repairs 修理

Do you do repairs?
修理はできますか。
shuuri wa dekimas(u) ka

Can you repair it?
直せますか。
naose mas(u) ka

Please make only essential repairs.
必要な修理だけしてください。
hitsuyoo na shuuri dake sh(i)te kudasai

Can I wait for it?
待っていていいですか。
matte ite iides(u) ka

Can you repair it today?
今日、できますか。
kyoo dekimas(u) ka

When will it be ready?
いつ直りますか。
itsu naorimas(u) ka

How much will it cost?
いくらかかりますか。
ikura kakari mas(u) ka

That's outrageous!
そんな馬鹿な！
son-na bakana

Can I have a receipt for my insurance?
保険申請のためにレシートをください *hoken shinsee no tame ni reshiito o kudasai*

…が壊れています。	The … isn't working.
必要な部品がありません。	I don't have the necessary parts.
部品を注文しなければ なりません。	I will have to order the parts.
応急の修理しか出来ません。	I can only repair it temporarily.
この車は手の付けようが ありません。	Your car is beyond repair.
修理不可能です。	It can't be repaired.
…直ります。	It will be ready …
今日、後ほどには	later today
明日には	tomorrow
…日で	in … days

DAYS OF THE WEEK ➤ 218; NUMBERS ➤ 217

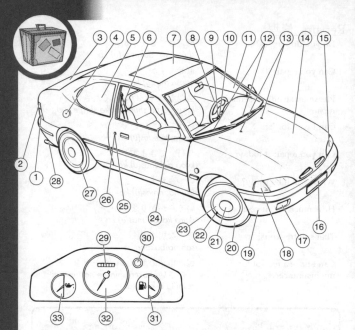

1. taillights [back lights] テールランプ teeru ranpu
2. brakelights 制動灯/ブレーキライト seedoo too/bureeki raito
3. trunk [boot] トランク toranku
4. gas tank door [petrol cap] 燃料タンクの蓋 nenryoo tanku no futa
5. window 窓 mado
6. seat belt シートベルト shiito beruto
7. sunroof サンルーフ san ruufu
8. steering wheel ハンドル handoru
9. ignition イグニション igunishon
10. ignition key イグニション・キー igunishon kii
11. windshield [windscreen] フロントガラス furonto garasu
12. windshield [windscreen] wipers ワイパー waipaa
13. windshield [windscreen] washer ウィンドウォッシャー uindo wosshaa
14. hood [bonnet] ボンネット bon-netto
15. headlights ヘッドランプ heddo ranpu
16. license [number] plate ナンバープレート nanbaa pureeto

17. fog lamp フォグランプ fogu ranpu
18. turn signals [indicators] 方向指示器/インジケータ hookoo shijiki/injikeetaa
19. bumper バンパー banpaa
20. tires [tyres] タイヤ taiya
21. hubcap ホイールキャップ hoiiru kyappu
22. valve バルブ barubu
23. wheels ホイール hoiiru
24. outside [wing] mirror サイドミラー saido miraa
25. central locking セントラルロック sentoraru rokku
26. lock ロック rokku
27. wheel rim リム rimu
28. exhaust pipe 排気管 haiki kan
29. odometer [milometer] オドメーター odomeetaa
30. warning light 警告灯 keekok(u) too
31. fuel gauge 燃料計 nenryoo kee
32. speedometer スピードメーター s(u)piido meetaa
33. oil gauge オイルゲージ oiru geeji

90

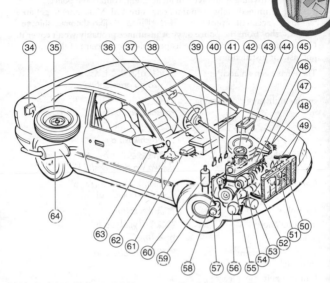

34 backup [reversing] lights バックライト
   bakku raito
35 spare wheel スペアタイヤ supea taiya
36 choke チョーク chooku
37 heater ヒーター hiitaa
38 steering column ステアリングコラム
   s(u)tearingu koramu
39 accelerator アクセル ak(u)seru
40 pedal ペダル pedaru
41 clutch クラッチ kuratchi
42 carburetor キャブレター kyaburetaa
43 battery バッテリー batterii
44 alternator オルタネータ orutaneeta
45 camshaft カムシャフト kamushafuto
47 distributor ディストリビュータ
   dis(u)toribyuuta
48 points ポイント pointo
49 radiator hose (top/bottom) ラジエータのホ
   ース（上/下）rajieeta no hoosu (ue/sh(i)ta)
50 radiator ラジエータ rajieeta
51 fan ファン fan

52 engine エンジン enjin
53 oil filter オイルフィルタ oiru furuta
54 starter motor スタータモーター
   sutaata mootaa
55 fan belt ファンベルト fan beruto
56 horn クラクション kurak(u)shon
57 brake pads ブレーキパッド bureeki paddo
58 transmission [gearbox] ギアボックス
   gia bokkusu
59 brakes ブレーキ bureeki
60 shock absorbers ショックアブソーバー
   shokku abuzoobaa
61 fuses ヒューズ hyuuzu
62 gear shift [lever] ギアレバー gia rebaa
63 handbrake サイドブレーキ
   saido bureeki
64 muffler [silencer] サイレンサー/マフラー
   sairensaa/mafuraa

Accidents 交通事故

If you are involved in an accident, contact the police immediately, even if no one is injured. Make sure to get an accident report form (事故証明申請書/**jiko shoomee shinsee sho**) from the police or your insurance probably won't cover it. Contact the rental office as soon as possible upon receipt of the report and ask for instructions.

There has been an accident ...	...事故がありました。
	... jiko ga arimash(i)ta
on the highway [motorway]	高速道路で
	koosoku dooro de
near ...	...の近くで
	... no chikaku de
Where's the nearest telephone?	電話はどこですか。
	denwa wa doko des(u) ka
Call ...	...を呼んでください。
	... o yonde kudasai
the police	警察　*keesatsu*
an ambulance	救急車　*kyuukyuusha*
a doctor	医者　*isha*
the fire department [brigade]	消防車　*shooboosha*
Can you help me, please?	助けてください。
	tas(u)kete kudasai

Injuries けが

There are people injured.	けが人がいます。
	keganin ga imas(u)
No one is hurt.	けが人はいません。
	keganin wa imasen
He's seriously injured.	重傷です。*juushoo des(u)*
She's unconscious.	意識がありません。
	ish(i)ki ga arimasen
He can't breathe.	息ができません。*iki ga deki masen*
He can't move.	動けません。*ugoke masen*
Don't move him.	動かさないでください。

Legal matters 法的必要事項

What's your insurance company?	保険会社はどこですか。 *hoken-gaisha wa doko des(u) ka*
What's your name and address?	名前と住所を教えてください。 *namae to juusho o oshiete kudasai*
That car ran into me.	あの車が、ぶつかってきました。 *ano kuruma ga buts(u)katte kimash(i)ta*
That car was going too fast/ too close.	あの車はスピードを出しすぎていました/接近しすぎていました。 *ano kuruma wa s(u)piido o dashisugite imash(i)ta/sekkin shisugite imash(i)ta*
I had the right of way.	私の方が優先でした。 *watashi no hoo ga yuusen desh(i)ta*
I was (only) driving at … kmph.	…キロで走っていました。 *… kiro de hashitte imash(i)ta*
I'd like an interpreter.	通訳をお願いします。 *tsuuyaku o onegai shimas(u)*
I didn't see the sign.	標識が見えませんでした。 *hyoosh(i)ki ga miemasen desh(i)ta*
This person saw it happen.	この人が見ていました。 *kono hito ga mite imash(i)ta*
The registration number was …	ナンバーは…でした。 *nanbaa wa … desh(i)ta*

…を見せてください。	Can I see your …, please?
運転免許証	driver's license [licence]
自動車保険証	insurance card
自動車登録証	vehicle registration document
いつ、起こりましたか。	What time did it happen?
どこで、起こりましたか。	Where did it happen?
他に、事故にあった人はいますか。	Was anyone else involved?
証人はいますか。	Are there any witnesses?
スピード違反です。	You were speeding.
ライトが故障しています。	Your lights aren't working.
(ここで) 罰金を払ってください。	You'll have to pay a fine (on the spot).
警察署で陳述してください。	We need you to make a statement at the station.

TIME ➤ 221

Asking directions
行き方をたずねる

Excuse me, please.	すみません。 *sumimasen*
How do I get to …?	どうしたら…に行けますか。 *doosh(i)tara … ni ikemas(u) ka*
Where is …?	…はどこですか。 *… wa doko des(u) ka*
Can you show me on the map where I am?	ここは地図ではどこですか。 *koko wa chizu dewa doko des(u) ka*
I've lost my way.	道に迷いました。 *michi ni mayoi mash(i)ta*
Could you repeat that, please?	もう一度、言ってください。 *moo ichido itte kudasai*
More slowly, please.	ゆっくり、言ってください。 *yukkurito itte kudasai*
Thanks for your help.	どうもありがとう。 *doomo arigatoo*

Traveling by car ドライブ

Is this the right road for …?	に行くのは、この道でいいんですか。 *ni ikuno wa kono michi de iin des(u) ka*
How far is it to … from here?	…まで、どのくらいありますか。 *… made dono kurai arimas(u) ka*
Where does this road lead?	この道は、どこに通じていますか。 *kono michi wa doko ni tsuujite imas(u) ka*
How do I get on to the highway [motorway]?	どうしたら高速道路に出られますか。 *doosh(i)tara koosoku dooro ni derare mas(u) ka*
What's the next town called?	次の町は、何といいますか。 *tsugi no machi wa nan to iimas(u) ka*
How long does it take by car?	車でどのくらいかかりますか。 *kuruma de dono kurai kakari mas(u) ka*

> – sumimasen. eki wa doko des(u) ka?
> – *san-bon me no michi o hidari ni magatte massugu des(u).*
> – san-bon me no michi o hidari des(u) ne. zuibun arimas(u) ka?
> – *aruite juppun kurai des(u).*
> – doomo arigatoo.
> – *doo itashi mash(i)te.*

COMMUNICATION DIFFICULTIES ➤ 11

Location 場所

...です。	It's ...
まっすぐ	straight ahead
左側	on the left
右側	on the right
突き当たり	at the end of the street
角	on the corner
道を曲がったところ	around the corner
...の方向	in the direction of ...
...の向かい/後ろ	opposite .../behind ...
...のとなり/後	next to .../after ...
...に入ってください。	Go down the ...
横道/大通り	side street/main street
...を渡ってください。	Cross the ...
橋	bridge
3本目の道を右に曲がってください。	Take the third right.
...左に曲がってください。	Turn left...
最初の信号を越えたら	after the first traffic lights
2番目の交差点で	at the second intersection [crossroad]

By car 車で

ここから...です。	It's ... of here.
北/南	north/south
東/西	east/west
...への道を進んでください。	Take the road for ...
道を間違えたようです。	You're on the wrong road.
...まで戻ってください。	You'll have to go back to ...
...行きの標識を辿ってください。	Follow the signs for ...

How far? どのくらい

...です。	It's ...
近く/遠く	close/a long way
歩いて5分	5 minutes on foot
車で10分	10 minutes by car
この道を100メートルほど行ったところ	about 100 meters down the road
10キロほど	about 10 kilometers away

TIME ➤ 221; NUMBERS ➤ 217

Road signs 道路標識

まわり道	detour [diversion]
一方通行	one-way street
通行止め	road closed
通学路	school zone [path]
止まれ	stop
追越禁止	no passing [overtaking]
徐行	drive slowly

Town plans 町の地図

空港	airport
銀行	bank
寺	Buddhist temple
バス路線	bus route
バス停留所/バス停	bus stop
教会	church
デパート	department store
病院	hospital
大通り/商店街	main [high] street/shopping street
映画館	movie theater [cinema]
案内所	information office
公園	park
駐車場	parking lot [car park]
横断歩道	pedestrian crossing
歩行者天国	pedestrian zone [precinct]
交番	police sub-station
警察署	police station
郵便局	post office
運動場	playing field [sports ground]
学校	school
神社	Shinto shrine
駅	rail station
スタジアム	stadium
地下鉄	subway [metro] station
地下道	underpass
タクシーのりば	taxi stand [rank]
劇場	theater
現在地	you are here

Sightseeing

Tourist information office	97	Tourist glossary	102
Excursions	98	Who/What/When?	104
Sights	99	In the countryside	106
Admission	100	Organized walks	106
Impressions	101	Geographic features	107

Tourist information office
観光案内所

The Japan National Tourist Organization (JNTO) operates the Tourist Information Centers (TIC) in Japan and also overseas offices. It provides a wealth of information, including free maps, brochures, tour itineraries, and advice on travel to and within Japan. They will also give advice on the 'goodwill guide' (free guide service) and professional guide services.
In Tokyo, at Tokyo and Shinjuku rail stations, you will find special centers (Information for Foreigners/外国人案内所/**gaikoku-jin an-nai jo**) providing foreigners with all sorts of information: places of interest, how to get to other areas of Japan, living in Tokyo, and much more.

Where's the tourist office?	観光案内所はどこですか。 *kankoo an-nai-jo wa doko des(u) ka*
What are the main points of interest?	観光名所はどこですか。 *kankoo meesho wa doko des(u) ka*
We're here for ...	ここには...います。 *koko niwa ... imas(u)*
a few hours	2〜3時間 *ni san jikan*
a day/week	1日/1週間 *ichi nichi/isshuukan*
Can you recommend ...?	...はありますか。 *... wa arimas(u) ka*
a sightseeing tour	観光ツアー *kankoo tsuaa*
an excursion	エクスカーション *ek(u)sukaashon*
a boat trip	遊覧船 *yuuransen*
Do you have any information on ...?	...の案内はありますか。 *... no an-nai wa arimas(u) ka*
Are there any trips to ...?	...へのツアーはありますか。 *... e no tsuaa wa arimas(u) ka*

Excursions エクスカーション

How much does the tour cost?	そのツアーはいくらですか。 *sono tsuaa wa ikura des(u) ka*
Is lunch included?	昼食付きですか。 *chuushoku tsuki des(u) ka*
Where do we leave from?	どこから出ますか。 *doko kara demas(u) ka*
What time does the tour start?	何時に出発しますか。 *nan-ji ni shuppats(u) shimas(u) ka*
What time do we get back?	何時に戻りますか。 *nan-ji ni modori mas(u) ka*
Do we have free time in …?	…で自由時間はありますか。 *… de jiyuu jikan wa arimas(u) ka*
Is there an English-speaking guide?	英語ができるガイドはいますか。 *eego ga dekiru gaido wa imas(u) ka*

On tour ツアーで

Are we going to see …?	…は見ますか。 *… wa mimas(u) ka*
We'd like to have a look at the …	…を見たいんですが。 *… o mitain des(u) ga*
Can we stop here …?	…ここで止まれますか。 *… koko de tomare mas(u) ka*
to take photographs	写真を撮りたいんですが、 *shashin o toritain des(u) ga*
to buy souvenirs	お土産を買いたいんですが、 *o-miyage o kaitain des(u) ga*
to use the bathrooms [toilets]	トイレに行きたいんですが、 *toire ni ikitain des(u) ga*
Would you take a photo of us, please?	写真を撮ってください。 *shashin o totte kudasai*
How long do we have here/in …?	ここで/…では、どのくらい時間があ りますか。 *koko/… dewa dono kurai* *jikan ga arimas(u) ka*
Wait! … isn't back yet.	待ってください。…がまだ戻ってい ません。 *matte kudasai. … ga mada* *modotte imasen*

Sights 観光地

The JNTO provides free tourist maps of Japan, Tokyo, Kyoto/Nara, Fuji, Osaka, and Hokkaido, as well as guides (including location maps) to hotels, **ryokan**, hostels and railways. All these are available in English.

Where is the ...?	...はどこですか。
	... wa doko des(u) ka
art gallery	美術館 bijutsu-kan
battle site	戦場跡 senjoo ato
botanical garden	植物園 shokubutsu-en
Buddhist temple	お寺 o-tera
castle	お城 o-shiro
castle remains	城跡 shiro ato
cemetery	墓地 bochi
church	教会 kyookai
downtown area	繁華街 hankagai
fountain	噴水 funsui
historic site	史跡 shiseki
(war) memorial	(戦争) 記念碑 (sensoo) kinen hi
museum	博物館 hakubutsu kan
five-story [storey] pagoda	五重塔 yojuu no too
Imperial palace	皇居 kookyo
park	公園 kooen
parliament building	国会議事堂 kokkai gijidoo
Shinto shrine	神社 jinja
shopping area	商店街 shootengai
statue	銅像 doozoo
theater [theatre]	劇場 gekijoo
town hall	市役所 shiyak(u)sho
viewpoint	展望台 tenboo dai
Can you show me on the map?	この地図で教えてください。
	kono chizu de oshiete kudasai

DIRECTIONS ➤ 94

Admission 入場

Museums are usually open from 9 a.m. to 4.30 p.m. on week-days and a little longer on Sundays and national holidays. Most are closed on Mondays. Temples keep similar opening and closing times.

Is the … open to the public?	…に入れますか。 *… ni haire mas(u) ka*
Can we look around?	見てもいいですか。 *mitemo ii des(u) ka*
What are the opening hours?	開館時間は何時ですか。 *kaikan jikan wa nan-ji des(u) ka*
When does it close?	何時に閉まりますか。 *nan-ji ni shimari mas(u) ka*
Is … open on Sundays?	…は日曜日に開いていますか。 *… wa nichi-yoobi ni aite imas(u) ka*
When's the next guided tour?	次のガイド付ツアーは何時ですか。 *tsugi no gaido tsuki tsuaa wa nan-ji des(u) ka*
Do you have you a guidebook (in English)?	（英語の）ガイドブックはありますか。 *(eego no) gaido-bukku wa arimas(u) ka*
Can I take photos?	写真を撮っていいですか。 *shashin o totte ii des(u) ka*
Is there access for the disabled?	身体障害者は入れますか。 *shintai shogai-sha wa haire mas(u) ka*
Is there an audioguide in English?	英語の案内テープはありますか。 *eego no an-nai teepu wa arimas(u) ka*

Paying/Tickets 入場料/入場券

How much is the entrance fee?	入場料はいくらですか。 *nyuujoo-ryoo wa ikura des(u) ka*
Are there any discounts for …?	…割引はありますか。 *… waribiki wa arimas(u) ka*
children/students	子供の/学生 *kodomo no/gak(u)see*
the disabled	身体障害者の *shintai shoogai-sha no*
groups/senior citizens	団体/高齢者 *dantai/kooreesha*
1 adult and 2 children, please.	大人1人と子供2人、お願いします。 *otona hitori to kodomo futari onegai shimas(u)*
I've lost my ticket.	入場券をなくしました。 *nyuujoo-ken o nakushi mash(i)ta*

TIME ➤ 221

– go-nin des(u). waribiki wa arimas(u) ka?
– *kodomo to otoshiyori wa go-hyaku en des(u).*
– otona futari to kodomo san-nin onegai shimas(u).
– *hai, san-zen go-hyaku en ni narimas(u).*

入場無料	admission free
閉館	closed
売店/ギフトショップ	gift shop
最終入場時間は午後5時です。	latest entry at 5 p.m.
次のツアーは…時です。	next tour at …
立入禁止	no entry
フラッシュお断り	no flash photography
写真撮影禁止	no photography
開館	open
開館時間	visiting hours

Impressions 印象

It's …	…ですね。 … *des(u) ne*
amazing	すごい *sugoi*
beautiful	美しい *utsukushii*
bizarre	気持ち悪い *kimochi warui*
boring	つまらない *tsumaranai*
breathtaking	息を飲むほど *iki o nomu hodo*
incredible	すてき *suteki*
interesting	おもしろい *omoshiroi*
lots of fun	とても楽しい *totemo tanoshii*
magnificent	立派 *rippa*
romantic	ロマンチック *romanchikku*
strange	変 *hen*
superb	素晴らしい *subarashii*
terrible/ugly	恐ろしい/醜い *osoroshii/minikui*
It's good value/a rip-off.	安いです。/高すぎます。 *yasui des(u)/taka sugimas(u)*
I like it.	好きです。 *suki des(u)*
I don't like it.	好きではありません。 *suki dewa arimasen*

Tourist glossary
観光用語集

寺	*tera*	Buddhist temple
本堂	*hondoo*	main hall (Buddhist temple)
仏像	*butsuzoo*	statue of Buddha
禅寺	*zen dera*	Zen temple
神社	*jinja*	Shinto shrine
三重塔	*sanjuu no too*	3-story [storey] pagoda
五重塔	*gojuu no too*	5-story [storey] pagoda
史跡	*shiseki*	historical site
皇居	*kookyo*	Imperial Palace
日本庭園	*nihon tee-en*	Japanese garden
石庭	*sekitee*	rock garden
博物館	*hakubutsu-kan*	museum
茶屋	*chaya*	teahouse
鳥居	*torii*	gate (Shinto shrine)

建築	*kenchiku*	architecture
美術	*bijutsu*	visual art
芸術	*geejutsu*	art
書画	*shoga*	calligraphy and ink drawing
陶磁器	*toojiki*	ceramics/pottery
生け花	*ikebana*	flower arranging
手工芸	*shu-koogee*	handicrafts
漆器	*shikki*	lacquerware
絵画	*kaiga*	painting
紙細工	*kamizaiku*	papercrafts
織物	*orimono*	textiles
浮世絵	*ukiyoe*	ukiyoe prints
木工	*mokkoo*	woodcrafts
襖絵	*fusuma e*	painting on sliding doors
屏風	*byoobu*	screens

Who/What/When? だれ/何/いつ?

What's that building?	あの建物は何ですか。 *ano tatemono wa nan des(u) ka*
When was it built?	いつ建てられましたか。 *itsu taterare mash(i)ta ka*
Who was the architect?	だれの設計ですか。 *dare no sekkee des(u) ka*
What style is that?	何の様式ですか。 *nan no yooshiki des(u) ka*

There are three major forms of traditional theater that are unique to Japan. They are **noh**, **kabuki**, and **bunraku**.

Noh, the oldest of the Japanese stage arts dating back to the thirteenth century, is performed in slow motion by an all-male cast wearing colorful, stiff-brocade costumes and wooden masks. The stage has no scenery except for a backdrop of painted pine trees and is open to the audience on three sides. It is not necessarily to everyone's taste.

Kabuki, originated in the sixteenth century, is just the opposite of **noh**. The stage is vast, costumes and settings gorgeous, the action fast and continuous. All the players are men, and the female characters are played by actors who have been specially trained since early childhood. Shows, comprising several parts, last up to four hours, but you can buy tickets for just a part of the program.

Bunraku is a form of puppet theater found only in Japan and uses the same dramatic themes, stories, and conventions as **noh** and **kabuki**. It isn't always easy for foreigners to appreciate. Each doll, three to four feet high, is manipulated by a master puppeteer and two black-clad assistants. The dolls move along a waist-high platform on stage.

Periods 年代

What period is that?　　　　　何時代のですか。 *nani jidai no des(u) ka*

Asuka period (C6 – early 8)	飛鳥時代
Nara period (C8)	奈良時代
Heian period (C9 – 12)	平安時代
Kamakura period (C late 12 – early 14)	鎌倉時代
Muromachi period (C14 – 16)	室町時代
Momoyama period (C late 16)	桃山時代
Edo period (C17 – mid 19)	江戸時代
Meiji period (1868 – 1912)	明治時代
Taisho period (1912 – 1926)	大正時代
Showa period (1926 – 1989)	昭和時代

Religion 宗教

Shinto is a religion unique to Japan, and its beliefs have influenced Japanese history and the Japanese character. Shinto has its origins in the myths of the tribal people of ancient Japan. Followers of Shinto worship the spirit of the gods, **kami**, whose nature is manifest in all natural things, such as rivers, mountains, trees, rocks, and animals.

Shinto shrines, known as **jinja**, are to be found throughout Japan in cities and the countryside alike. They are constructed from unpainted wood and often have thatched roofs. The Japanese make offerings at a **jinja** either to their ancestors or to the guardian spirits of the particular shrine. The entrance to a **jinja** is identified by a gate with two uprights and two cross-bars, known as a **torii** gate.

There are no fixed scriptures in Shinto. Its rituals and ceremonies are directed at receiving a blessing from the gods for a particular function or event. Shinto priests are called upon to officiate at all manner of occasions. Confucianism, brought to Japan by Chinese merchants, had an important influence on Shinto beliefs. Confucianism was a code of ethics which emphasized loyalty to the family, including ancestors. These ideas, coupled with the Shinto teaching that the emperor was a living **kami** and that the spirits of the dead lived on, produced the patriarchal, ancestor-worshipping culture of traditional Japan.

The Japanese use rituals from both Shinto and Buddhism to mark important events in their lives. Marriage is usually a Shinto ceremony and burial a Buddhist one.

Places of worship 教会

There are many Christians in Japan so there are churches in most towns. However, few services are in English. For the times of Protestant, Catholic, Greek and Russian Orthodox, Muslim, and Jewish services, look in the English-language newspapers or ask at the local Tourist Information Center.

Catholic/Protestant church	カトリック/プロテスタント教会 *katorikku/purotes(u)tanto kyookai*
mosque	回教寺院 *kaikyoo jiin*
synagogue	ユダヤ教会 *yudaya kyookai*
What time is …?	…は何時ですか。 … *wa nan-ji des(u) ka*
mass/the service	ミサ/礼拝式 *misa/reehai-shiki*
Buddhist temple	寺 *tera*
Shinto shrine	神社 *jinja*

In the countryside 田舎で

I'd like a map of …	…の地図をください。 *… no chizu o kudasai*
this region	この地域 *kono chiiki*
walking routes	ハイキングコース *haikingu koosu*
cycle routes	サイクリングコース *saikuringu koosu*
How far is it to …?	…まで、どのくらいありますか。 *… made dono kurai arimas(u) ka*
Is there a right of way?	通れますか。 *toore mas(u) ka*
Is there a trail/scenic route to …?	…に行くハイキング/眺めの良いコースはありますか。 *… ni iku haikingu/ nagame no ii koosu wa arimas(u) ka*
Can you show me on the map?	地図で教えてください。 *chizu de oshiete kudasai*
I'm lost.	道に迷いました。 *michi ni mayoi mash(i)ta*

Organized walks ハイキングツアー

When does the guided walk start?	ハイキングツアーは、いつ出発しますか。 *haikingu tsuaa wa itsu shuppats(u) shimas(u) ka*
When will we return?	いつ戻りますか。 *itsu modori mas(u) ka*
Is it a hard course?	大変ですか。 *taihen des(u) ka*
gentle/medium/tough	楽/普通/大変 *raku/futsuu/taihen*
I'm exhausted.	疲れました。 *tsukare mash(i)ta*
How long are we resting here?	ここで、何分休憩しますか。 *koko de nan-pun kyuukee shimas(u) ka*
What kind of … is that?	何の…ですか。 *nan no … des(u) ka*
animal/bird	動物/鳥 *doobutsu/tori*
flower/tree	花/木 *hana/ki*

Geographic features 地形

beach	海岸 *kaigan*
bridge	橋 *hashi*
cave	洞窟 *dook(u)tsu*
canal	運河 *unga*
cliff	崖 *gake*
farmhouse	農家 *nooka*
field	野原 *nohara*
forest	森 *mori*
hill	丘 *oka*
island	島 *shima*
lake	湖 *mizuumi*
mountain	山 *yama*
mountain pass	山道 *yama michi*
mountain range	山脈 *sanmyaku*
nature reserve	自然保護区域 *shizen hogo kuiki*
panorama	展望/パノラマ *tenboo/panorama*
park	公園 *kooen*
peak	山頂 *sanchoo*
plain	平野 *heeya*
pond	池 *ike*
rapids	急流 *kyuuryuu*
river	川 *kawa*
sea	海 *umi*
hot spring	温泉 *onsen*
stream	小川 *ogawa*
valley	谷間 *tanima*
viewpoint	展望台 *tenboo dai*
village	村 *mura*
waterfall	滝 *taki*
wood	林 *hayashi*

Leisure

Events	108	Nightlife	112
Tickets	109	Admission	112
Movies [Cinema]	110	Children	113
Theater	110	Sports	114
Opera/Ballet/Dance	111	At the beach	116
Music/Concerts	111	Skiing	117

Events 催し

Do you have a program of events?	催し物の案内はありますか。 *moyooshi mono no an-nai wa arimas(u) ka*
Can you recommend a good …?	何か良い…はありますか。 *nanika ii … wa arimas(u) ka*
ballet/concert	バレエ/コンサート *baree/konsaato*
movie [film]	映画 *eega*
opera	オペラ *opera*
Kabuki	歌舞伎 *kabuki*
Noh play	能 *noo*
play	芝居 *shibai*

Availability チケットを買う

When does it start?	何時に始まりますか。 *nan-ji ni hajimari mas(u) ka*
When does it end?	何時に終わりますか。 *nan-ji ni owari mas(u) ka*
Are there any seats for tonight?	今晩の席はありますか。 *konban no seki wa arimas(u) ka*
Where can I get tickets?	チケットはどこで買えますか。 *chiketto wa doko de kaemas(u) ka*
There are … of us.	…人分ください。 *… nin bun kudasai*

Tickets　チケット

How much are the seats?	その席はいくらですか。 *sono seki wa ikura des(u) ka*
Do you have anything cheaper?	もっと安い席はありますか。 *motto yasui seki wa arimas(u) ka*
I'd like to reserve ...	...予約したいんですが。 *... yoyaku sh(i)tain des(u) ga*
three tickets for Sunday evening	日曜日の夜、3枚 *nichi-yoobi no yoru san-mai*
one ticket for the Friday matinée	金曜日のマチネ、1枚 *kin-yoobi no machine ichi-mai*

クレジットカードの...は何ですか。	What's your credit card ...?
番号	number
種類	type
有効期限	expiration [expiry] date
チケットは...受け取りに来てください。	Please pick up the tickets ...
午後...時までに	by ... p.m.
予約窓口まで	at the reservations desk

| May I have a program, please? | プログラムをください。
puroguramu o kudasai |
| Where's the coatcheck [cloakroom]? | クロークルームはどこですか。
kurooku ruumu wa doko des(u) ka |

- *irasshaimase.*
- *konban no konsaato no chiketto o ni-mai hoshiin des(u) ga.*
- *kash(i)komari mash(i)ta.*
- *kurejitto kaado wa tsukae mas(u) ka?*
- *hai.*
- *sorenara biza de onegai shimas(u).*
- *arigatoo gozaimas(u). koko ni sain o onegai itashimas(u).*

売切れ	sold out
当日券	tickets for today
予約	advance reservations

NUMBERS ➤ 217

Movies [Cinema] 映画

Foreign films are usually shown in their original language with Japanese subtitles. You will find video rental stores everywhere. Again, films are not dubbed but subtitled.

However, with some very popular films you will find two versions: one with Japanese dubbing, the other subtitled.

FEN (810 KHz) is the American forces radio network and broadcasts in English. Television programs are mostly Japanese, but news and foreign films are broadcast bilingually on TV sets with a stereo facility, and major hotels have English-language cable and satellite TV.

Is there a multiplex cinema near here?	この近くにマルチプレックスの映画館はありますか。 *kono chikaku ni maruchi purekk(u)su no eega kan wa arimas(u) ka*
What's playing at the movies [on at the cinema] tonight?	今晩、どんな映画をやっていますか。 *konban don-na eega o yatte imas(u) ka*
Is the film dubbed?	吹替えしてありますか。 *fukikae sh(i)te arimas(u) ka*
Is the film subtitled?	字幕はありますか。 *jimaku wa arimas(u) ka*
Is the film in the original English?	映画は英語ですか。 *eega wa eego des(u) ka*
A …, please.	…ひとつください。 *… hitotsu kudasai*
box [carton] of popcorn	ポップコーン *poppukoon*
chocolate ice cream [choc-ice]	チョコアイス *choko aisu*
hot dog	ホットドッグ *hotto doggu*
soft drink	ソフトドリンク *sof(u)to dorinku*
small/regular/large	S/M/L *es(u)/emu/eru*

Theater 劇場

What's playing at the … theater?	…劇場では、何をやっていますか。 *… gekijoo dewa nani o yatte imas(u) ka*
Who's the playwright?	だれの作品ですか。 *dare no sak(u)hin des(u) ka*
Do you think I'd enjoy it?	私でも楽しめますか。 *watashi demo tanoshime mas(u) ka*
I don't know much Japanese.	日本語はあまり分かりません。 *nihongo wa amari wakarimasen*

Opera/Ballet/Dance
オペラ/バレエ/舞踊

Where's the theater?	劇場はどこですか。 *gekijoo wa doko des(u) ka*
Who is the composer/soloist?	作曲者/ソリストはだれですか。 *sakkyok(u)sha/soris(u)to wa dare des(u) ka*
Is formal dress expected?	正装は必要ですか。 *seesoo wa hitsuyoo des(u) ka*
Who's dancing?	だれが踊っていますか。 *dare ga odotte imas(u) ka*
I'm interested in contemporary dance.	現代舞踊が好きなんですが。 *gendai buyoo ga suki nandes(u) ga*

Music/Concerts 音楽/コンサート

Where's the concert hall?	コンサートホールはどこですか。 *konsaato hooru wa doko des(u) ka*
Which orchestra/band is playing?	どのオーケストラ/バンドが演奏していますか。 *dono ookes(u)tora/bando ga ensoo sh(i)te imas(u) ka*
What are they playing?	何を演奏していますか。 *nani o ensoo sh(i)te imas(u) ka*
Who is the conductor/soloist?	指揮者/ソリストはだれですか。 *shikisha/soris(u)to wa dare des(u) ka*
Who is the support band?	バックはどのバンドですか。 *bakku wa dono bando des(u) ka*
I really like …	…がとても好きです。 *… ga totemo suki des(u)*
karaoke	カラオケ *karaoke*
folk music/country music	フォーク/カントリー *fooku/kantorii*
music of the sixties	60年代の音楽 *rokujuu-nendai no ongaku*
pop/rock music	ポップス/ロック *poppusu/rokku*
jazz/soul music	ジャズ/ソウル *jazu/sooru*
Have you ever heard of her/him?	名前を聞いたことはありますか。 *namae o kiita koto wa arimas(u) ka*
Are they popular?	人気がありますか。 *ninki ga arimas(u) ka*

<u>Nightlife</u> ナイトライフ

If you are looking for popular music and dancing you'll find good quality jazz clubs and conventional discos, even country-and-western bars, all in Tokyo's cosmopolitan restaurant districts of Akasaka and Roppongi. Teenagers might like to join in the open-air disco dancing at Harajuku, near Yoyogi Park.

What is there to do in the evenings?	夜は何がありますか。 *yoru wa nani ga arimas(u) ka*
Can you recommend a ...?	良い…を教えてください。 *ii ... o oshiete kudasai*
Is there a ...?	…はありますか。 *... wa arimas(u) ka*
bar/restaurant	バー/レストラン *baa/res(u)toran*
cabaret	キャバレー *kyabaree*
discotheque	ディスコ *dis(u)ko*
gay club	ゲイバー *gee baa*
nightclub	ナイトクラブ *naito kurabu*
What type of music do they play?	どんな音楽をやっていますか。 *donna ongaku o yatte imas(u) ka*
How do I get there?	どうやって行けますか。 *dooyatte ikemas(u) ka*

<u>Admission</u> 入場

What time does the show start?	ショーは何時に始まりますか。 *shoo wa nan-ji ni hajimari mas(u) ka*
Is there a cover charge?	カバーチャージはありますか。 *kabaa chaaji wa arimas(u) ka*
Is a reservation necessary?	予約は要りますか。 *yoyaku wa irimas(u) ka*
Do we need to be members?	会員制ですか。 *kaiin-see des(u) ka*
Can you have dinner there?	そこで食事はできますか。 *soko de shokuji wa dekimas(u) ka*
How long will we have to stand in line [queue]?	どのくらい並びますか。 *dono kurai narabi mas(u) ka*
I'd like a good table.	良い席をお願いします。 *ii seki o onegai shimas(u)*

Children 子供

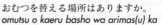

Can you recommend something for the children?	子供が楽しめるところを教えてください。 *kodomo ga tanoshimeru tokoro o oshiete kudasai*
Are there changing facilities here for babies?	おむつを替える場所はありますか。 *omutsu o kaeru basho wa arimas(u) ka*
Where are the bathrooms [toilets]?	トイレはどこですか。 *toire wa doko des(u) ka*
amusement arcade	ゲームセンター *geemu sentaa*
fairground	遊園地 *yuuenchi*
kiddie [paddling] pool	子供用のプール *kodomo yoo no puuru*
playground	公園 *kooen*
play group	託児所 *takuji-sho*
zoo	動物園 *doobutsu-en*

Baby-sitting ベビーシッター

Can you recommend a reliable baby-sitter?	信頼できるベビーシッターを教えてください。 *shinrai dekiru bebii shittaa o oshiete kudasai*
Is there constant supervision?	目を離さないでくれますか。 *me o hanasanai de kuremas(u) ka*
Is the staff properly trained?	ちゃんと訓練を受けていますか。 *chanto kunren o ukete imas(u) ka*
When can I drop them off?	いつ預けに行けますか。 *itsu azuke ni ikemas(u) ka*
I'll pick them up at …	…に迎えに行きます。 *… ni mukae ni ikimas(u)*
We'll be back by …	…までに戻ります。 *… made ni modori mas(u)*
She's 3 and he's 18 months.	女の子は3歳で、男の子は18ヶ月です。 *on-na no ko wa san-sai de, otoko no ko wa juu-hakkagetsu des(u)*

Sports　スポーツ

Most sports that are popular in the West – such as golf, tennis, football, basketball, etc. – are also popular in Japan. Many cities have martial arts halls in which you can watch **kendoo**, **juudoo**, **aikidoo** and **karate**. Japan's real national sport is **sumoo** (wrestling). This is an ancient, highly ritualized sport providing a true spectacle. There are six tournaments a year, each lasting 15 days. These are held in January, May, and September in Tokyo; in March in Osaka; July in Nagoya; November in Fukuoka. Skiing is very popular in this mountainous country, and there are numerous ski resorts. However, it is best to reserve accommodations before you leave.

Spectating　観戦

Is there a soccer [football] game [match] this Saturday?	今度の土曜日にサッカーの試合はありますか。 *kondo no do-yoobi ni sakkaa no shiai wa arimas(u) ka*
Which teams are playing?	どのチームが出ますか。 *dono chiimu ga demas(u) ka*
Can you get me a ticket?	切符を手配できますか。 *kippu o tehai dekimas(u) ka*
What's the admission charge?	入場料はいくらですか。 *nyuujoo-ryoo wa ikura des(u) ka*
Where's the racetrack [race course]?	競馬場はどこですか。 *keeba-joo wa doko des(u) ka*
Where can I place a bet?	どこで賭け金を払いますか。 *doko de kakekin o harai mas(u) ka*
What are the odds on …?	…の賭け率は何ですか。 *… no kake-ritsu wa nan des(u) ka*
athletics	陸上競技 *rikujoo kyoogi*
basketball	バスケットボール *bas(u)ketto booru*
golf	ゴルフ *gorufu*
horseracing	競馬 *keeba*
karate/kendo	空手/剣道 *karate/kendoo*
soccer [football]	サッカー *sakkaa*
sumo/judo/aikido	相撲/柔道/合気道 *sumoo/juudoo/aikido*
swimming/tennis	水泳/テニス *suiee/tenisu*
volleyball/baseball	バレーボール/野球 *bareebooru/yakyuu*

Playing 参加

Is there a … nearby?	この近くに…はありますか。 kono chikaku ni … wa arimas(u) ka
golf course	ゴルフ場 gorufu-joo
sports club	スポーツクラブ s(u)pootsu kurabu
Are there tennis courts?	テニスコートはありますか。 tenisu kooto wa arimas(u) ka
What's the charge per …?	使用料は、…いくらですか。 shiyoo-ryoo wa … ikura des(u) ka
day/round/hour	1日/1ラウンド/1時間 ichi-nichi/ichi-raundo/ichi-jikan
Do I need to be a member?	会員制ですか。 kaiin-see des(u) ka
Where can I rent [hire] …?	どこで…を借りられますか。 doko de … o karirare mas(u) ka
boots	ブーツ buutsu
clubs	クラブ kurabu
equipment	道具 doogu
a racket	ラケット raketto
Can I get lessons?	コーチはいますか。 koochi wa imas(u) ka
Do you have a fitness room?	フィットネスルームはありますか。 fittonesu ruumu wa arimas(u) ka
Can I join in?	参加できますか。 sanka dekimas(u) ka

申し訳ございませんが、満員です。	I'm sorry, we're booked up.
…の前金をいただきます。	There is a deposit of …
サイズは何ですか。	What size are you?
パスポート写真が要ります。	You need a passport-size photo.

更衣室	changing room

At the beach 海岸で

Beaches close to Tokyo and Osaka can be very crowded in the summer up to September 1, when summer officially ends. Okinawa and the Amakusa Islands are good for snorkeling and scuba diving.

Is the beach pebbly/sandy?	このビーチは砂利/砂浜ですか。 *kono biichi wa jari/suna hama des(u) ka*
Is there a … here?	…はありますか。 *… wa arimas(u) ka*
children's pool	子供用のプール *kodomo yoo no puuru*
swimming pool	プール *puuru*
indoor/open-air	屋内/屋外 *okunai/okugai*
Is it safe to swim/dive here?	ここで泳いでも/飛び込んでも大丈夫ですか。*kokode oyoidemo/tobikondemo daijoobu des(u) ka*
Is it safe for children?	子供でも大丈夫ですか。 *kodomo demo daijoobu des(u) ka*
Is there a lifeguard?	救助員はいますか。 *kyuujoin wa imas(u) ka*
I want to rent [hire] a/some …	…を借りたいんですが。 *… o karitain des(u) ga*
deck chair	デッキチェア *dekki chea*
jet-ski	ジェットスキー *jetto s(u)kii*
motorboat	モーターボート *mootaa booto*
diving equipment	ダイビング用具 *daibingu yoogu*
umbrella [sunshade]	パラソル *parasoru*
surfboard	サーフボード *saafuboodo*
water skis	水上スキー *suijoo s(u)kii*
For … hours.	…時間 *… jikan*

Skiing スキー

You will find opportunities for both downhill and cross-country skiing in Japan. You may also be lucky enough to combine skiing with sampling the delights of a **ryokan** or **minshuku** offering a hot spa.

Is there much snow?	雪は十分ありますか。 *yuki wa juubun arimas(u) ka*
What's the snow like?	どんな雪ですか。 *don-na yuki des(u) ka*
heavy/icy	重い/凍つた *omoi/kootta*
powdery/wet	さらさらした/濡れた *sarasara sh(i)ta/nureta*
I'd like to rent [hire] some …	…を借りたいんですが。 *… o karitain des(u) ga*
poles	ストック *s(u)tokku*
skates	スケート靴 *s(u)keeto gutsu*
ski boots	スキー靴 *s(u)kii gutsu*
skis	スキー *s(u)kii*
These are too …	…すぎます。 *… sugimas(u)*
big/small	大き/小さ *ooki/chiisa*
They're uncomfortable.	合いません。 *aimasen*
A lift pass for a day/ five days, please.	1日/5日分のリフト券、お願いします。 *ichi-nichi/itsuka-bun no rifuto-ken onegai shimas(u)*
I'd like to join the ski-school.	スキースクールに入りたいんですが。 *s(u)kii s(u)kuuru ni hairitain des(u) ga*
I'm a beginner.	初心者です。 *shoshinsha des(u)*
I'm experienced.	経験者です。 *keekensha des(u)*

ケーブルカー	cable car/gondola
リフト	lift

Making Friends

Introductions	118	Enjoying your trip?	123
Where are you from?	119	Invitations	124
Who are you with?	120	Encounters	126
What do you do?	121	Telephoning	127

Introductions 紹介

According to Japanese practice the surname comes first, though more recently when meeting foreigners many Japanese will give their surname last. It is customary to use the suffix **-san** (Mr., Mrs., or Ms.) after the family name, e.g. Kenji Honda (or Honda Kenji) would be addressed as Honda-san.

Visiting cards. The exchange of cards is the Japanese equivalent of shaking hands, together with a bow. Bowing is not expected of foreign visitors. Visiting cards (**meeshi**) printed on one side in English and on the other in Japanese can be obtained rapidly at most major hotels. Include your occupation or position, or it will be assumed to be a lowly one.

Hello, we haven't met.	こんにちは。はじめまして。 *kon-nichi-wa. hajime mash(i)te*
My name is …	…です。 *… des(u)*
May I introduce …?	こちらは…さんです。 *kochira wa … san des(u)*
Pleased to meet you.	よろしくお願いします。 *yorosh(i)ku onegai shimas(u)*
What's your name?	お名前は。*o-namae wa*
How are you?	お元気ですか。*o-genki des(u) ka*
Fine, thank you.	はい、おかげさまで。 *hai, o-kage sama de.*

– *kon-nichi wa. o-genki des(u) ka?*
– *hai, o-kage sama de.*

Where are you from?
どちらからですか。

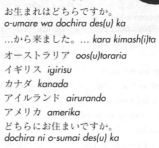

Where are you from?	どちらからですか。 *dochira kara des(u) ka*
Where were you born?	お生まれはどちらですか。 *o-umare wa dochira des(u) ka*
I'm from …	…から来ました。 *… kara kimash(i)ta*
Australia	オーストラリア *oos(u)toraria*
Britain	イギリス *igirisu*
Canada	カナダ *kanada*
Ireland	アイルランド *airurando*
U.S.	アメリカ *amerika*
Where do you live?	どちらにお住まいですか。 *dochira ni o-sumai des(u) ka*
What part of … are you from?	…のどちらからですか。 *… no dochira kara des(u) ka*
Japan	日本 *nihon*
South Korea/North Korea	韓国/北朝鮮 *kankoku/kita choosen*
China	中国 *chuugoku*
We come here every year.	毎年来ています。 *maitoshi kite imas(u)*
It's my/our first visit.	初めて来ました。 *hajimete kimash(i)ta*
Have you ever been to …?	…へ行ったことはありますか。 *… e itta koto wa arimas(u) ka*
Britain/the U.S.	イギリス/アメリカ *igirisu/amerika*
Do you like it here?	ここはいかがですか。 *koko wa ikaga des(u) ka*
What do you think of the …?	…をどう思いますか。 *… o doo omoi mas(u) ka*
I love the … here.	ここの…が好きです。 *koko no … ga suki des(u)*
I don't really like the … here.	ここの…は、あまり好きではありません。 *koko no … wa amari suki dewa arimasen*
food/people	食べ物/人 *tabemono/hito*

Who are you with?
どなたとご一緒ですか/家族

In Japanese words for members of the family vary according to the relationship of the speaker to the person. Therefore **chichi** is *father* when this speaker is talking about his/her own father, but **otoosan** when talking about someone else's father. The words here are for talking about your own family members.

Who are you with?	どなたとご一緒ですか。 *donata to go-issho des(u) ka*
I'm on my own.	ひとりです。*hitori des(u)*
I'm with a friend.	友人と一緒です。*yuujin to issho des(u)*
I'm with my …	…と一緒です。 *… to issho des(u)*
husband/wife/family	主人/家内/家族 *shujin/kanai/kazoku*
children/parents	子供/両親 *kodomo/ryooshin*
boyfriend/girlfriend	ボーイフレンド/ガールフレンド *booifurendo/gaarufurendo*
father/son	父/息子 *chichi/mus(u)ko*
mother/daughter	母/娘 *haha/musume*
older brother/younger brother/brothers	兄/弟/兄弟 *ani/otooto/kyoodai*
older sister/younger sister/sisters	姉/妹/姉妹 *ane/imooto/shimai*
uncle/aunt	伯父/伯母 *oji/oba*
What's your son's/wife's name?	息子さん/奥さんのお名前は。 *mus(u)ko-san/ok(u)san no o-namae wa*
Are you married?	結婚していますか。*kekkon sh(i)te imas(u) ka*
I'm married.	結婚しています。*kekkon sh(i)te imas(u)*
I'm single.	独身です。*dok(u)shin des(u)*
I'm engaged.	婚約しています。*kon-yaku sh(i)te imas(u)*
Do you have any children?	お子さんはいますか。 *o-kosan wa imas(u) ka*
We have two boys and a girl.	男の子2人と女の子1人です。*otoko no ko futari to on-na no ko hitori des(u)*
How old are they?	何歳ですか。*nan-sai des(u) ka*
They're ten and twelve.	10歳と12歳です。*jissai to juuni-sai des(u)*

What do you do?
何をしていますか。

What do you do?	何をしていますか。 *nani o sh(i)te imas(u) ka*
What are you studying?	何を勉強していますか。 *nani o benkyoo sh(i)te imas(u) ka*
I'm studying …	…を勉強しています。 *… o benkyoo sh(i)te imas(u)*
I'm a/an …	…です。 *… des(u)*
businessman	サラリーマン *sarariiman*
engineer	エンジニア *enjinia*
teacher	教師 *kyooshi*
salesman	セールスマン *seerusuman*
Who do you work for …?	どちらにお勤めですか。 *dochira ni o-tsutome des(u) ka*
I work for …	…に勤めています。 *… ni tsutomete imas(u)*
I'm (a/an) …	…です。 *… des(u)*
accountant	会計士 *kaikeeshi*
housewife	主婦 *shufu*
student	学生 *gak(u)see*
self-employed	自営業 *jieegyoo*
between jobs	求職中 *kyuushoku chuu*
I'm retired.	退職しました。 *taishoku shimash(i)ta*
What are your interests/ hobbies?	趣味は何ですか。 *shumi wa nan des(u) ka*
I like …	…が好きです。 *… ga suki des(u)*
music	音楽 *ongaku*
reading	読書 *dok(u)sho*
sports	スポーツ *s(u)pootsu*
I play …	…をします。 *… o shimas(u)*
Would you like to play …?	…をしますか。 *… o shimas(u) ka*
cards	トランプ *toranpu*
chess	チェス *chesu*

What weather! 天気

What a lovely day!	良い天気ですね。 *ii tenki des(u) ne*
What awful weather!	ひどい天気ですね。 *hidoi tenki des(u) ne*
It's cold/hot today!	今日は寒い/暑いですね。 *kyoo wa samui/atsui des(u) ne*
Is it usually this warm?	いつもこんなに暑いんですか。 *itsumo kon-na ni atsuin des(u) ka*
Do you think it's going to … tomorrow?	明日は…になると思いますか。 *ash(i)ta wa … ni naru to omoi mas(u) ka*
be a nice day	晴れ *hare*
rain	雨 *ame*
snow	雪 *yuki*
What's the weather forecast for tomorrow?	明日の予報は何ですか。 *ash(i)ta no yohoo wa nan des(u) ka*
It's …	…です。 … *des(u)*
cloudy	曇り *kumori*
foggy	霧 *kiri*
icy	氷点下 *hyootenka*
stormy	雷 *kaminari*
windy	風が強い *kaze ga tsuyoi*
It's frosty.	霜が降りています。 *shimo ga orite imas(u)*
It's raining.	雨が降っています。 *ame ga futte imas(u)*
It's snowing.	雪が降っています。 *yuki ga futte imas(u)*
It's sunny.	晴れています。 *harete imas(u)*
Has the weather been like this for long?	ずっとこの天気でしたか。 *zutto kono tenki desh(i)ta ka*
What's the pollen count?	花粉量はどのくらいですか。 *kafun ryoo wa dono kurai des(u) ka*
high/medium/low	多い/中ぐらい/少ないです。 *ooi/chuu-gurai/s(u)kunai des(u)*
Will it be good weather for skiing?	スキー日和になりますか。 *s(u)kii biyori ni narimas(u) ka*

天気予報	weather forecast

122

Enjoying your trip?
旅行はいかがですか。

ホリデーですか。	Are you on vacation?
ここには、何で来られましたか。	How did you get/travel here?
どこにお泊まりですか。	Where are you staying?
いつからここにいらっしゃいますか。	How long have you been here?
後、どのくらいいらっしゃいますか。	How long are you staying?
今までに、何をされましたか。	What have you done so far?
次はどこへ行くのですか。	Where are you going next?
旅行はいかがですか。	Are you enjoying your vacation?

I'm here on …	…で来ました。 … de kimash(i)ta
business	出張 shutchoo
vacation [holiday]	ホリデー horidoo
We came by …	…で来ました。 … de kimash(i)ta
train/bus/plane	列車/バス/飛行機 ressha/basu/hikooki
car/ferry	車/フェリー kuruma/ferii
I have a rental [hire] car.	レンタカーがあります。 rentakaa ga arimas(u)
We're staying in/at …	…に泊まっています。 … ni tomatte imas(u)
a hotel/a campsite	ホテル/キャンプ場 hoteru/kyanpu-joo
a youth hostel	ユースホステル yuusu hos(u)teru
traditional Japanese hotel/ guest house	旅館/民宿 ryokan/minshuku
with friends	友人の家 yuujin no ie
Can you suggest …?	…はありますか。 … wa arimas(u) ka
things to do	ここでできること koko de dekiru koto
places to eat	食べるところ tameru tokoro
places to visit	観光名所 kankoo meesho
We're having a great time.	楽しんでいます。 tanoshinde imas(u)
We're having an awful time.	大変です。 taihen des(u)

Invitations 招待

Would you like to have dinner with us on …?
…一緒に食事をしませんか。
… issho ni shokuji o shimasen ka

May I invite you to lunch?
一緒にお昼を食べませんか。
issho ni ohiru o tabe masen ka

Can you come for a drink this evening?
今晩、一緒に飲みませんか。
konban issho ni nomi masen ka

We are having a party. Can you come?
パーティーを開きますが、いらっしゃいませんか。 *paatii o hiraki mas(u) ga irasshai masen ka*

May we join you?
ご一緒できますか。
go-issho dekimas(u) ka

Would you like to join us?
いらっしゃいませんか。
irasshai masen ka

Going out 外出

What are your plans for …?
…予定はありますか。
… yotee wa arimas(u) ka

today/tonight
今日/今晩
kyoo/konban

tomorrow
明日 *ash(i)ta*

Are you free this evening?
今晩、お暇ですか。
konban o-hima des(u) ka

Would you like to …?
…行きませんか。
… iki masen ka

go dancing
踊りに *odori ni*

go for a drink
飲みに *nomi ni*

go out for a meal
食事に *shokuji ni*

go for a walk
散歩に *sanpo ni*

go shopping
買い物に *kaimono ni*

I'd like to go to …
…に行きたいです。
… ni ikitai des(u)

I'd like to see …
…が見たいです。
… ga mitai des(u)

Do you enjoy …?
…は好きですか。
… wa suki des(u) ka

Accepting/Declining 承諾/お断り

Thank you. I'd love to.	喜んで。 yorokonde
Thank you, but I'm busy.	申し訳ありませんが、約束があります。 mooshiwake arimasen ga yak(u)soku ga arimas(u)
May I bring a friend?	友達を連れてきていいですか。 tomodachi o tsurete kite iides(u) ka
Where shall we meet?	どこで待ち合わせますか。 doko de machiawase mas(u) ka
I'll meet you ...	…迎えに行きます。 ... mukae ni ikimas(u)
in front of your hotel	ホテルの前に hoteru no mae ni
I'll call for you at 8.	8時に迎えに行きます。 hachi-ji ni mukae ni ikimas(u)
Could we make it a bit later/ earlier?	もう少し遅く/早くできますか。 moo s(u)koshi osoku/hayaku dekimas(u) ka
How about another day?	他の日はどうですか。 hoka no hi wa doo des(u) ka
That will be fine.	それなら大丈夫です。 sore nara daijoobu des(u)

Dining out/in 食事

While Japanese society is generally formal, you may well be approached by people eager to practice their English and mix with a foreigner, or by those offering help. In bars you may find yourself being offered drinks and food by friendly customers. It is less likely that you will be invited to a person's home (the Japanese tend to entertain outside the home more often than Westerners), but if you do receive an invitation you should consider taking a gift with you.

Let me buy you a drink.	飲物をおごらせてください。 nomimono o ogorasete kudasai
Do you like ...?	…は好きですか。 ... wa suki des(u) ka
What are you going to have?	何にしますか。 nan ni shimas(u) ka
That was a lovely meal.	ごちそうさまでした。 goch(i)soo sama desh(i)ta

TIME ➤ 221

Encounters 出会い

Do you mind if ...?	...いいですか。 ... *ii des(u) ka*
I sit here/I smoke	ここに座っても/煙草を吸っても *koko ni suwattemo/tabako o suttemo*
Can I get you a drink?	何か飲みますか。 *nani ka nomi mas(u) ka*
I'd love to have some company.	ご一緒していただけると嬉しいです。 *goissho sh(i)te itadakeruto ureshii des(u)*
What's so funny?	何がおかしいんですか。 *nani ga okashiin des(u) ka*
Is my Japanese that bad?	私の日本語は、そんなに下手ですか。 *watashi no nihongo wa son-na ni heta des(u) ka*
Shall we go somewhere quieter?	もっと静かなところへ行きませんか。 *motto shizukana tokoro e iki masen ka*
Leave me alone, please!	構わないでください。 *kamawanaide kudasai*
Would you like to come to my home?	家に来ませんか。 *uchi ni kimasen ka*
I'm not ready for that.	今は、まだだめです。 *ima wa mada dame des(u)*
I'm afraid we've got to leave now.	もう行かなければなりません。 *moo ikanakereba narimasen*
Thanks for the evening.	どうもありがとう。 *doomo arigatoo*
It was great.	楽しかったです。 *tanosh(i)katta des(u)*
Can I see you again tomorrow?	明日も会えますか。 *ash(i)ta mo aemas(u) ka*
See you soon.	じゃあ、また。 *jaa mata*
Can I have your address?	住所を教えてください。 *juusho o oshiete kudasai*

Telephoning 電話をかける

Most public telephones are now green and can be used for both international and domestic calls. Green telephones take coins (¥10 and ¥100) and prepaid telephone cards. In a few rural areas you may still come across small pink or yellow phones that can only be used for domestic calls. Telephone cards can be bought everywhere in stores and kiosks and also from vending machines next to the public telephones. They come in a variety of denominations. You may also see gray telephones that have ports for modem connection (both ISDN and analog) and a few telephones (red or gray) that take credit cards.

Can I have your telephone number?	電話番号を教えてください。 *denwa-bangoo o oshiete kudasai*
Here's my number.	これが私の電話番号です。 *korega watashi no denwa bangoo des(u)*
Please call me.	電話してください。 *denwa sh(i)te kudasai*
I'll give you a call.	電話します。*denwa shimas(u)*
Where's the nearest telephone booth?	電話ボックスはどこですか。 *denwa bokkusu wa doko des(u) ka*
May I use your phone?	電話を貸してください。 *denwa o kash(i)te kudasai*
It's an emergency.	緊急です。*kinkyuu des(u)*
I'd like to call someone in England.	イギリスに電話したいんですが。 *igirisu ni denwa sh(i)tain des(u) ga*
What's the area [dialling] code for …?	…の市外局番は何ですか。 … *no shigai kyokuban wa nan des(u) ka*
I'd like a phonecard, please.	テレホンカードをください。 *terehon kaado o kudasai*
What's the number for Information [Directory Enquiries]?	番号案内は何番ですか。 *bangoo an-nai wa nanban des(u) ka*
I'd like the number for …	…の番号を教えてください。 … *no bangoo o oshiete kudasai*
I'd like to call collect [reverse the charges].	コレクトコールでお願いします。 *korek(u)to kooru de onegai shimas(u)*

Speaking 電話で話す

Hello. This is …	もしもし。…ですが。 *moshi moshi. … des(u) ga*
I'd like to speak to …	…さん、お願いします。 *… san onegai shimas(u)*
Extension …	内線… *naisen … ban*
Speak louder, please.	もっと大きい声で話してください。 *motto ookii koe de hanash(i)te kudasai*
Speak more slowly, please.	ゆっくり話してください。 *yukkuri hanash(i)te kudasai*
Could you repeat that, please?	もう一度言ってください。 *moo ichido itte kudasai*
I'm afraid he/she's not in.	すみません。今、出ています。 *sumimasen. ima dete imas(u)*
You have the wrong number.	番号をお間違えです。 *bangoo o o-machigae des(u)*
Just a moment, please.	少々お待ちください。 *shoo shoo o-machi kudasai*
Hold on, please.	少々お待ちください。 *shoo shoo o-machi kudasai*
When will he/she be back?	いつ戻られますか。 *itsu modorare mas(u) ka*
Will you tell him/her that I called?	電話があったとお伝えください。 *denwa ga atta to o-tsutae kudasai*
My name is …	私は…です。*watashi wa … des(u)*
Would you ask him/her to call me?	電話をくださいと、お伝えください。 *denwa o kudasai to o-tsutae kudasai*
I must go now.	もう、行かなくてはなりません。 *moo ikanak(u)tewa narimasen*
Thank you for calling.	お電話、ありがとうございました。 *o-denwa arigatoo gozaimash(i)ta*
I'll be in touch.	また、電話します。 *mata denwa shimas(u)*
Bye.	ごめんください。 *gomen kudasai*

Stores & Services

Stores and services	130	Hairdresser	147
Opening hours	132	Household articles	148
Service	133	Jeweler	149
Preference	134	Newsstand [News-	
Decision	135	agent]/Tobacconist	150
Paying	136	Photography	151
Complaints	137	Police	152
Repairs/Cleaning	137	Lost property/Theft	153
Bank/Changing		Post office	154
money	138	Souvenirs	156
Pharmacy	140	Gifts	156
Toiletries	142	Music	157
Clothing	143	Toys and games	157
Color	143	Antiques	157
Size	146	Supermarket/	
Health and beauty	147	Minimart	158

Japan is a paradise for shoppers with every type of store imaginable.
In the cities there are large department stores and supermarkets offering
almost everything. There are also numerous smaller stores specializing in
everything from electronic goods to futons. You will find no difficulty in
spending hours browsing and wondering at the array of goods for sale.

ESSENTIAL

I'd like ...	...をください。 ... o kudasai
Do you have ...?	...は、ありますか。
	... wa arimas(u) ka
How much is that?	いくらですか。 ikura des(u) ka
Thank you.	どうも。 doomo

営業中	open
閉店	closed
大売り出し/セール	sale

129

Stores and services 商店
Where is …? どこですか。

Where's the nearest …?	いちばん近い…はどこですか。 *ichiban chikai … wa doko des(u) ka*
Is there a good …?	良い…はありますか。 *ii … wa arimas(u) ka*
Where's the main shopping mall [centre]?	ショッピングセンターはどこですか。 *shoppingu sentaa wa doko des(u) ka*
Is it far from here?	ここからずいぶんありますか。 *koko kara zuibun arimas(u) ka*
How do I get there?	どうやって行けますか。 *dooyatte ike mas(u) ka*

Stores 店

Most department stores have an information desk near the entrance with a list in English explaining what you can find on each floor. Many salespeople will also speak some English.

bakery	パン屋 *pan-ya*
bank	銀行 *ginkoo*
bookstore	本屋 *hon-ya*
butcher	肉屋 *niku-ya*
camera store	カメラ屋 *kamera-ya*
cigarette kiosk [tobacconist]	タバコ屋 *tabako-ya*
clothing store [clothes shop]	洋服屋 *yoofuku-ya*
convenience store	コンビニ *konbini*
department store	デパート *depaato*
drugstore	薬局/ドラッグストア *yakkyoku/doraggu sutoa*
fish store [fishmonger]	魚屋 *sakana-ya*
florist	花屋 *hana-ya*

gift store	ギフトショップ *gifuto shoppu*
greengrocer	八百屋 *yaoya*
health food store	健康食品店 *kenkoo shok(u)hin ten*
jeweler	宝石店 *hooseki ten*
liquor store [off-licence]	酒屋 *saka-ya*
newsstand [newsagent]	キオスク *kios(u)ku*
pastry store	ケーキ屋 *keeki-ya*
pharmacy [chemist]	薬局 *yakkyoku*
produce store	食料品店 *shokuryoohin ten*
record [music] store	レコード屋 *rekoodo-ya*
shoe store	靴屋 *kutsu-ya*
souvenir store	お土産屋 *omiyage-ya*
sporting goods store	スポーツ用品店 *s(u)pootsu yoohin ten*
supermarket	スーパー *suupaa*
toy store	おもちゃ屋 *omocha-ya*

Services サービス業

clinic	総合病院 *soogoo byooin*
dentist	歯医者 *ha-isha*
doctor	医者 *isha*
dry cleaner	ドライクリーニング店 *dorai kuriiningu ten*
hairdresser/barber	美容院/床屋 *biyooin/tokoya*
hospital	病院 *byooin*
laundromat	コインランドリー *koin randorii*
optician	眼鏡店 *megane ten*
police station	警察署 *keesatsusho*
police sub-station	交番 *kooban*
post office	郵便局 *yuubin-kyoku*
travel agency	旅行代理店 *ryokoo dairi-ten*

Opening hours 営業時間

Stores usually open between 9 and 11 a.m. and close between 8 and 9 p.m., except department stores, which close at around 7 p.m. Convenience stores are generally open 24 hours a day.

Many stores close one day a week, but most are open on Saturdays and Sundays. Department stores close for two days a month, often on a Wednesday or Thursday. These closing days are displayed within the store.

When does the … open/shut?	…はいつ開きます/閉まりますか。 *… wa itsu akimas(u)/shimarimas(u) ka*
Are you open in the evening?	夜は開いていますか。 *yoru wa aite imas(u) ka*
Where is the …	…はどこですか。 *… wa doko des(u) ka*
cashier [cash desk]	会計 *kaikee*
escalator	エスカレーター *es(u)kareetaa*
elevator [lift]	エレベーター *erebeetaa*
store guide	店内の案内 *ten-nai no an-nai*
first [ground *(Brit.)*] floor	一階 *ikkai*
second [first *(Brit.)*] floor	二階 *ni-kai*
Where's the … department?	…売場はどこですか。 *… uriba wa doko des(u) ka*

営業時間	business hours
入口	entrance
エスカレーター	escalator
出口	exit
非常口	emergency/fire exit
エレベーター	elevator
階段	stairs
化粧室	restroom [toilet]

Service サービス

Can you help me?	お願いします。
	onegai shimas(u)
I'm looking for …	…を探しているんですが。
	… o sagash(i)te irun des(u) ga
I'm just browsing.	見ているだけです。
	miteiru dake des(u)
It's my turn.	私の番です。
	watashi no ban des(u)
Do you have any …?	…はありますか。
	… wa arimas(u) ka
I'd like to buy …	…が欲しいんですが。
	… ga hoshiin des(u) ga
Could you show me …?	…を見せてください。
	… o misete kudasai
How much is this/that?	これ/あれはいくらですか。
	kore/are wa ikura des(u) ka
That's all, thank you.	それで全部です。
	sore de zenbu des(u)

いらっしゃいませ。	Good morning/afternoon madam/sir.
何かお探しですか。	What would you like?
これで全部ですか。	Is that everything?
他に何かございますか。	Anything else?

– *nani ka o-sagashi des(u) ka?*
– iie, miteiru dake des(u).
– *kash(i)komari mash(i)ta.*
– sumimasen.
– *hai, nan de shoo?*
– *are wa ikura des(u) ka?*
– *shooshoo omachi kudasai … ni-sen en des(u).*

セルフサービス	self-service
特別奉仕	clearance

Preference 好み

I want something …	…のが欲しいんですが。
	… no ga hoshiin des(u) ga
It must be …	…のでなければ困ります。
	… no de nakereba komari mas(u)

big/small	大きい/小さい	*ookii/chiisai*
cheap/expensive	安い/高い	*yasui/takai*
dark/light (color)	濃い/薄い(色)	*koi/usui (iro)*
light/heavy	軽い/重い	*karui/omoi*
oval/round/square	楕円形の/丸い/四角い	
	daenkee no/marui/shikakui	
genuine/imitation	本物/イミテーション	
	honmono/imiteeshon	
I don't want anything too expensive.	あまり高いのは要りません。	
	amari takai no wa iri masen	
In the region of … yen.	…円くらいのもの。 *… en kurai no mono*	

どんな…がよろしいですか。	What … would you like?
色/形	color/shape
いくつご入用ですか。	How many would you like?
どんな種類がよろしいですか。	What sort would you like?
ご予算は、いくらぐらいですか。	What price range are you thinking of?

Do you have anything …?	…のはありますか。	
	… no wa arimas(u) ka	
larger/smaller	もっと大きい/もっと小さい	
	motto ookii/motto chiisai	
better quality/cheaper	もっと質の良い/もっと安い	
	motto shitsu no ii/motto yasui	
Can you show me …?	…を見せてください。	
	… o misete kudasai	
this one/these	これ	*kore*
that one/those	あれ	*are*
the one in the window/ display case	ウインドー/ショーケースの	
	uindoo/shoo-keesu no	
some others	他の	*hoka no*

Conditions of purchase 購入条件

| Is there a guarantee? | 保証は付いていますか。 |
| | *hoshoo wa tsuite imas(u) ka* |

| Are there any instructions with it? | 説明書は付いていますか。 |
| | *setsumee-sho wa tsuite imas(u) ka* |

Out of stock 売り切れ

申し訳ございませんが、。今、切らしております	I'm sorry, we haven't any.
売り切れです。	We're out of stock.
他のもの/違うタイプをご覧になりますか。	Can I show you something else/ a different sort?
注文いたしましょうか。	Shall we order it for you?

| Can you order it for me? | 注文してください。 |
| | *chuumon sh(i)te kudasai* |

| How long will it take? | どのくらいかかりますか。 |
| | *dono kurai kakari mas(u) ka* |

| Is there another store that sells … | …を売っている店は、他にありますか。 |
| | *… o utte iru mise wa hoka ni arimas(u) ka* |

Decision 買います/買いません

| That's not quite what I want. | 私が欲しいのと少し違います。 |
| | *watashi ga hoshii no to s(u)koshi chigaimas(u)* |

| No, I don't like it | あまり好きではありません。 |
| | *amari s(u)ki dewa arimasen* |

| That's too expensive. | 高すぎます。 *taka sugimas(u)* |

| I'd like to think about it. | 考えさせてください。 |
| | *kangae sasete kudasai* |

| I'll take it. | それにします。 *sore ni shimas(u)* |

– sumimasen. toreenaa ga hoshiin des(u) ga.
– hai. nani iro ga yoroshii des(u) ka?
– orenji-iro o kudasai. ookii no ga hoshiin des(u) ga.
– kochira ni gozaimas(u). ni-sen go-hyaku en ni narimas(u).
– sumimasen. watashi ga hoshii no to s(u)koshi chigaimas(u).

Paying 支払い

A sales tax of 5% is added to nearly all goods and services. However, many articles can be purchased free of tax at stores that display a *tax-free* sign. You will need to produce your passport and fill in a *Record of Purchase of Consumption Tax Exempt for Export* form.

Where do I pay?	どこで払うんですか。 *doko de haraun des(u) ka*
How much is that?	いくらですか。 *ikura des(u) ka*
Could you write it down, please?	紙に書いてください。 *kami ni kaite kudasai*
Do you accept traveler's checks [cheques]?	トラベラーズチェックは使えますか。 *toraberaazu chekku wa tsukae mas(u) ka*
I'll pay by …	…で払います。 *… de harai mas(u)*
cash	現金 *genkin*
credit card	（クレジット）カード *(kurejitto) kaado*
I don't have any smaller change.	小銭がありません。 *kozeni ga arimasen*
Sorry, I don't have enough money.	すみません。お金が足りません。 *sumimasen. o-kane ga tarimasen*

お支払いはどうなさいますか。	How are you paying?
このカードは使えません。	This transaction has not been approved/accepted.
このカードは有効期限を過ぎています。	This card is not valid.
他に身分証明はお持ちですか。	May I have further identification?
小銭はございますか。	Do you have any smaller change?

Could I have a receipt please?	レシートをください。 *reshiito o kudasai*
I think you've given me the wrong change.	お釣りが間違っています。 *otsuri ga machigatte imas(u)*

会計	please pay here

Complaints 苦情

This doesn't work.	壊れています。 *kowarete imas(u)*
Can you exchange this, please?	取り替えてください。 *torikaete kudasai*
I'd like a refund.	払い戻ししてください *harai modoshi sh(i)te kudasai*
Here's the receipt.	これがレシートです。 *kore ga reshiito des(u)*
I don't have the receipt.	レシートはありません。 *reshiito wa arimasen*
I'd like to see the manager.	店長を呼んでください。 *tenchoo o yonde kudasai*

Repairs/Cleaning 仕立て直し/クリーニング

Your hotel may well have a laundry service. You will also find that there are plenty of dry cleaners who do an excellent job.

This is broken. Can you repair it?	これが壊れています。直せますか。 *kore ga kowarete imas(u). naose mas(u) ka*
Do you have … for this?	…はありますか。*… wa arimas(u) ka*
a battery	電池 *denchi*
replacement parts	部品 *buhin*
There's something wrong with …	… がおかしいんですが。 *… ga okashiin des(u) ga*
Can you clean this?	クリーニングできますか。 *kuriiningu deki mas(u) ka*
Can you press this?	アイロンをかけられますか。 *airon o kakerare mas(u) ka*
Can you patch this?	継を当てられますか。 *tsugi o aterare mas(u) ka*
Could you alter this?	直せますか。*naose mas(u) ka*
When will it be ready?	いつできますか。*itsu dekimas(u) ka*
This isn't mine.	これは私のではありません。 *kore wa watashi no dewa arimasen*
There's … missing.	…がありません。*… ga arimasen*

TIME ➤ 221; DATE ➤ 219

Bank/Currency exchange
銀行/両替所

Banks are open from 9 a.m. to 3 p.m. Monday through Friday. All banks are closed on Saturdays and Sundays, except the bank at Tokyo Airport, which is open 24 hours a day.

When you go into a bank find the appropriate window – most banks have a foreign currency section. You will need to show your passport to change foreign currency or traveler's checks. You will usually be invited to sit down while the transaction is conducted. This may take as long as 15 minutes. Your name will be called when your money is ready.

両替所	currency exchange
営業中/閉店	open/closed
会計	cashiers

Where's the nearest …?	…はどこですか。 *… wa doko des(u) ka*
bank	銀行 *ginkoo*
currency exchange office [bureau de change]	両替所 *ryoogae-jo*

Changing money 両替

Can I exchange foreign currency here?	外国通貨の両替はできますか。 *gaikok(u) tsuuka no ryoogae wa dekimas(u) ka*
I'd like to change some dollars/pounds into yen.	ドル/ポンドを円に替えたいんですが。 *doru/pondo o en ni kaetain des(u) ga*
I want to cash some traveler's checks [cheques].	トラベラーズチェックを換金したいんですが。 *toraberaazu chekku o kankin sh(i)tain des(u) ga*
What's the exchange rate?	（為替）レートはいくらですか。 *(kawase) reeto wa ikura des(u) ka*
How much commission do you charge?	手数料はいくらですか。 *tesuuryoo wa ikura des(u) ka*
Could I have some small change, please?	小銭をください。 *kozeni o kudasai*
I've lost my traveler's checks. These are the numbers.	トラベラーズチェックをなくしました。これが番号です。 *toraberaazu chekku o nakushi mash(i)ta. kore ga bangoo des(u)*

Security 警備

…をお見せください。	Could I see …?
パスポート	your passport
身分証明	some identification
キャッシュカード	your bank card
ご住所はどこですか。	What's your address?
どこにお泊まりですか。	Where are you staying?
この用紙にご記入ください。	Fill in this form, please.
ここにご署名ください。	Please sign here.

ATMs [Cash machines] キャッシュコーナー

You will not be able to use foreign credit cards to obtain cash from ATM machines, except those run by Citibank (the only foreign bank operating in Japan at present). In rural areas the banks may not have currency exchange facilities. The safest solution is to have cash with you at all times.

Can I withdraw money on my credit card here?	このカードで現金を引き出せますか。 *kono kaado de genkin o hikidase mas(u) ka*
Where are the ATMs [cash machines]?	キャッシュコーナーはどこですか。 *kyasshu koonaa wa doko des(u) ka*
Can I use my … card in the cash machine?	私の…カードは、この機械で使えますか。 *watashi no … kaado wa kono kikai de tsukae mas(u) ka*
The cash machine has eaten my card.	カードが機械から出てきません。 *kaado ga kikai kara dete kimasen*

キャッシュコーナー	automated teller [cash machine]

Currency The monetary system is the yen (円), abbreviated to ¥.

Coins: ¥1, ¥5, ¥10, ¥50, ¥100, and ¥500
Notes: ¥1,000, ¥5,000, and ¥10,000

Pharmacy 薬局

You will find a large selection of imported medications at the American Pharmacy in Tokyo (Hibiya Park Bldg 1, 1-8-1 Yurakucho, Chiyoda-ku; tel (03) 3271.4034). These are much more expensive than at home, so if you have any special medical needs it is best to bring an ample supply with you.

Where's the nearest (all-night) pharmacy?	（夜間営業の）薬局はどこですか。 *(yakan eegyoo no) yakkyoku wa doko des(u) ka*
What time does the pharmacy open/close?	薬局は何時に開き／閉まりますか。 *yakkyoku wa nan-ji ni aki/shimari mas(u) ka*
Can you make up this prescription for me?	この薬をください。 *kono kusuri o kudasai*
Shall I wait?	待っていましょうか。 *matte imashoo ka*
I'll come back for it.	後で取りに来ます。 *ato de tori ni kimas(u)*

Dosage instructions 用法と用量

How much should I take?	どのくらい飲むんですか。 *dono kurai nomun des(u) ka*
How many times a day should I take it?	一日何回飲むんですか。 *ichi-nichi nan-kai nomun des(u) ka*
Is it suitable for children?	子供でも飲めますか。 *kodomo demo nomemas(s) ka*

…服用してください。	take …
…錠	… tablets
食前／食後	before/after meals
水と一緒に	with water
まるごと	whole
朝／晩	in the morning/at night
…日間	for … days

外用薬	For external use only
飲まないでください。	Not to be taken internally.
服用後は自動車等の運転を しないでください。	Do not drive after taking the medication.

Asking advice 相談

I'd like some medicine for ...	…の薬をください。
	… no kusuri o kudasai
a cold	風邪 kaze
a cough	咳 seki
diarrhea	下痢 geri
a hangover	二日酔い futsuka yoi
hay fever	花粉症 kafun-shoo
insect bites	虫刺され mushi sasare
a sore throat	喉の痛み nodo no itami
sunburn	日焼け hiyake
motion [travel] sickness	乗物酔 norimono yoi
an upset stomach	胃 i
Can I get it without a prescription?	処方箋なしで買えますか。
	shohoosen nashi de kaemas(u) ka
Can I have ...?	…をください。
	… o kudasai
antiseptic cream	傷薬
	kizu gusuri
aspirin (headache tablets)	頭痛薬
	zutsuuyaku
gauze [bandages]	包帯 hootai
condoms	コンドーム
	kondoomu
cotton [cotton wool]	脱脂綿
	dasshimen
insect repellent	虫除け
	mushi yoke
pain killers	痛み止め
	itami dome
vitamin tablets	ビタミン剤
	bitamin zai

Toiletries 化粧品

I'd like some …	…をください。	… o kudasai
after shave	アフターシェーブ	afutaa sheebu
after-sun lotion	アフターサン・ローション	afutaa san rooshon
deodorant	デオドラント	deodoranto
sanitary napkins [towels]	生理用ナプキン	seeri-yoo nap(u)kin
razor blades	カミソリの刃	kamisori no ha
soap	石鹸	sekken
sun block	日焼け止めクリーム	hiyake dome kuriimu
suntan lotion	サンタン・ローション	santan rooshon
factor …	SPF …	es(u) pii efu …
tampons	タンポン	tanpon
tissues	ティッシュペーパー	tisshu peepaa
toilet paper	トイレットペーパー	toiretto peepaa
toothpaste	歯磨き粉	hamigaki-ko

Haircare ヘアケア

comb	櫛	kushi
conditioner	コンディショナー/リンス	kondishonaa/rinsu
hair mousse/gel	ムース/ジェル	muusu/jeru
hair spray	ヘアスプレー	hea supuree
shampoo	シャンプー	shanpuu

For the baby ベビー用品

baby food	ベビーフード	bebii fuudo
baby wipes	ウェットティッシュ	wetto tisshu
diapers [nappies]	(紙)おむつ	(kami) omutsu
sterilizing solution	消毒液	shoodoku-eki

Clothing 衣類

If you want to buy clothing in Japan, note that the Japanese
have shorter arms and legs than many Westerners. However,
clothes for the Western figure are becoming more available in
Tokyo and other major cities.

General 一般

I'd like …	…をください。 … o kudasai
Do you have any …?	…はありますか。 … wa arimas(u) ka

婦人服	ladieswear
紳士服	menswear
子供服	childrenswear

Color 色

I'm looking for something in …	…のを探しているんですが。 … no o sagashite irun des(u) ga
beige	ベージュ beeju
black/white	黒/白 kuro/shiro
blue/green	ブルー buruu
green	グリーン guriin
brown	茶色 chairo
gray [grey]	グレー guree
orange	オレンジ色 orenji iro
purple	紫 murasaki
red	赤 aka
pink	ピンク pinku
yellow	黄色 kiiro
light …	薄い… usui …
dark …	濃い… koi …
I want a darker/lighter shade.	もっと濃い/薄い色が欲しいんですが。 motto koi/usui iro ga hoshiin des(u) ga
Do you have the same in …?	同じもので…はありますか。 onaji mono de … wa arimas(u) ka

Clothes and accessories 衣類と雑貨

belt	ベルト	*beruto*
bikini	ビキニ	*bikini*
blouse	ブラウス	*burausu*
bra/briefs	ブラジャー/パンティー	*burajaa/pantii*
cap	帽子	*booshi*
coat	コート	*kooto*
dress	ワンピース	*wanpiisu*
handbag	ハンドバッグ	*handobaggu*
hat	帽子	*booshi*
jacket	ジャケット/上着	*jeketto/uwagi*
jeans	ジーパン/ジーンズ	*jiipan/jiinzu*
leggings	スパッツ	*s(u)pattsu*
pants (U.S.)	ズボン/パンツ	*zubon*
panty hose [tights]	パンスト	*pans(u)to*
raincoat	レーンコート	*reenkooto*
scarf	スカーフ	*s(u)kaafu*
shirt (men's)	ワイシャツ	*waishatsu*
shorts	半ズボン/ショートパンツ	*han zubon/shooto pantsu*
skirt	スカート	*s(u)kaato*
socks	靴下/ソックス	*kutsush(i)ta/sokk(u)su*
stockings	ストッキング	*s(u)tokkingu*
suit	スーツ	*suutsu*
sweater	セーター	*seetaa*
sweatshirt	トレーナー	*toreenaa*
swimming trunks/swimsuit	海水パンツ/水着	*kaisui pantsu/mizugi*
T-shirt	Tシャツ	*tii shatsu*
tie	ネクタイ	*nek(u)tai*
trousers	ズボン/パンツ	*zubon*
underpants	パンツ/ブリーフ	*pantsu/buriifu*
with long/short sleeves	長袖/半袖の…	*nagasode/hansode no …*
with a V-/round neck	Vネック/丸首の…	*bui nekku/marukubi no …*

Shoes 靴

boots	ブーツ *buutsu*
flip-flops	ビーチサンダル *biichi sandaru*
running [training] shoes	スニーカー *s(u)niikaa*
sandals	サンダル *sandaru*
shoes	靴 *kutsu*
slippers	スリッパ *surippa*

Walking/hiking gear ハイキング用品

knapsack	ナップザック *nappuzakku*
hiking boots	登山靴 *tozan-gutsu*
waterproof jacket/anorak	アノラック *anorakku*
windbreaker [cagoule]	ウインドブレーカー *uindobureekaa*

Fabric 生地

I want something in …	…のが欲しいんですが *… no ga hoshiin des(u) ga*
cotton	綿/コットン *men/kotton*
denim	デニム *denimu*
lace	レース *reesu*
leather	革 *kawa*
linen	麻 *asa*
wool	ウール *uuru*
Is this …?	これは…ですか。 *kore wa … des(u) ka*
pure cotton	綿100% *men hyak(u) paasento*
synthetic	合成繊維 *goosee sen-i*
Is it hand/machine washable?	手/洗濯機で洗えますか。 *te/sentakki de arae mas(u) ka*

ドライクリーニングのみ	dry clean only
手洗いのみ	handwash only
アイロン掛け禁止	do not iron
ドライクリーニング禁止	do not dry clean

Does it fit? 試着

Can I try this on?	これを試着できますか。
	kore o shichaku dekimas(u) ka
Where's the fitting room?	試着室はどこですか。
	shichaku shitsu wa doko des(u) ka
It fits well. I'll take it.	ぴったりです。これにします。
	pittari des(u). kore ni shimas(u)
It doesn't fit.	身体に合いません。 *karada ni aimasen*
It's too…	…すぎます。 *… sugimas(u)*
short/long	短/長 *mijika/naga*
tight/loose	きつ/ゆる *kitsu/yuru*
Do you have this in size …?	これで…サイズのはありますか。
	korede … saizu no wa arimas(u) ka
What size is this?	このサイズは何ですか。
	kono saizu wa nan des(u) ka
Could you measure me, please?	サイズを測ってください。
	saizu o hakatte kudasai
I don't know Japanese sizes.	日本のサイズは分かりません。
	nihon no saizu wa wakari masen

Size サイズ

	Dresses/Suits						Women's shoes			
American	8	10	12	14	16	18	5	6	7	7$^{1/2}$
British	10	12	14	16	18	20	3	4	5	5$^{1/2}$
Japanese	9	11	13	15	17	19	22.5	23.5	24.5	25

	Men's shirts				Men's shoes								
American } British	15	16	17	18	5	6	7	8	8$^{1/2}$	9	9$^{1/2}$	10	11
Japanese	38	41	43	45	23	24	25	26	26$^{1/2}$	27	27$^{1/2}$	28	29

XL	extra large (XL)
L	large (L)
M	medium (M)
S	small (S)

1 centimeter (cm.) = 0.39 in. 1 inch = 2.54 cm.
1 meter (m.) = 39.37 in. 1 foot = 30.5 cm.
10 meters = 32.81 ft. 1 yard = 0.91 m.

Health and beauty 美容と健康

I'd like a ...	...をお願いします。 ... o onegai shimas(u)
facial	フェーシャル feesharu
manicure	マニキュア manikyua
massage	マッサージ massaaji
waxing	ワックス wakk(u)su

Hairdresser/Hairstylist 美容院

Japanese barbers and hairdressers give excellent service. Hotel hairdressers are used to non-Japanese hair. If you ask the barber for **futsuu ni** (as usual), you'll get a head and neck massage too. Ladies hairdressers usually close on Tuesdays, barbers on Mondays; both are open on Sundays.

I'd like to make an appointment for ...	...の予約をしたいんですが。 ... no yoyaku o sh(i)tain des(u) ga
Can you make it a bit earlier/later?	もう少し早く/遅くできますか。 moo s(u)koshi hayaku/osoku dekimas(u) ka
I'd like a ...	...をお願いします。 ... o onegai shimas(u)
cut and blow-dry	カットとブロードライ katto to buroo dorai
shampoo and set	シャンプーとセット shanpuu to setto
trim	トリム torimu
I'd like my hair highlighted.	髪にハイライトを入れたいんですが。 kami ni hairaito o iretain des(u) ga
I'd like my hair permed.	パーマをかけたいんですが。 paama o kaketain des(u) ga
Don't cut it too short.	切りすぎないでください。 kiri suginai de kudasai
A little more off the ...	...をもう少しカットしてください。 ... o moo s(u)koshi katto shite kudasai
back/front	後ろ/前 ushiro/mae
neck/sides	首筋/横 kubisuji/yoko
top	上 ue
That's fine, thanks.	これで結構です。korede kekkoo des(u).

Household articles 日用品

I'd like a(n)/some … ….をください。 … o kudasai

adapter	アダプター	adap(u)taa
alumin(i)um foil	アルミホイル	arumi hoiru
bottle-opener	栓抜き	sen-nuki
can [tin] opener	缶切り	kankiri
clothes pins [pegs]	洗濯ばさみ	sentaku basami
corkscrew	コルクスクリュー	koruku s(u)kuryuu
light bulb	電球	denkyuu
matches	マッチ	matchi
paper napkins	紙ナプキン	kami nap(u)kin
plastic wrap [cling film]	ラップ	rappu
plug	プラグ	puragu
scissors	はさみ	hasami
screwdriver	ドライバー	doraibaa

Cleaning items 洗剤・洗濯用品

bleach	漂白剤	hyoohaku zai
dishcloth	布巾	fukin
dishwashing [washing-up] liquid	中性洗剤	tyuusee senzai
garbage [refuse] bags	ごみ袋	gomi bukuro
detergent [washing powder]	洗剤	senzai
sponge	スポンジ	s(u)ponji

Crockery/Cutlery 食器類

bowls	ボール	booru
chopsticks	箸	hashi
cups	カップ	kappu
glasses	グラス/コップ	gurasu/koppu
knives/forks	ナイフ/フォーク	naifu/fooku
mugs	マグカップ	magukappu
plates	皿	sara
rice bowls	茶碗	chawan
soup dish	スープ皿	suupu zara
spoons	スプーン	s(u)puun

Jeweler 宝石店

Could I see …?	…を見せてください。 *… o misete kudasai*
this/that	これ/あれ *kore/are*
It's in the window/display cabinet.	ウインドー/ショーケースに あります。 *uindoo/shookeesu ni arimas(u)*
alarm clock	目覚まし時計 *mezamashi dokee*
battery	電池 *denchi*
bracelet	ブレスレット *buresuretto*
brooch	ブローチ *buroochi*
chain	チェーン *cheen*
clock	時計 *tokee*
earrings	イヤリング *iyaringu*
necklace	ネックレス *nekkuresu*
ring	指輪/リング *yuhiwa/ringu*
watch	腕時計 *ude-dokee*

Materials 材質

Is this real silver/gold?	これは本物の銀/金ですか。 *kore wa honmono no gin/kin des(u) ka*
Is there a certificate for it?	証書はありますか。 *shoosho wa arimas(u) ka*
Do you have anything in …?	…のはありますか。 *… no wa arimas(u) ka*
copper	銅 *doo*
crystal (quartz)	水晶 *suishoo*
cut glass	カットグラス *katto gurasu*
diamond	ダイアモンド *daiamondo*
enamel	七宝 *shippoo*
gold	金 *kin*
gold plate	金メッキ *kin mekki*
pearl	真珠 *shinju*
platinum	プラチナ *purachina*
silver	銀 *gin*
silver plate	銀メッキ *gin mekki*
stainless steel	ステンレス *s(u)tenresu*

Newsstand [Newsagent]/ Tobacconist キオスク/タバコ屋

Foreign books, magazines, and newspapers can be found in large bookstores, department stores, and hotels. Several newspapers are published in English – *Asahi Evening News*, *Mainichi Daily News*, *Japan Times*, *Daily Yomiuri* – and are sold at hotels and many newsstands.

Do you sell English-language books/newspapers?	英語の本/新聞はありますか。 *eego no hon/shinbun wa arimas(u) ka*
I'd like a(n)/some …	…をください。 *… o kudasai*
book	本 *hon*
candy [sweets]	キャンデー *kyandee*
chewing gum	ガム *gamu*
chocolate bar	チョコレート *chokoreeto*
cigarettes (packet of)	タバコ *tabako*
cigars	葉巻 *hamaki*
dictionary	辞書 *jisho*
English-Japanese	英和 *eewa*
envelopes	封筒 *fuutoo*
guidebook of …	…のガイドブック *… no gaido bukku*
lighter	ライター *raitaa*
magazine	雑誌 *zasshi*
map	地図 *chizu*
map of the town	市街地図 *shigai chizu*
matches	マッチ *matchi*
newspaper	新聞 *shinbun*
American/English	アメリカの/イギリスの *amerika no/igirisu no*
writing paper	便箋 *binsen*
pen	ボールペン *boorupen*
road map of …	…の道路地図 *… no dooro chizu*
stamps	切手 *kitte*
tobacco	刻みタバコ *kizami tabako*

Photography 写真撮影

I'm looking for a … camera.	…カメラを探しているんですが。 … kamera o sagash(i)te irun des(u) ga
automatic	オートマチック ootomachikku
compact	コンパクト konpakuto
disposable	使い捨て tsukais(u)te
SLR	一眼レフ ichigan refu
I'd like a(n)/some …	…をください。 … o kudasai
battery	電池 denchi
camera case	カメラのケース kamera no keesu
electronic flash	フラッシュ furasshu
filter	フィルター firutaa
lens	レンズ renzu
lens cap	レンズのキャップ renzu no kyappu

Film/Processing フィルム/現像

I'd like a … film.	…フィルムをください。 … firumu o kudasai
black and white	白黒 shirokuro
color	カラー karaa
24/36 exposures	24/36枚撮り nijuu-yon/sanjuu-roku mai dori
I'd like this film developed, please.	このフィルムを現像してください。 kono firumu o genzoo sh(i)te kudasai
Would you enlarge this, please?	これを引き伸ばしてください。 kore o hiki nobash(i)te kudasai
How much do … exposures cost?	…枚撮りは、いくらですか。 … mai dori wa ikura des(u) ka
When will the photos be ready?	写真はいつできますか。 shashin wa itsu dekimas(u) ka
I'd like to collect my photos.	写真を取りに来ました。 shashin o tori ni kimash(i)ta
Here's the receipt.	これが引換券です。 kore ga hikikae ken des(u)

Police 警察

Theft is not common in Japan, although bicycles and umbrellas often go missing! Japan is generally a safe country and violent crime is rare. However, beware of pickpockets and gropers (**chikan**) in crowded trains.

Where's the nearest police sub-station?	交番はどこですか。 *kooban wa doko des(u) ka*
Does anyone here speak English?	英語ができる人はいますか。 *eego ga dekiru hito wa imas(u) ka*
I was attacked.	襲われました。 *osoware mash(i)ta*
I was mugged.	強盗にあいました。 *gootoo ni aimash(i)ta*
I was raped.	強姦されました。 *gookan sare mash(i)ta*
My child is missing.	子供がいなくなりました。 *kodomo ga inaku nari mash(i)ta*
Here's a photo of him/her.	これが子供の写真です。 *kore ga kodomo no shashin des(u)*
Someone's following me.	だれかに後を付けられています。 *dareka ni ato o tsukerarete imas(u)*
I need an English-speaking lawyer.	英語ができる弁護士を呼んでください。 *eego ga dekiru bengoshi o yonde kudasai*
I need to make a phone call.	電話をかけさせてください。 *denwa o kakesasete kudasai*
I need to contact the ... Consulate.	...領事館に知らせてください。 *... ryoojikan ni shirasete kudasai*
American/British	アメリカ/イギリス *amerika/igirisu*

どんな子/人ですか。	Can you describe him/her?
男/女	male/female
ブロンド/ブルネット	blond/brunette
赤毛/白髪頭	red-headed/gray [grey] haired
ロングヘア/ショートヘア/禿げ上がっている	long/short hair/balding
身長は...くらい	approximate height ...
年齢は... (くらい)	aged (approximately) ...
...を着ていました。	He/She was wearing ...

CLOTHES ➤ 144; COLORS ➤ 143

Lost property/Theft 落し物/盗難

I want to report a theft.	盗難にあいました。 *toonan ni aimash(i)ta*
My bag was snatched.	バッグをすられました。 *baggu o surare mash(i)ta*
My ... has been stolen from my car.	車から...が盗まれました。 *kuruma kara ... ga nusumare mash(i)ta*
I've been robbed/mugged.	強盗にあいました。 *gootoo ni aimash(i)ta*
I've lost my ...	...をなくしました。 *... o nak(u)shi mash(i)ta*
My ... has been stolen.	...を盗まれました。 *... o nusumare mash(i)ta*
bicycle	自転車 *jitensha*
camera	カメラ *kamera*
car	車 *kuruma*
rental car	レンタカー *renta kaa*
credit cards	クレジットカード *kurejitto kaado*
handbag	ハンドバッグ *hando baggu*
money	お金 *o-kane*
passport	パスポート *pas(u)pooto*
purse/wallet	財布 *saifu*
ticket	チケット *chiketto*
watch	腕時計 *ude-dokee*
What shall I do?	どうしましょうか。 *doo shimashoo ka*
I need a police report for my insurance claim.	保険の申請に警察の証明書が要ります。 *hoken no shinsee ni keesatsu no shoomee-sho ga irimas(u)*

何がなくなりましたか。	What's missing?
何を盗られましたか。	What's been taken?
いつ盗まれましたか。	When was it stolen?
いつ、起こりましたか。	When did it happen?
どこにお泊まりですか。	Where are you staying?
どこから盗まれましたか。	Where was it taken from?
その時、どこにいましたか。	Where were you at the time?
通訳を呼んできます。	We're getting an interpreter for you.
調査します。	We'll look into the matter.
この用紙に記入してください。	Please fill out this form.

Post office 郵便局

Main post offices are open from 8 a.m. to 7 p.m. on weekdays, 9 a.m. to 5 p.m. on Saturdays and from 9 a.m. to 12.30 p.m. on Sundays. Local post offices are not open on Sundays and only from 9 a.m. to 5 p.m. on weekdays, and from 9 a.m. to 12.30 p.m. on Saturdays. Tokyo International Post Office is open round the clock for urgent mail. Stamps are also sold at hotels and some tobacconists.

Mailboxes, usually red, are found on street corners. You can also mail letters at hotel desks.

General queries 一般的質問

Where is the post office?	郵便局はどこですか。 *yuubin-kyoku wa doko des(u) ka*
What time does the post office open/close?	郵便局は、何時に開き/閉まりますか。 *yuubin-kyoku wa nan-ji ni aki/ shimari mas(u) ka*
Where's the mailbox [postbox]?	郵便ポストはどこですか。 *yuubin pos(u)to wa doko des(u) ka*
Is there any mail for me?	私に手紙は来ていますか。 *watashi ni tegami wa kite imas(u) ka*

Buying stamps 切手を買う

A stamp for this postcard/letter, please.	この葉書/手紙用の切手をください。 *kono hagaki/tegami yoo no kitte o kudasai*
A … yen stamp, please.	…円切手をください。 *… en kitte o kudasai*
What's the postage for a letter to …?	…宛の手紙はいくらかかりますか。 *… ate no tegami wa ikura kakari mas(u) ka*

---

*kore o amerika ni okuritain des(u) ga
nan-mai des(u) ka?
kyuu-mai des(u).
hyaku-en ga kyuu-mai de kyuuhyaku-en ni narimas(u).*

Sending parcels 小包を送る

I want to send this package [parcel] by …	この小包を…で送りたいんですが。 kono kozutsumi o … de okuritain des(u) ga
airmail	航空便 kookuubin
special delivery [express]	速達 sok(u)tatsu
registered mail	書留 kakitome
It contains …	中は…です。 naka wa … des(u)

税関申告書に記入してください。	Please fill in the customs declaration.
どのくらいの値段のものですか。	What is the value?
中には何が入っていますか。	What's inside?

Telecommunications 電話

I'd like a phonecard, please.	テレホンカードをください。 terehon kaado o kudasai
200/500/1,000 yen card, please.	200/500/1,000円のカード、お願いします。 ni-hyaku/go-hyaku/sen en no kaado, onegai shimas(u)
Do you have a photocopier?	コピー機はありますか。 kopii-ki wa arimas(u) ka
I'd like to send a message …	…メッセージを送りたいんですが。 … messeeji o okuritain des(u) ga
by e-mail/fax	電子メール/ファックスで denshi-meeru/fakk(u)su de
What's your e-mail address?	電子メールのアドレスは何ですか。 denshi-meeru no adoresu wa nan des(u) ka
Can I access the Internet here?	インターネットにアクセスできますか。 intaanetto ni ak(u)sesu dekimas(u) ka
What are the charges per hour?	料金は1時間いくらですか。 ryookin wa ichi-jikan ikura des(u) ka

packages	小包
international money orders	外国為替
general delivery [poste restante]	局留め
stamps	切手
telegrams	電報

155

Souvenirs お土産

You will have no difficulty in finding any number of souvenirs and presents to take home. There is something for everybody and in every price range. If you are buying electrical goods, remember that Japan uses 100 volts and that television/video systems may not be compatible. The following are just a few suggestions.

dolls	人形	*ningyoo*
electrical goods	電気製品	*denki seehin*
fans	扇子	*sensu*
furoshiki*	風呂敷	*furosh(i)ki*
handicrafts	工芸品	*koogee-hin*
kimono	着物	*kimono*
lacquerware	漆器	*shikki*
ornaments	置物	*okimono*
paper crafts	紙細工	*kami zaiku*
pearls	真珠	*shinju*
porcelain	磁器	*jiki*
pottery	陶器/焼き物/瀬戸物	*tooki/yakimono/setomono*
prints	版画	*hanga*
sake (rice wine)	日本酒	*nihonshu*
woodblock prints	木版	*mok(u)han*
yukata (cotton bathrobe)	浴衣	*yukata*

*A cloth wrap tradionally used instead of a handbag for carrying things.

Gifts 贈り物

wine	ワイン	*wain*
chocolates	チョコレート	*chokoreeto*
calendar	カレンダー	*karendaa*
key ring	キーホルダー	*kii horudaa*
picture postcard	絵葉書	*e-hagaki*
souvenir guide	ガイドブック	*gaido bukku*
scarf	スカーフ	*s(u)kaafu*
T-shirt	Tシャツ	*tii shatsu*

Music 音楽

I'd like a …	…をください。 … o kudasai
cassette	カセット kasetto
compact disc	CD shii dii
videocassette	ビデオテープ bideo teepu
Who are the popular native singers/bands?	今はやりの日本の歌手/バンドは、だれですか。 ima hayari no nihon no kashu/bando wa dare des(u) ka

Toys and games おもちゃとゲーム

I'd like a toy/game …	…おもちゃ/ゲームが欲しいんですが。 … omocha/geemu ga hoshiin des(u) ga
for a boy	男の子用の otoko no ko yoo no
for a 5-year-old girl	5歳の女の子用の go-sai no on-na no ko yoo no
ball	ボール booru
chess set	チェスのセット chesu no setto
doll	人形 ningyoo
electronic game	コンピューターゲーム konpyuutaa geemu
pail and shovel [bucket and spade]	バケツとシャベル baketsu to shaberu

Antiques 骨董品

How old is this?	いつの品ですか。 itsu no shina des(u) ka
Do you have anything of the … era?	…時代のものはありますか。 … jidai no mono wa arimas(u) ka
Can you send it to me?	送ってもらえますか。 okutte morae mas(u) ka
Will I have problems with customs?	税関で問題になりますか。 zeekan de mondai ni narimas(u) ka
Is there a certificate of authenticity?	鑑定書はありますか。 kantee-sho wa arimas(u) ka

ARTISTIC PERIODS ➤ 104

Supermarket/Minimart
スーパー/コンビニ

There are plenty of large supermarkets that often sell household articles, toiletries, and clothing, too. In addition, most department store chains have a supermarket or food-hall section.

Even if you are not planning to buy food, it is an experience just to wander around the supermarkets, and especially the food halls: you will be amazed at the marvelous variety and strangeness of the items on sale.

There are also plenty of late-opening minimarts, called *convenience stores*. These sell a limited range of general food items and also ready-to-eat foods. They generally sell tobacco and alcohol as well.

At the supermarket スーパーで

Excuse me. Where can I find (a) …?	すみません。…はどこですか。 *sumimasen. … wa doko des(u) ka*
Do I pay for this here?	お金はここで払うんですか。 *o-kane wa koko de haraun des(u) ka*
Where are the carts [trolleys]/baskets?	カート/かごはどこですか。 *kaato/kago wa doko des(u) ka*
Is there a … here?	…はありますか。 *… wa arimas(u) ka*
pharmacy	薬局 *yakkyoku*

缶詰類	canned foods
乳製品	dairy products
鮮魚	fresh fish
鮮肉	fresh meat
生鮮食品	fresh produce
冷凍食品	frozen foods
家庭用品	household goods
鶏肉	poultry

Weights and measures
- **1 kilogram** or **kilo (kg)** = **1000 grams (g)**; **100 g** = 3.5 oz.; **1 kg** = 2.2 lb.; 1 oz. = **28.35 g**; 1 lb. = **453.60 g**
- **1 liter (l)** = 0.88 imp. quart or 1.06 U.S. quart; 1 imp. quart = **1.14 l**; 1 U.S. quart = **0.951 l**; 1 imp. gallon = **4.55 l**; 1 U.S. gallon = **3.8 l**

Food hygiene 食品衛生

開封後...日以内にお召し上がりください。	eat within ... days of opening
要冷蔵	keep refrigerated
賞味期限...	best before ...

At the minimart コンビニで

I'd like some of that/those.	それを少しください。 *sore o s(u)koshi kudasai*
I'd like ...	...をください。... *o kudasai*
this one/these	これ *kore*
that one/those	あれ *are*
to the left/right	左/右の *hidari/migi no*
over there/here	あそこ/ここの *asoko/koko no*
Where is/are the ...?	...はどこですか。 *... wa doko des(u) ka*
beer	ビール *biiru*
bread	パン *pan*
cheese	チーズ *chiizu*
cookies [biscuits]	クッキー *kukkii*
eggs	卵 *tamago*
ham	ハム *hamu*
jam	ジャム *jamu*
packed lunch (box)	お弁当 *o-bentoo*
milk	牛乳 *gyuunyuu*
potato chips [crisps]	ポテトチップス *poteto chippusu*
cola	コーラ *koora*
A cup of coffee, please.	コーヒーを一杯ください。 *koohii o ippai kudasai*
Could you warm this up?	これを温めてください。 *kore o atatamete kudasai*
That's all.	それで全部です。 *sore de zenbu des(u)*

– ano hamu go-hyaku guramu kudasai.
– *kore des(u) ka?*
– ee, roosu hamu des(u).
– *kash(i)komari mash(i)ta. … hoka ni nani ka?*
– korokke yon-ko onegai shimas(u).
– *doozo.*

Provisions/Picnic 常備食/ピクニック

butter	バター	*bataa*
cheese	チーズ	*chiizu*
cookies [biscuits]	クッキー	*kukkii*
eggs	卵	*tamago*
French fries [chips]	ポテトフライ	*poteto furai*
grapes	ぶどう	*budoo*
ice cream	アイスクリーム	*ais(u) kuriimu*
instant coffee	インスタントコーヒー	*ins(u)tanto koohii*
(loaf of) bread	パン	*pan*
margarine	マーガリン	*maagarin*
milk	牛乳	*gyuunyuu*
potato chips [crisps]	ポテトチップス	*poteto chippusu*
rolls	ロールパン	*rooru pan*
sausages	ソーセージ	*sooseeji*
beer	ビール	*biiru*
soft drinks	ソフトドリンク	*sof(u)to dorinku*
tea bags	ティーバッグ	*tii baggu*
wine	ワイン	*wain*

Japanese bakeries sell loaves of bread and rolls. However, there is a limited choice of brown/wholewheat bread. Sliced white loaves come in all thicknesses, including the enormously thick slices that are part of the modern Japanese breakfast. You will also find a large variety of rolls with interesting fillings cooked within the roll, for example potato and mayonnaise, tuna and spring onion. These are delicous hot. You will also find sandwiches with interesting fillings, like strawberries and cream! Many bakeries are self-service, so you can inspect and choose at your leisure. They also have an excellent selection of cakes and pastries, many of which you will recognize. In addition, there are a lot of small stores that sell a variety of delicious cakes and sweets, and often serve tea and coffee too.

Health

Doctor/General	161	Gynecologist	167	
Accident and injury	162	Hospital	167	
Symptoms	163	Optician		167
Health conditions	163	Dentist		168
Doctor's inquiries	164	Payment and		
Parts of the body	166	insurance		168

The Japanese health system is good, but health insurance is a must as doctors and dentists are expensive. For minor ailments your hotel or the Tourist Information Centre (TIC) can contact an English-speaking doctor. Hospitals with English-speaking staff include St Lukes International Hospital, the International Catholic Hospital in Tokyo; the Baptist Hospital in Kyoto; the Yodogawa Chioba Hospital in Osaka; and the Kaisei Hospital in Kobe.

You will find a large selection of imported medicines and toiletries at the American Pharmacy in Tokyo. For urgent dental treatment go to Oyama Dental Clinic, Tokyo ☎ (03)3221.4182.

Doctor/General 医者/一般

Where can I find a hospital/dental office [surgery]?	病院/歯医者はどこですか。 *byooin/ha-isha wa doko des(u) ka*
Is there a doctor/dentist who speaks English?	英語ができる医者/歯医者はいますか。 *eego ga dekiru isha/ha-isha wa imas(u) ka*
What are the office [surgery] hours?	診療時間は何時ですか。 *shinryoo jikan wa nan-ji des(u) ka*
Could the doctor come to see me here?	往診してくれますか。 *ooshin sh(i)te kure mas(u) ka*
Can I make an appointment for …?	…予約したいんですが。 *… yoyaku sh(i)tain des(u) ga*
today/tomorrow	今日/明日 *kyoo/ash(i)ta*
as soon as possible	できるだけ早く *dekirudake hayaku*
It's urgent.	至急お願いします。 *sh(i)kyuu onegai shimas(u)*
I've got an appointment with Doctor …	…先生に予約しました。 *… sensee ni yoyaku shimash(i)ta*

Accident and injury 事故とけが

My ... is hurt/injured.	...が、けがをしました。 *... ga kega o shimash(i)ta*
husband/wife	主人/家内 *shujin/kanai*
son/daughter	息子/娘 *mus(u)ko/musume*
friend	友人 *yuujin*
child	子供 *kodomo*
He/She is unconscious.	意識がありません。*ish(i)ki ga arimasen*
He/She is (seriously) injured.	(ひどい) けがです。*(hidoi) kega des(u)*
He/She is bleeding (heavily).	(かなり) 出血しています。 *(kanari) shukketsu sh(i)te imas(u)*
I have a blister.	水脹れができました。 *mizubukure ga dekimash(i)ta*
I have a boil.	できものがあります。 *dekimono ga arimas(u)*
I have a bruise.	打撲しました。*daboku shimash(i)ta*
I have a burn.	火傷しました。*yakedo shimash(i)ta*
I have a cut.	切り傷があります。 *kirikizu ga arimas(u)*
I have a graze.	擦り傷があります。*surikizu ga arimas(u)*
I have an insect bite.	虫に刺されました。 *mushi ni sasare mash(i)ta*
I have a lump.	こぶがあります。*kobu ga arimas(u)*
I have a rash.	発疹があります。*hasshin ga arimas(u)*
I have a strained muscle.	筋を違えました。*suji o chigae mash(i)ta*
I have a swelling.	腫れ物があります。 *haremono ga arimas(u)*
My ... hurts.	...が痛みます。*... ga itami mas(u)*

Symptoms 一時的症状

I've been feeling ill for … days.	…日くらい、具合が悪いんですが。… nichi kurai guai ga waruin des(u) ga
I feel faint.	めまいがします。memai ga shimas(u)
I have a fever.	熱があります。netsu ga arimas(u)
I've been vomiting.	もどしました。modoshi mash(i)ta
I've got diarrhea.	下痢しています。geri sh(i)te imas(u)
It hurts here.	ここが痛みます。koko ga itami mas(u)
I have a backache.	腰が痛みます。koshi ga itami mas(u)
I have cramps in my leg.	足がつりました。ashi ga tsuri mash(i)ta
I have an earache.	耳が痛みます。mimi ga itami mas(u)
I have a headache.	頭痛がします。zutsuu ga shimas(u)
I have a sore throat.	のどが痛みます。nodo ga itamimas(u)
I have a stomachache.	お腹が痛みます。o-naka ga itami mas(u)
I have sunstroke.	日射病にかかりました。nisshabyoo ni kakari mash(i)ta

Health conditions 健康状態

I have arthritis.	関節炎をわずらっています。kansetsuen o wazuratte imas(u)
I have asthma.	喘息です。zensoku des(u)
I am …	私は… watashi wa …
deaf	耳が聞こえません。mimi ga kikoe masen
diabetic	糖尿病です。toonyoo-byoo des(u)
epileptic	てんかん持ちです。tenkan mochi des(u)
handicapped	身体が不自由です。karada ga fujiyuu des(u)
(… months) pregnant	(…ケ月) 妊娠しています。(… kagetsu) ninshin sh(i)te imas(u)
I have a heart condition.	心臓が弱いです。shinzoo ga yowai des(u)
I have high blood pressure.	高血圧です。koo ketsuatsu des(u)
I had a heart attack … years ago.	…年前、心臓発作を起こしました。… nen mae shinzoo hossa o okoshi mash(i)ta

Doctor's inquiries 診察

いつからこの状態が 続いていますか。	How long have you been feeling like this?
こうなったのは、 初めてですか。	Is this the first time you've had this?
他に薬を飲んでいますか。	Are you taking any other medication?
何かのアレルギーはありますか。	Are you allergic to anything?
破傷風の予防注射は受け ましたか。	Have you been vaccinated against tetanus?
食欲はありますか。	Is your appetite OK?

Examination 検査

熱/血圧を計ります。	I'll take your temperature/ blood pressure.
袖をまくってください。	Roll up your sleeve, please.
腰まで服を脱いでください。	Please undress to the waist.
横になってください。	Please lie down.
口を開けてください。	Open your mouth.
深呼吸してください。	Breathe deeply.
咳をしてください。	Cough, please.
どこが痛みますか。	Where does it hurt?
ここが痛みますか。	Does it hurt here?

Diagnosis 診断

レントゲンを撮りましょう。	I want you to have an X-ray.
血液/大便/尿の検査を しましょう。	I want a specimen of your blood/stools/urine.
専門医に診てもらってください。	I want you to see a specialist.
病院に行ってください。	I want you to go to hospital.
骨折/捻挫しています。	It's broken/sprained.
脱臼/裂傷しています。	It's dislocated/torn.

これは…です。	You've got (a/an) …
盲腸炎	appendicitis
膀胱炎	cystitis
インフルエンザ	flu
食中毒	food poisoning
骨折	fracture
胃炎	gastritis
痔	hemorrhoids
ヘルニア	hernia
…の炎症	inflammation of …
はしか	measles
肺炎	pneumonia
座骨神経痛	sciatica
扁桃炎	tonsilitis
腫瘍	tumor
性病	venereal disease
化膿しています。	It's infected.
これは感染します。	It's contagious.

Treatment 治療

…をあげましょう。	I'll give you …
化膿止め	an antiseptic
痛み止め	a painkiller
…を処方します。	I'm going to prescribe …
抗生物質	a course of antibiotics
座薬	some suppositories
薬のアレルギーはありますか。	Are you allergic to any medication?
…1錠飲んでください。	Take one pill …
…時間毎に	every … hours
一日…回	… times a day
食前/食後に	before/after each meal
痛い時に	in case of pain
…日間	for … days
家へ帰られたら、ご自分の主治医に診ていただいてください。	Consult a doctor when you get home.

appendix	盲腸	*moochoo*
arm	腕	*ude*
back	背中	*senaka*
bladder	膀胱	*bookoo*
bone	骨	*hone*
breast	乳房	*chibusa*
chest	胸	*mune*
ear	耳	*mimi*
eye	目	*me*
face	顔	*kao*
finger/thumb	指/親指	*yubi/oya-yubi*
foot	足	*ashi*
gland	腺	*sen*
hand	手	*te*
head	頭	*atama*
heart	心臓	*shinzoo*
jaw	顎	*ago*
joint	関節	*kansetsu*
kidney	腎臓	*jinzoo*
knee	膝	*hiza*
leg	脚	*ashi*
lip	唇	*kuchibiru*
liver	肝臓	*kanzoo*
mouth	口	*kuchi*
muscle	筋肉	*kin-niku*
neck	首	*kubi*
nose	鼻	*hana*
rib	肋骨	*rokkotsu*
shoulder	肩	*kata*
skin	皮膚	*hifu*
stomach	胃	*i*
thigh	腿	*momo*
throat	喉	*nodo*
toe	足の指	*ashi no yubi*
tongue	舌	*sh(i)ta*
tonsils	扁桃腺	*hentoosen*
vein	血管	*kekkan*

Gynecologist 婦人科

I have abdominal pains.	腹痛がします。 fuk(u)tsuu ga shimas(u)
I have period pains.	生理痛がします。 seeritsuu ga shimas(u)
I have a vaginal infection.	膣炎があります。 chitsuen ga arimas(u)
I haven't had my period for ... months.	生理が...ヶ月間ありません。 seeri ga ... ka-getsu kan arimasen
I'm on the Pill.	ピルを飲んでいます。 piru o nonde imas(u)

Hospital 病院

Please notify my family.	家族に知らせてください。 kazoku ni shirasete kudasai
I'm in pain.	痛みます。itamimas(u)
I can't eat/sleep.	食べられ/眠れません。 taberare/nemure masen
When will the doctor come?	医者はいつ来ますか。 isha wa itsu kimas(u) ka
Which ward is ... in?	...はどの病室ですか。 ... wa dono byooshitsu des(u) ka
I'm visiting ...	...の見舞いに来ました。 ... no mimai ni kimash(i)ta

Optician 眼鏡店

I'm short-sighted / far- [long-] sighted.	私は近眼/遠視です。 watashi wa kingan/enshi des(u)
I've lost ...	...をなくしました。 ... o nakushi mash(i)ta
one of my contact lenses	片方のコンタクトレンズ katahoo no kontakuto renzu
my glasses/a lens	眼鏡/レンズ　megane/renzu
Could you give me a replacement?	代わりのをください。 kawari no o kudasai

Dentist 歯医者

I have toothache.	歯が痛みます。	*ha ga itami mas(u)*
This tooth hurts.	この歯が痛みます。	*kono ha ga itami mas(u)*
I've lost a filling/tooth.	詰物/歯が取れました。	*tsumemono/ha ga tore mash(i)ta*
Can you repair this denture?	この入れ歯を直せますか。	*kono ireba o naose mas(u) ka*
I don't want it extracted.	抜かないでください。	*nukanaide kudasai*

Payment and insurance 支払いと保険

注射をします/麻酔をかけます。	I'm going to give you an injection/ a anesthetic.
詰物/クラウンが必要です。	You need a filling/cap (crown).
抜かなければなりません。	I'll have to take it out.
応急の治療しかできません。	I can only fix it temporarily.
…時間、物を食べないで ください。	Don't eat anything for … hours.

How much do I owe you?	いくらですか。	*ikura des(u) ka*
I have insurance.	保険に入っています。	*hoken ni haitte imas(u)*
Can I have a receipt for my insurance?	保険の払い戻し用に、領収書をください。	*hoken no harai modoshi yoo ni ryooshuu-sho o kudasai*
Would you fill in this insurance form, please?	この保険用紙に記入してください。	*kono hoken yooshi ni kinyuu sh(i)te kudasai*

Dictionary
English - Japanese

To enable correct usage, most terms in this dictionary are either followed by an expression or cross-referenced to pages where the word appears in a phrase. The notes below provide some basic grammar guidelines.

Nouns

Japanese nouns have no articles. Plurals do not exist either. All nouns have one single form which does not change according to the noun's role in a sentence.

Adjectives

Japanese adjectives are very different from their English counterparts and in fact behave more like verbs. It may be helpful to think of the adjective as having *to be* attached to it. The past tense of most adjectives is formed by adding **-katta** to the basic stem:

takai	expensive	**yasui**	cheap
takakatta	(was) expensive	**yasukatta**	(was) cheap

Verbs

At first glance Japanese verbs are very straightforward having only present and past tenses and no special form to indicate person or number. Future meaning is gauged from the context.

However, verbs are subject to other changes to express a complexity of degrees of politeness and mood. The two basic verb forms are:

taberu	to eat	**nomu**	to drink
tabemasu	to eat (polite form)	**nomimasu**	to drink (polite form)

This phrase book uses the polite form throughout.

tabemasu	(I, you, he, she, we, they) eat
tabemasen	(I, you, he, she, we, they) don't/doesn't eat
tabemashita	(I, you, he, she, we, they) ate
tabemasen deshita	(I, you, he, she, we, they) didn't eat

Particles

Japanese uses a number of particles which mark the use of/add to the meaning of the word they follow in a sentence.

ga	subject marker	**nodo ga itai desu** *literal meaning*: The throat is sore.
wa	attention-directing marker	**watashi wa nodo ga itai desu** *literal meaning*: As for me the throat is sore.
o	object marker	**gohan o tabemasu** *literal meaning*: I eat rice.

a bit earlier
もう少し早く
moo s(u)koshi hayaku 147
a bit later もう少し遅く
moo s(u)koshi osoku 147
a cup of ... ...を一杯 o ippai 159
a few 少し s(u)koshi 15
a little 少し s(u)koshi 15
a lot たくさん tak(u)san 15
a.m. 午前 gozen
about (*approximately*) くらい kurai 15
abroad 海外 kaigai
accept: do you accept ...? ...を使え
ますか ... o tsukae mas(u) ka 42, 136
access, to (*Internet*) アクセスする
ak(u)sesu suru 155
access: no access 立入禁止
tachi-iri kinshi 81
accessories 雑貨 zakka 144
accident (*road*) 交通事故
kootsuu jiko 92
accidentally 間違って machigatte 28
accompaniments 付け合わせ
tsuke awase 38
accompany, to 連れていく
tsurete iku 65
accountant 会計士 kaikeeshi 121
acne にきび nikibi
acrylic アクリル akuriru
actor/actress 俳優/女優 haiyuu/joyuu
adapter アダプタ adap(u)ta 148
address 住所 juusho 84, 93, 126, 139
adjoining room 続きの部屋
tsuzuki no heya 22
admission charge 入場料
nyuujoo ryoo 114
admission free 入場無料
nyuujoo muryoo 101
adult 大人 otona 81, 100, 101
advance reservations 予約
yoyaku 109
advance, in 前もって mae motte 21
advice 相談 soodan 141
after (*place*) ...の後 ... no ato 95;
(*time*) 後 ato 13

after lunch 昼食後 chuushok(u) go
222; **~ meals** 食後 shokugo 140
after shave アフターシェーブ
afutaa sheebu 142
after-sun lotion アフターサン・ローショ
ン afutaa san rooshon 142
afternoon 午後 gogo 222
age 年齢 nenree 152
ago 前に mae ni 222
agree: I don't agree そうは思いません
soo wa omoi masen
aikido 合気道 aikidoo 114
air conditioning エアコン eakon 22, 25
air mattress エアマットレス
(ea) mattoresu 31
air pump エアポンプ eaponpu 87
air sickness bag ごみ袋
gomi bukuro 70
airmail 航空便 kookuubin 155
airport 空港 kuukoo 96
aisle seat 通路側の席
tsuuro gawa no seki 69, 74
alarm 警報 keehoo 21
alarm clock 目覚まし時計
mezamashi dokee 149
alcoholic (*drink*) 酒 sake
all-night pharmacy 夜間営業の薬局
yakan eegyoo no yakkyoku 140
allergic アレルギー arerujii 164
allowance (*duty*) 免税の範囲
menzee no han-i 67
almost ほとんど hotondo
alone ひとり hitori
also また mata
alter, to 直す naosu 137
alumin(i)um foil アルミホイル
arumi hoiru 148
always いつも itsumo 13
am: I am ... ...です ... desu
amazing すごい sugoi 101
ambassador 大使 taishi
ambulance 救急車 kyuukyuu sha 92
American (*adj*) アメリカ
amerika 150, 152
amount 金額 kingaku 42
amusement arcade ゲームセンター
geemu sentaa 113

HUDSON NEWS
Terminal C - North
Houston Intercontinental Airport

128238 Reg17 ID 23 10:30 am 07/17/00

S BERLITZ PHRASE BK	1 @ 7.95	7.95
SUBTOTAL		7.95
SALES TAX - 8.25%		.66
TOTAL		8.61
CASH PAYMENT		10.00
CHANGE		1.39

Thank you for your patronage.

an extra *(adj)* もう一つ
moo hitotsu 27
anaesthetic 麻酔 masui
and と to
anesthetic 麻酔 masui 168
animal 動物 doobutsu 106
anorak アノラック anorakku 145
another 他の hoka no 21, 125
antacid 制酸薬 seesan-yaku
antifreeze 不凍液 futooeki
antique 骨董品 kottoohin 157
antiseptic cream 傷薬 kizu gusuri 141
anyone: does anyone speak English?
英語ができる人はいますか。
eego ga dekiru hito wa imas(u) ka 11
apartment マンション manshon 28
apologize: I apologize すみません
sumimasen
appetite 食欲 shokuyoku 164
appointment 予約 yoyaku 161;
to make an ~ 予約をする
yoyaku o suru 147
approximately くらい gurai 152
April 四月 shi-gatsu 219
architect 設計者 sekkeesha 104
area code 市外局番
shigai kyokuban 127
around ... *(time)* ...ころ ... goro 13
arrivals 到着 toochaku 69, 73
arrive in, to 着く tsuku 76
arrive, to 到着する
toochaku suru 68, 70
art gallery 美術館 bijutsu kan 99
arthritis 関節炎 kansetsu en 163
artificial sweetener ダイエットシュガー
daietto shugaa 38
ashtray 灰皿 haizara 39
ask: I asked for ... ...を注文しました
... o chuumon shimashita 41
aspirin 頭痛薬
zutsuuyaku *(headache tablets)* 141
asthma 喘息 zensoku 163
at ... *(place)* ...で ... de 12;
(time) ...に ... ni 13
at last! やっと yatto 19
at least 最低 saitee 23
athletics 陸上競技 rikujoo kyoogi 114

ATM/cash machine
キャッシュコーナー
kyasshu koonaa 139
attack, to 襲う osou 152
attractive 魅力的 miryoku
teki
audioguide 案内テープ
an-nai teepu 100
August 八月 hachi-gatsu 219
aunt 伯母 oba 120
Australia オーストラリア
oos(u)toraria 119
authentic: is it authentic? 本物ですか
honmono des(u) ka
automatic *(car)* オートマチック
ootomachikku 86; **~ camera**
オートマチックカメラ ootomachikku
kamera 151; **~ automatic doors**
自動ドア jidoo doa 77
automobile 車 kuruma
autumn 秋 aki 219
avalanche なだれ nadare
awful ひどい hidoi 122

B **baby** 赤ちゃん aka chan 39,
113; **~ food** ベビーフード bebii
fuudo 142; **~ wipes** ウェットティッシ
ュ wetto tisshu 142; **~-sitter**
ベビーシッター bebii shittaa 113
back *(of body)* 後ろ ushiro 147
back by, to be ...までに戻る ...
made ni modoru 113
back, to be 戻る modoru 98, 222
backache, to have a 腰が痛む
koshi ga itamu 163
backpacking バックパッキング
bakku pakkingu
bad 悪い warui 14
bad *(at)* 下手 heta 126
bag バッグ baggu 67, 153
baggage 荷物 nimotsu 32, 69, 71
baggage check 手荷物一時預り所
tenimotsu ichiji azukari jo 71, 73
bakery パン屋 pan-ya 130
balcony ベランダ beranda 29
balding 禿げ上がっている
hageagatte iru 152

ball ボール booru 157
ballet バレエ baree 108, 111
band (musical group) バンド bando 111, 157
bandages 包帯 hootai 141
bank 銀行 ginkoo 96, 130, 138
bar (hotel) バー baa 26, 112
barber 床屋 tokoya 131
baseball 野球 yakyuu 114
basement 地下 chika
basket かご kago 158
basketball バスケットボール bas(u)ketto booru 114
bath バス basu 21
bath towel バスタオル basu taoru 27
bathroom 風呂場 furoba 29
bathroom (toilet) トイレ toire 26, 98, 113
battery 電池 denchi 137, 149, 151
battery (car) バッテリー batterii 88
battle site 戦場跡 senjoo ato 99
be back, to 戻る modoru 135
beach 海岸/ビーチ kaigan/biichi 107, 116
beard 髭 hige
beautiful 美しい utsukushii 14, 101
because ... ...から ... kara 15;
because of ... ...のため ... no tame 15
bed ベッド beddo 21
bed and breakfast 朝食込み chooshok(u) komi 24
bedroom 寝室 shinshitsu 29
beer ビール biiru 40, 159, 160
before (time) 前 mae 13
before lunch 昼食前 chuushok(u) mae 222
before meals 食前 shokuzen 140
begin, to 始める hajimeru
beginner 初心者 shoshinsha 117
beige ベージュ beeju 143
belong: this belongs to me これは私のです kore wa watashi no des(u)
belt ベルト beruto 144
berth 寝台 shindai 74, 77
best 一番良い ichiban ii

best before ... 賞味期限 shoomi kigen 159
best: all the best 頑張って ganbatte 220
better もっと良い motto ii 14
better quality もっと質の良い motto shitsu no ii 134
between ... and ... (time) ...から...の間 ... kara ... no aida 222
between jobs (unemployed) 求職中 kyuushok(u)chuu 121
bib よだれ掛け yodare kake
bicycle 自転車 jitensha 75, 83, 153
bidet ビデ bide
big 大きい ookii 14, 117, 134
bigger もっと大きい motto ookii 24
bikini ビキニ bikini 144
bill (hotel) 会計 kaikei 32
bill (restaurant) お勘定 o-kanjoo 42
bin liner ゴミ袋 gomi bukuro
binoculars 双眼鏡 soogankyoo
bird 鳥 tori 106
birthday 誕生日 tanjoobi 220
biscuits クッキー kukkii 159, 160
bite (insect) 虫刺され mushi sasare
bitten: I've been bitten by a dog 犬に噛まれました inu ni kamare mashita
bitter (taste) 苦い nigai 41
bizarre 気持ち悪い kimochi warui 101
black 黒 kuro 143
black (of coffee) ブラック burakku 40
black and white film (camera) 白黒フィルム shirokuro firumu 151
blanket 毛布 moofu 27
bleach 漂白剤 hyoohaku zai 148
bleeding (n) 出血 shukketsu 162
blinds ブラインド buraindo 25
blister (n) 水脹れ mizubukure 162
blocked, to be つまる tsumaru 25
blond ブロンド burondo 152
blood 血液 ketsueki 164; **~ group** 血液型 ketsueki gata; **~ pressure** 血圧 ketsuatsu 163, 164

blouse ブラウス burauzu 144

blow-dry ブロードライ
 buroo dorai 147

blue ブルー buruu 143

board, on 車内 shanai 78

boarding card 搭乗券 toojoo ken 70

boat trip 遊覧船 yuuransen 97, 81

boil (n) できもの dekimono 162

boiled 茹で yude

boiler ボイラー boiraa 29

book 本 hon 150

book, to 予約する yoyaku suru 21

booked up, (to be) 満員 man-in 115

booked: fully booked いっぱい
 ippai 162

booklet of tickets 回数券 kaisuu-ken 79

bookshop 本屋 hon-ya 130

boots (for sport) ブーツ buutsu 115, 145

boring つまらない tsumaranai 101

born: I was born in ...
 ...で生まれました
 ... de umare mash(i)ta

borrow: may I borrow your ...?
 ...を貸してください
 ... o kash(i)te kudasai

botanical garden 植物園
 shokubutsu en 99

bottle (counter) 本 hon (pon, bon) 37

bottle-opener 栓抜き sen-nuki 148

bottled (beer) 瓶入り bin-iri 40

bowel 結腸 ketchoo

bowls ボール booru 148

boy 男の子 otoko no ko 120, 157

boyfriend ボーイフレンド
 booifurendo 120

bra ブラジャー burajaa 144

bracelet ブレスレット buresuretto 149

bread パン pan 38, 159, 160

break, to 壊す kowasu 28

break down, to 壊れる kowareru 28

breakdown (of vehicle) 故障 koshoo 88

breakdown truck 牽引車 ken-in-sha 88

breakdown, have a (of vehicle) 壊れる
 kowareru 88

breakfast 朝食
 chooshoku
 23, 26, 27

breathe, to 息をする
 iki o suru 92

breathtaking 息を飲むほど
 iki o nomu hodo 101

bridge 橋 hashi 107

briefs (ladies) パンティー pantii 144

bring, to (a friend) 連れてくる
 tsurete kuru 125

Britain イギリス igirisu 119, 152

brochure パンフレット panfuretto

broken (bone) 骨折 kossetsu 164

broken, to be 壊れる
 kowareru 25, 137

bronchitis 気管支炎
 kikanshi en

brooch ブローチ buroochi 149

brother (older) 兄 ani 120

brother (younger) 弟 otooto 120

brothers (plural) 兄弟 kyoodai 120

brown 茶色 chairo 143

browse, to 見る miru 133

bruise (n) 打撲 daboku 162

brunette ブルネット
 burunetto 152

bucket バケツ baketsu 157

Buddhist temple 寺 tera 96, 99, 105

building ビル/建物 biru/tatemono

built, to be 建てられる taterareru 104

bulletin board 掲示板 keeji ban 26

bureau de change 両替所
 ryoogae jo 138

burger ハンバーガー hanbaagaa 40

burger stand ハンバーガーの店
 hanbaagaa no mise 35

burn (n) 火傷 yakedo 162

bus バス basu 70, 71, 78, 79, 123;
 ~ route バス路線 basu rosen 96;
 ~ station バスターミナル basu
 taaminaru 78; **~stop** バス停留所/
 バス停 bas(u) teeryuujo/bas(u) tee
 65, 78, 96

business: on ~ 仕事で shigoto de 66; **~ class** ビジネスクラス bijinesu kurasu 68; **~ hours** 営業時間 eegyoo jikan 132; **~ trip** 出張 shutchoo 123; **~man** サラリーマン sararii man 121

busy, to be *(occupied)* 約束がある yak(u)soku ga aru 125; *(restaurant)* 込み合う komiau 36

butane gas ブタンガス butan gasu 30, 31

butcher shop 肉屋 niku-ya 130

butter バター bataa 38, 160

button ボタン botan

buy, to 買う kau 97, 98

by ... *(time)* …までに ... made ni 13, 222; **~ car** 車で kuruma de 17, 94; **~ cash** 現金で genkin de 17; **~ credit card** (クレジット) カードで (kurejitto) kaado de 17

by the window 窓際 madogiwa 36

bye さよなら sayonara 10

C

cabaret キャバレー kyabaree 112

cabin キャビン kyabin 81

cable car ケーブルカー keeburu kaa 117; **~ TV** 有線テレビ yuusen terebi 22

café 喫茶店 kissaten 35, 40

cagoule ウインドブレーカー uindobureekaa 145

cake ケーキ keeki 40

calendar カレンダー karendaa 156

call for somebody, to *(person)* 迎えに行く mukae ni iku 125

call the police! 警察を呼んで keesatsu o yonde 92

call, to 呼ぶ yobu 92

call, to *(on phone)* 電話する denwa suru 127, 128

camera カメラ kamera 151, 153; **~ case** カメラのケース kamera no keesu 151; **~ shop** カメラ屋 kamera-ya 130

camp, to キャンプする kyanpu suru

campbed キャンプベッド kyanpu beddo 31

camping キャンプ kyanpu 30

camping equipment キャンプ用品 kyanpu yoohin 31

campsite キャンプ場 kyanpu joo 30, 123

can opener 缶切り kankiri 148

can you help me? 手伝ってください tetsudatte kudasai 18

can you recommend ...? …を教えてください ... o oshiete kudasai 112

Canada カナダ kanada 119

canal 運河 unga 107

cancel, to キャンセルする kyanseru suru 68

cancer *(disease)* 癌 gan

candy キャンデー kyandee 150

canned food 缶詰類 kanzume rui 158

cap 帽子 booshi 144

cap *(dental)* クラウン kuraun 168

car *(train compartment)* 車両 sharyoo 75

car 車 kuruma 81, 86, 88, 89, 123, 153; **by ~** 車で kurumade 95; **~ ferry** カーフェリー kaa ferii 81; **~ hire** レンタカー renta kaa 70, 86; **~ park** 駐車場 chuusha joo 26, 87, 96; **~ rental** レンタカー renta kaa 70, 86, 153

caravan キャンピングカー kyanpingu-kaa 30, 81

card *(phone)* カード kaado 155

cards *(playing)* トランプ toranpu 121

careful: be careful! 気をつけて ki o tsukete

carpet *(rug)* カーペット/絨毯 kaapetto/juutan

carrier bag 袋 fukuro

cases スーツケース suutsukeesu 69

cash 現金 genkin 136

cash card キャッシュカード kyasshu kaado 139

cash desk 会計 kaikee 132, 136

cash machine/ATM キャッシュコーナー kyasshu koonaa 139

cash, to 換金する kankin suru 138

cashier 会計 kaikee 132, 138

casino (illegal in Japan) カジノ kajino

cassette カセット kasetto 157

castle お城 o-shiro 99

castle remains 城跡 shiro ato 99

catch, to (bus) 乗る noru

Catholic カトリック katorikku 105

cave 洞窟 dook(u)tsu 107

CD CD shii dii; ~ **player** CDプレーヤー shii dii pureeyaa

cemetery 墓地 bochi 99

central heating セントラルヒーティング sentoraru hiitingu

ceramics 陶磁器 toojiki

certificate 証書 shoosho 149

certificate of authenticity 鑑定書 kantee sho 157

chain チェーン cheen 149

change (coins) 小銭 kozeni 87, 136

change (n) (payment) お釣り otsuri 136

change, to (baby) おむつを替える omutsu o kaeru 39

change, to (bus, train) 乗り換える norikaeru 75, 76, 78, 79, 80

change, to (money) 替える kaeru 138

change, to (reservation) 変更する henkoo suru 68

change: keep the change お釣りは結構 です otsuri wa kekkoo des(u) 84

changing facilities おむつを替える場所 omutsu o kaeru basho 113

changing room 更衣室 kooi shitsu 115

charcoal 炭 sumi 31

charge 料金/使用料 ryookin/ shiyoo-ryoo 30, 115, 155

charter flight チャーター便 chaataa bin

cheap 安い yasui 14, 134

cheaper もっと安い motto yasui 21, 24, 109, 134

check in, to チェックインする chekku-in suru 68

check-in desk チェックイン・デスク chekku-in desuku 69

check out, to (hotel) チェックアウト する chekku auto suru

checkout チェックアウト chekkuauto 32

cheers! 乾杯！ kanpai

cheese チーズ chiizu 159, 160

chemist 薬局 yakkyoku 131

chess チェス chesu 121; ~ **set** チェスのセット chesu no setto 157

chewing gum ガム gamu 150

child 子供 kodomo 152, 162

child's seat 子供用のイス kodomo yoo no isu 39; ~ **seat** (in car) チャイルド シート chairudo shiito; ~**minder** ベビーシッター bebii shittaa

children (your own) 子供 kodomo 22, 24, 39, 66, 74, 81, 100, 101, 113, 116, 120, 140; (another person's) お子さん okosan 120

children's menu 子供用のメニュー kodomo yoo no menyuu 39

childrenswear 子供服 kodomo fuku 143

China 中国 chuugoku 119

Chinese (cuisine) 中華料理 chuuka ryoori 35

chips ポテトフライ poteto furai 160

choc-ice チョコアイス choko aisu 110

chocolate (flavour) チョコレート chokoreeto 40; ~ **bar** チョコレート chokoreeto 150; ~ **ice** チョコアイス choko aisu 110

chocolates チョコレート chokoreeto 156

chopsticks 箸 hashi 39, 41, 148

Christmas クリスマス kurisumasu 220

church 教会 kyookai 96, 99, 105

cigarette kiosk タバコ屋 tabako-ya 130

cigarettes, packet of タバコ tabako 150

cigars 葉巻 hamaki 150

cinema 映画館 eega kan 96, 110

claim check (baggage) 荷物引換証 nimotsu hikikae shoo 71

claim form 紛失届用紙 funshitsu todoke yooshi 71

clean きれい kiree 14, 39, 41

clean, to クリーニングする kuriiningu suru 137

clearance (special offer) 特別奉仕 tokubetsu hooshi 133

cliff 崖 gake 107

cling film ラップ rappu 148

clinic 総合病院 soogoo byooin 131

cloakroom クロークルーム kurooku ruumu 109

clock 時計 tokee 149

close (near) 近く chikaku 95

close, to 閉まる shimaru 100, 140, 154

closed 閉館/閉店 heekan/heeten 101, 138

clothes 衣類 irui 144; **~ pins** 洗濯ばさみ sentaku basami 148

clothing 衣類 irui 143; **~ store** 洋服屋 yoofuku-ya 130

cloudy 曇り kumori 122

clubs (golf) クラブ kurabu 115

coach 長距離バス chookyori basu 78; **~ bay** バス停 bas(u) tee 78; **~ station** バスターミナル bas(u) taaminaru 78

coach (train compartment) 車両 sharyoo 75

coast 海岸 kaigan

coat コート kooto 144

coatcheck クロークルーム kurooku ruumu 109

coathanger ハンガー hangaa

cockroach ゴキブリ gokiburi

code (area, dialling) 市外番号 shigai bangoo

coffee コーヒー koohii 40, 159

coin コイン koin

cola コーラ koora 159

cold 冷たい tsumetai 14

cold (flu) 風邪 kaze 141

cold (weather) 寒い samui 122

cold, to be (food) 冷める sameru 41

collapse: he's collapsed 倒れました taore mash(i)ta

collect call コレクトコール korek(u)to kooru 127

collect, to 取りに来る tori ni kuru 151

color 色 iro 134, 143; **~ film** (camera) カラーフィルム karaa firumu 151

color, to (hair) 染める someru 147

comb 櫛 kushi 142

come, to 来る kuru 126

come back, to 戻る modoru 36

commission (charge) 手数料 tesuuryoo 138

compact camera コンパクトカメラ konpakuto kamera 151

compact disc CD shii dii 157

company (business) 会社 kaisha

company man 会社員 kaishain 121

complaint 苦情 kujoo 41, 137

composer 作曲者 sakkyok(u)sha 111

computer コンピュータ konpyuuta

concert コンサート konsaato 108, 111; **~ hall** コンサートホール konsaato hooru 111

concession 割引 waribiki

concussion: he has concussion 脳震とうです nooshintoo des(u)

conditioner コンディショナー/リンス kondishonaa/rinsu 142

condoms コンドーム kondoomu 141

conductor 指揮者 shikisha 111

confirm, to 確認する kakunin suru 22, 68

congratulations! おめでとう omedetoo

connection 連絡 renraku 76

conscious: he's conscious 意識があります ish(i)ki ga arimas(u)

constipation 便秘 benpi

consulate 領事館 ryoojikan 152

contact lens コンタクトレンズ kontakuto renzu 167

contact, to 連絡する renraku suru 28

contain, to 入っている haitte iru 39, 69

contemporary dance 現代舞踊 gendai buyoo 111

contraceptive 避妊薬 hinin-yaku

convenience store コンビニ konbini 130

cook (chef) コック kokku

cook, to 料理する ryoori suru

cooker コンロ konro 28

cookies クッキー kukkii 159, 160

cooking (cuisine) 料理 ryoori

cooking facilities 炊事場 suiji-ba 30

coolbox アイスボックス aisu bokkusu

copper 銅 doo 149

copy コピー kopii

corkscrew コルクスクリュー
koruku s(u)kuryuu 148

corner 角 kado 95

correct 正しい tadashii

cosmetics 化粧品 keshoohin

cot ベビーベッド bebii beddo 22

cottage (house) 家 ie 28

cotton 綿/コットン men/kotton 145

cotton (cotton wool) 脱脂綿
dasshimen 141

cough (n) 咳 seki 141, 164

country (nation) 国 kuni

country music カントリー kantorii 111

countryside 田舎 inaka 106

courier (guide) 添乗員 tenjooin

course (meal) コース koosu

cousin 従兄 itoko

cover charge カバーチャージ
kabaa chaaji 112

craft shop クラフトショップ
kurafuto shoppu

cramps in the leg, to have 足がつる
ashi ga tsuru 163

cream クリーム kuriimu 40

crèche 託児所 takuji sho

credit card （クレジット）カード
(kurejitto) kaado 42, 109, 136, 153

crib ベビーベッド bebii beddo 22

crisps ポテトチップス
poteto chippusu 159, 160

crockery and cutlery 食器 shokki 29

cross (crucifix) 十字架 juujika

cross, to (road) 渡る wataru 95

crossroad 交差点 koosaten 95

crowded 込み合う komiau 31

crown (dental) クラウン kuraun 168

cruise (n) クルーズ kuruuzu

crutches 松葉杖 matsuba zue

crystal (quartz) 水晶
suishoo 149

cup カップ kappu
39, 148

cupboard 戸棚 todana

curlers カーラー kaaraa

currency 通貨 tsuuka 67, 138;
~ exchange 両替所 ryoogae jo 70, 138

curtains カーテン kaaten

customs 税関 zeekan 67, 157

customs declaration 税関申告書
zeekan shinkoku sho 155

cut (n) 切り傷 kirikizu 162

cut and blow-dry カットとブロードライ
katto to buroo dorai 147

cut glass カットグラス
katto gurasu 149

cut, to 切る kiru 147

cutlery 食器類 shokki rui 148

cycle helmet サイクリング用ヘルメット
saikuringu-yoo herumetto

cycle path 自転車道 jitensha doo

cycle route サイクリングコース
saikuringu koosu 106

D daily 毎日 mainichi
dairy products 乳製品
nyuu seehin 158

damaged, to be 壊れる
kowareru 28, 71

damp (n) 湿気 shikke

dance (performance) 舞踊 buyoo 111

dance, to 踊る odoru 111

dancing, to go 踊りに行く
odori ni iku 124

danger 危険 kiken

dark (no light) 暗い kurai 14, 24

dark (color) 濃い koi 134, 143; darker
もっと濃い motto koi 143

date 日付 hizuke 23, 219

date of birth 生年月日 seenen gappi 23

daughter 娘 musume 120, 162

dawn 夜明け yoake 222

day 日 nichi/hi 97, 122

days (of the week) 曜日 yoobi 218

day trip 日帰り旅行 higaeri ryokoo

dead *(battery)* 上がる
agaru 88

deaf, to be
耳が聞こえない
mimi ga kikoenai 163

December 十二月
juu-ni-gatsu 219

deck chair デッキチェア
dekki chea 116

declare, to 申告する shinkoku suru 67

deduct, to *(money)* 差し引く sashihiku

deep 深い fukai

deep freeze *(freezer)* 冷凍庫 reetooko

deep fried 揚げ age

defrost, to 解凍する kaitoo suru

degrees *(temperature)* 度 do

delay: is there any delay
遅れていますか
okurete imas(u) ka 70

delicious おいしい oishii 14

deliver, to 配達する haitatsu suru

denim デニム denimu 145

dental floss デンタルフロス
dentaru furosu

dentist 歯医者 ha-isha 131, 161, 168

dentures 入れ歯 ireba 168

deodorant デオドラント
deodoranto 142

depart, to *(train, bus)* 出発する
shuppatsu suru

department *(section)* 売場 uriba 132;
~ store デパート depaato 96, 130

departure *(train)* 発車 hassha 76;
~ lounge 出発ロビー shuppats(u)
robii 69

departures 出発 shuppats(u) 69, 73

deposit 前金 maekin 24, 83, 115

destination 行先 ikisaki

details 詳細 shoosai

detergent 洗剤 senzai 148

detour まわり道
mawari michi 96

develop, to *(photos)*
現像する genzoo suru 151

diabetic 糖尿病
toonyoo byoo 39, 163

diagnosis 診断 shindan 164

dialling code 市外局番
shigai kyokuban 127

diamond ダイアモンド
daiamondo 149

diapers おむつ omutsu 142

diarrhea 下痢 geri 141, 163

diarrhoea: I have diarrhoea 下痢して
います geri shite imas(u)

dice サイコロ saikoro

dictionary 辞書 jisho 150

diesel ディーゼル diizeru 87

diet: I'm on a diet ダイエットしていま
す daietto shite imas(u)

different 違う chigau 135

difficult 難しい muzukashii 14

dining car *(train)* 食堂車
shokudoo-sha 75, 77

dining room 食堂/ダイニングルーム
shokudoo/dainingu ruumu 26, 29

dinner 食事 shokuji 112; **~ jacket**
タキシード takishiido

dinner, to have 食事をする
shokuji o suru 124

dipped beam ロービーム
roo biimu 86

direct *(of train)* 直通 chok(u)tsuu 75

direct, to: can you direct me to...?
...への行き方を教えてください ...
eno ikikata o oshiete kudasai 18

direction of , in the ...の方向
... no hookoo 95

directions 行き方 ikikata 94

director *(of company)* 役員 yakuin

directory *(telephone)* 電話帳
denwa-choo

Directory Enquiries 番号案内
bangoo an-nai 127

dirty 汚い kitanai 14

dirty: it's dirty 汚れています
yogorete imas(u) 28

disabled *(n)* 身体障害者
shintai shoogai sha 22, 100

discotheque ディスコ dis(u)ko 112

discount *(reduction)* 割引 waribiki 74,
100, 101

disgusting むかむかする
mukamuka suru

dish (meal) 料理 ryoori 37

dish cloth 布巾 fukin 148

dishwashing liquid 中性洗剤 tyuusee senzai 148

dislocated 脱臼 dakkyuu 164

display cabinet/case ショーケース shookeesu 134, 149

disposable camera 使い捨てカメラ tsukais(u)te kamera 151

disposable diapers [nappies] 紙おむつ kami omutsu 142

distilled water 蒸留水 jooryuusui

disturb: don't disturb 起こさないで ください okosanaide kudasai

dive, to 飛び込む tobikomu 116

diversion まわり道 mawari michi 96

dizzy: I feel dizzy くらくらします kurakura shimas(u)

do you have …? …はありますか。 … wa arimas(u) ka 37

do: things to do できること dekiru koto 123

doctor 医者 isha 92, 131, 161, 167

doll 人形 ningyoo 156, 157

dollar ドル doru 67, 138

door ドア doa 25

dosage 用量 yooryoo 140

double ダブル daburu 81; **~ bed** ダブルベッド daburu beddo 21; **~ room** ダブルルーム daburu ruumu 21

downstairs 下 sh(i)ta 12

downtown area 繁華街 hankagai 99

dozen, a 一ダースの… ichi-daasu no … 218

draft beer 生 nama 40

drain 下水 gesui

draught (wind) 隙間風 sukima kaze

draught beer 生 nama 40

dress ワンピース wanpiisu 144

drink (n) 飲物 nomimono 37, 70, 125

drink: can I get you a drink? 何か飲みますか nani ka nomi mas(u) ka 126

drinking water 飲料水 inryoosui 30

drive, to 運転する unten suru 141

driver 運転手 untenshu

driver's license 運転免許証 unten menkyo shoo 93

drop someone off, to 降ろす orosu 83

drowning: someone is drowning 誰かが溺れています dareka ga oborete imas(u)

drugstore 薬局／ドラッグストア yakkyoku/doraggu sutoa 130

drunk 酔っ払い yopparai

dry clean ドライクリーニング dorai kuriiningu 145; **~ cleaner** ドライクリーニング店 dorai kuriiningu ten 131

dubbed, to be 吹替えする fukikae suru 110

dummy (child's) おしゃぶり oshaburi

during … …の間 … no aida

dustbins ゴミ箱 gomi bako 30

duty free shop 免税店 menzee ten 67

duty: you must pay duty 関税がかかり ます kanzee ga kakari mas(u) 67

duvet 上掛け uwagake

E **e-mail** 電子メール denshi meeru 155; **~ address** 電子メールのアドレス denshi meeru no adoresu 155

ear drops 耳薬 mimi gusuri

earache, to have an 耳が痛む mimi ga itamu 163

early 早く hayaku 13, 125, 222

earrings イヤリング iyaringu 149

east 東 higashi 95

easy かんたん kantan 14

eat, to 食べる taberu 41, 167

eat: places to eat 食べるところ taberu tokoro 123

economy class エコノミー ekonomii 68

eggs 卵 tamago 159, 160

electric outlets 電源 dengen 30; **~ shaver** 電気かみそり denki kamisori

electricity 電気 denki 28; **~ meter** 電 気のメーター denki no meetaa 28

electronic equipment
電気製品 denki seehin 69,
156; ~ **flash** フラッシュ
furasshu 151; ~ **game**
コンピュータゲーム
konpyuuta geemu 157

elevator エレベーター
erebeetaa 26, 132

else: something else 何かほかの
nani ka hoka no

embassy 大使館 taishikan

emerald エメラルド emerarudo

emergency 緊急 kinkyuu 127

emergency brake
非常ブレーキ/緊急停止用ブレーキ
hijoo bureeki/kinkyuu teeshi yoo
bureeki 77; ~ **exit** 非常口
hijooguchi 78, 132

empty 空 kara 14

enamel 七宝 shippoo 149

end: at the end 突き当たり
tsukiatari 95

engaged, to be 婚約する
kon-yak(u) suru 120

engine エンジン enjin

engineer エンジニア enjinia 121

English (language) 英語 eego 11, 67,
100, 110, 150, 152, 161

English-speaking 英語ができる
eego ga dekiru 98, 152

enjoy, to 楽しむ tanoshimu 110

enlarge, to (photos) 引き伸ばす
hikinobasu 151

enough 十分 juubun 15

enough: to be enough 足りる
tariru 42, 136

entertainment guide 催し物案内
moyooshimono an-nai

entrance 入口 iriguchi 73, 132

entrance fee 入場料
nyuujoo ryoo 100

entry visa 入国ビザ nyuukoku biza

envelope 封筒 fuutoo 150

epileptic てんかん tenkan 163

equipment (sports) 道具 doogu 115

era 時代 jidai 157

error 間違い machigai

escalator エスカレーター
es(u)kareetaa 132

essential 必要な hitsuyoo na 89

estate agent 不動産屋 fudoosan-ya

EU 欧州連合 ooshuu rengoo

evening, in the 夕方 yuugata 222

events 催し物 moyooshi mono 108

every day 毎日 mainichi; ~ **hour**
1 時間に 1 本 ichi-jikan ni ippon 76;
~ **month** 毎月 mai tsuki 219; ~ **week**
毎週 mai shuu 13; ~ **year** 毎年
mai toshi 219

examination (medical) 検査 kensa

example, for 例えば tatoeba

except ... ...を除いて ... o nozoite

excess baggage 重量超過
juuryoo chooka 69

exchange rate (為替) レート
(kawase) reeto 138

exchange, to 取り替える
torikaeru 137

exchange, to (money) 両替する
ryoogae suru 138

excluding meals 食事抜き
shokuji nuki 24

excursion エクスカーション
ek(u)sukaashon 97, 98

excuse me (apology) すみません
sumimasen 10

excuse me (attention) すみません/
失礼します sumimasen/shitsuree
shimas(u) 10, 37, 94

exhausted, to be 疲れる
tsukareru 106

exit 出口 deguchi 70, 73, 78, 83, 132

expensive 高い takai 14, 134

experienced 経験者 keekensha 117

expiry date 有効期限
yuukoo kigen 109

exposure (photos) 枚撮り
mai dori 151

express 速達 sok(u)tatsu 155

extension 内線 naisen 128

extra night もう一泊 moo ippaku 23

extract, to 抜く nuku 168

F **fabric** 生地 kiji 145
facial フェーシャル
feesharu 147
facilities 設備 setsubi 22
factor ... SPF ... es(u) pii efu ... 142
faint めまい memai 163
fairground 遊園地 yuuenchi 113
fall (season) 秋 aki 219
family 家族 kazoku 66, 74, 120, 167
famous 有名 yuumee
fan (electric) 扇風機 senpuuki 25
fan (hand-held) 扇子 sensu 156
far-sighted 遠視 enshi 167
far: how far is it?
距離はどのくらいですか
kyori wa dono kurai des(u) ka 73
farm 農家 nooka 107
fast 速い hayai 93
fast, to be (clock) 進む susumu 222
fast food ファストフード faas(u)to
fuudo 40; **~ restaurant** ファスト
フードの店 faas(u)to fuudo no mise 35
fat 脂肪 shiboo 39
father 父 chichi 120
faucet 蛇口 jaguchi 25
faulty: this is faulty 壊れています
kowarete imas(u)
favorite [favourite] 大好きな daisuki na
fax ファックス fakkusu 155
February 二月 ni-gatsu 219
feed, to (baby): (breast milk) おっぱい
oppai; (formula milk) ミルクをあげる
miruku o ageru 39
feeding bottle 哺乳瓶 honyuubin
feel ill, to 具合が悪い
guai ga warui 163
female 女 on-na 152
ferry フェリー ferii 81, 123
fever 熱 netsu 163
fiancé(e) フィアンセ fianse
field 野原 nohara 107
fifth 五番 go-ban 218
fight (brawl) けんか kenka
fill in, to 記入する kinyuu suru
139, 155, 168
filling (dental) 詰物 tsumemono 168

film 映画 eega
108, 110
film (camera) フィルム
firumu 151
filter (camera)
フィルター firutaa 151
find, to: I'd like to find ...
... を探しているんですが
... o sagash(i)te irun des(u) ga 18
fine (good) 結構 kekkoo 19
fine (Fine, thank you.)
おかげさまで o-kage sama de 19, 118
fine (penalty) 罰金 bakkin 93
fire alarm 火災警報 kasai keehoo;
~ department [brigade] 消防車
shooboo sha 92; **~ escape**
非常階段 hijoo kaidan; **~ exit** 非常口
hijooguchi 132; **~ extinguisher** 消化器
shookaki
fire: There's a fire! 火事だ！ kaji da
firewood たきぎ takigi
first 最初/一番 saisho/ichi-ban
68, 75, 218
first class (plane) ファーストクラス
faas(u)to kurasu 68
first class (train) グリーン車
guriin-sha 74
first name 名 mee 23
fish restaurant 魚料理の店
sakana ryoori no mise 35
fish store 魚屋 sakana-ya 130
fishing rod 釣り竿 tsurizao
fishing, to go 釣りに行く tsuri ni iku
fishmonger 魚屋 sakana-ya 130
fit, to (clothes) 身体に合う
karada ni au 146
fitness room フィットネスルーム
fittonesu ruumu 115
fitting room 試着室
shichaku shitsu 146
fix, to 治療する chiryoo suru 168
flash (camera) フラッシュ furasshu 151
flashlight 懐中電灯 kaichuu dentoo 31
flat (tire/tyre) パンク panku 83, 88
flavor: what flavours do you have?
どの味がありますか dono aji ga
arimas(u) ka

flea のみ nomi

flight 便 bin 68, 70; **~ number** 便名 bin mee 68

flip-flops ビーチサンダル biichi sandaru 145

floor (level) 階 kai 132

florist 花屋 hana-ya 130

flour 小麦粉 komugiko 39

flower 花 hana 106

flush: the toilet won't flush トイレの水が流れません toire no mizu ga nagare masen

fly (insect) ハエ hae

foggy 霧 kiri 122

folk art 民芸 mingee; **~ music** フォーク fooku 111

follow, to (pursue) 後を付ける ato o tsukeru 152

food 食べ物 tabemono 119

food hygiene 食品衛星 shokuhin eesee 159

foot path 小道 komichi

football サッカー sakkaa 114

for a day 1日間 ichi-nichi kan 86

for a week 1週間 isshuukan 86

for ... days …日間 … nichi kan 140

for ... hours …時間 … jikan 13

forecast 予報 yohoo 122

foreign currency 外国通貨 gaikok(u) tsuuka 138

forest 森 mori 107

forget, to 忘れる wasureru 42

fork フォーク fooku 39, 41, 148

form 用紙 yooshi 23, 139, 153, 168

formal dress 正装 seesoo 111

fortnight 2週間 ni-shuukan

fortunately 幸い saiwai 19

fountain 噴水 funsui 99

four-door car 4ドア車 foo-doa sha 86

four-wheel drive 4輪駆動車 yon-rin kudoo sha 86

fourth 四番 yon-ban 218

foyer (hotel/theatre) ロビー robii

frame (glasses) フレーム fureemu

free (not busy) 暇 hima 124

free: to be free (available) 空いている aite iru 36

freezer 冷凍庫 reetooko 29

French dressing フレンチドレッシング furenchi doresshingu 38

French fries ポテトフライ poteto furai 160

frequent: how frequent? たくさんありますか tak(u)san arimas(u) ka 76

frequently 頻繁に hinpan ni

fresh 新鮮 shinsen 41; **~ fish** 鮮魚 sengyo 158; **~ meat** 鮮肉 sen-niku 158; **~ produce** 生鮮食品 seesen shokuhin 158

Friday 金曜日 kin-yoobi 218

fried 炒め itame

friend 友人 yuujin 162

friendly 親切な shinsetsu na

fries ポテトフライ poteto furai 38, 40

frightened, to be 怖がる kowagaru

fringe (hairstyle) 前髪 maegami 147

from ... (place) …から … kara 12, 119

from ... to ... (time) …から…まで … kara … made 13, 222

front 前 mae 147

front door 正面玄関 shoomen genkan 26

frosty, to be 霜が降りる shimo ga oriru 122

frozen foods 冷凍食品 reetoo shokuhin 158

frying pan フライパン furaipan 29

fuel (gas/petrol) ガソリン gasorin 86

full いっぱい ippai 14

full beam ハイビーム hai biimu 86

full board (American Plan [A.P.]) 3食込み san-shok(u) komi 24

full insurance 総合保険 soogoo hoken 109

full up (restaurant) 満席 manseki 36

fun, to have 楽しむ tanoshimu

funny おかしい okashii 126

furniture 家具 kagu

further (extra) 他に hoka ni 136

fuse ヒューズ hyuuzu 28; **~ box** ヒューズボックス hyuuzu bokkusu 28

game 試合 shiai 114; *(toy)*
ゲーム geemu 157

garage 修理工場 shuuri koojoo 88

garbage bags ごみ袋
gomi bukuro 148

garden 庭 niwa

gas ガソリン gasorin 87, 88;
~ bottle ガスタンク gas(u) tanku 28;
~ station ガソリンスタンド gasorin
s(u)tando 87

gas: I smell gas! ガス臭い！ gasu kusai

gate *(airport)* ゲート geeto 70

gauze 包帯 hootai 141

gay club ゲイバー gee baa 112

gel *(hair)* ジェル jeru 142

general delivery 局留め
kyoku dome 155

genuine 本物 honmono 134

get back, to 戻る modoru 98

get off, to 下りる oriru 79

get to, to *(find)* 行く iku 70

get to, to *(arrive)* 着く tsuku 77

get, to *(board bus, train)* 乗る
noru 78, 84

gift 贈り物 okurimono 67, 156;
~ shop 売店/ギフトショップ
baiten/gifuto shoppu 101, 131

girl 女の子 on-na no ko 120, 157

girlfriend ガールフレンド
gaarufurendo 120

glass グラス/コップ gurasu/koppu
39, 148

glasses *(optical)* 眼鏡 megane 167

glossy finish *(photos)* 光沢仕上げ
kootaku shiage

glove 手袋 tebukuro

go away! あっちへ行け atchi e ike

go back, to *(turn around)* 戻る
modoru 95

go for a walk, to 散歩に行く
sanpo ni iku 124

go out, to 出かける dekakeru

go shopping, to 買い物に行く
kaimono ni iku 124

go, to 行く iku 18

go: let's go! 行きましょう ikimashoo

**go: where does this
bus go?** このバスはどこ
行きですか kono basu
wa doko yuki des(u) ka

goggles ゴーグル
googuru

gold 金 kin 149

gold-plate 金メッキ kin mekki 149

golf ゴルフ gorufu 114; **~ course**
ゴルフ場 gorufu joo 115

good 良い ii 14; *(food)* おいしい
oishii 35, 42; **~ afternoon** こんにちは
kon nichi wa 10; **~ evening** こんばん
は konban wa 10; **~ morning** おはよ
うございます ohayoo gozaimas(u) 10;
~ night おやすみなさい oyasumi
nasai 10

good value 安い yasui 101

good-bye さようなら saoonara 10

grandparents *(your own)*
祖父母 sofubo

grapes ぶどう budoo 160

grass 芝生 shibafu

gratuity チップ chippu

gray [grey] グレー guree 143;
~ haired 白髪頭 shiraga atama 152

graze *(n)* 擦り傷 surikizu 162

greasy *(hair)* 脂性 aburashoo

great たいへん結構 taihen kekkoo 19

green グリーン guriin 143

greengrocer 八百屋 yaoya 131

greetings あいさつ aisatsu 220

grilled 焼き yaki

grocer *(grocery store)* 食料品店
shokuryoo-hin ten

ground *(earth)* 地面 jimen 31

groundcloth [groundsheet]
グランドシート gurando shiito 31

group グループ/団体
guruupu/dantai 66, 100

guarantee 保証 hoshoo 135

guest house 民宿 minshuku 123

guide *(tour)* ガイド gaido 98

guidebook ガイドブック
gaido bukku 100, 150

guided tour ガイド付ツアー
gaido tsuki tsuaa 100

guided walk ハイキングツアー haikingu tsuaa 106

guitar ギター gitaa

gum (dental) 歯ぐき haguki

guy rope ガイロープ gai roopu 31

gynecologist 婦人科 fujin-ka 167

H

haemorrhoids 痔 ji

hair 髪 kami 147; **~ mousse** ムース muusu 142; **~ spray** ヘアスプレー hea supuree 142

haircut ヘアカット heakatto

hairdresser 美容院 biyooin 131, 147

half a tank タンクの半分 tanku no hanbun 218

half an hour 三十分 sanjippun 218

half board (Modified American Plan [M.A.P.]) 2食込み ni-shok(u) komi 24

half past ... ...時半 ... ji han 221

half, a 半分 hanbun 218

ham ハム hamu 159

hammer ハンマー hanmaa 31

hand luggage 手荷物 tenimotsu 69

hand washable 手で洗える te de araeru 145

handbag ハンドバッグ hando baggu 144, 153

handicap (golf) ハンディ handi

handicapped 身体が不自由 karada ga fujiyuu 163

handicrafts 工芸品 koogee hin 156

handkerchief ハンカチ hankachi

handwash 手洗い te arai 145

hang-glider ハンググライダー hangu guraidaa

hanger ハンガー hangaa 27

hangover (n) 二日酔い futsuka yoi 141

happy: I'm not happy with the service サービスが良くありません saabisu ga yoku arimasen

harbor [harbour] 港 minato

hat 帽子 booshi 144

hatchback ハッチバック hatchibakku

have, to ある aru 133

have, to: can I have ...? ...をお願いします ... o onegai shimas(u) 18

hay fever 花粉症 kafun shoo 141

head, to (travel) 行く iku 83

headache 頭痛 zutsuu 163

health food store 健康食品店 kenkoo shok(u)hin ten 131

hear, to 聴く kiku

hearing aid 補聴器 hochooki

heart attack 心臓発作 shinzoo hossa 163

heart condition 心臓が弱い shinzoo ga yowai 163

hearts (cards) ハート haato

heat 暖房 danboo 25

heater ヒーター hiitaa

heating 暖房 danboo 25

heavy 重い omoi 34, 69, 134

height 身長 shinchoo 152

hello こんにちは kon-nichi-wa 10, 118

hello (on telephone) もしもし moshi moshi 128

help, to 手伝う tetsudau 18

help: can you help me? 助けてください tas(u)kete kudasai 92

her(s) 彼女の kanojo no 16

here ここ koko 12

hers: it's hers 彼女のです kanojo no des(u)

hi! こんにちは kon-nichi-wa 10

high 多い ooi 122

high beam ハイビーム hai biimu 86

high street 大通り oodoori 96

highlight, to ハイライトを入れる hairaito o ireru 147

highway 高速道路 koosoku dooro 88, 94

hiking ハイキング haikingu

hiking boots 登山靴 tozan gutsu 145

hill 丘 oka 107

hire, for 空車 kuusha 84

hire, to 借りる kariru 83, 86, 115, 116, 117

his 彼の kare no 16

his: it's his 彼のです kare no des(u)

historic site 史跡 shiseki 99

hitchhiking ヒッチハイク
hitchi haiku 83

HIV-positive HIV陽性
etchi-ai-bui yoosee

hobby (pastime) 趣味 shumi 121

hold on, to 待つ matsu 128

hole (in clothes) 穴 ana

holiday 観光/ホリデー
kankoo/horidee 66, 123

holiday resort リゾート rizooto

home 家 uchi 126

home address 現住所 genjuusho 23

home: we're going home 家へ帰ります
uchi e kaeri mas(u)

homosexual (adj) ホモ homo

honeymoon: we're on honeymoon
ハネムーンです hanemuun des(u)

horse 馬 uma

horseracing 競馬 keeba 114

hospital 病院 byooin 96, 131, 164, 167

hot 熱い atsui 14, 122

hot dog ホットドッグ
hotto doggu 110

hot spring 温泉 onsen 107

hot water お湯 oyu 25

hotel ホテル hoteru 21, 65, 123, 125

hour 時間 jikan 97

hour, in an 1時間後に
ichi-jikan go ni 84

house 家 ie

household articles 日用品
nichiyoo hin 148

housewife 主婦 shufu 121

how are things? いかがですか
ikaga des(u) ka 19

how are you? お元気ですか
o-genki des(u) ka 118

how long? どのくらい dono kurai 76,
78, 88, 94, 98, 135

how many times? 何回 nan-kai 140

how many? いくつ ik(u)tsu 15, 80

how much? (money) いくら ikura 15,
21, 79, 84, 98, 100, 109

how much? (quantity) どのくらい
dono kurai 140

how old? 何歳 nan-sai 120

how? 何で
nani de 17

hundred 百 hyaku 217

hungry: I'm hungry お腹
がすきました o-naka ga
suki mash(i)ta

hurry: I'm in a hurry 急いでいます
isoide imas(u)

hurt, to 痛む itamu 164

hurt: my ... hurts …が痛みます
... ga itami mas(u) 162

hurt: no one is hurt けが人はいません
keganin wa imasen 92

husband 主人 shujin 120, 162

hypermarket 大型スーパー
oogata suupaa

I **I don't mind.** 何でも結構です
nandemo kekkoo des(u) 19

I'd like (some) ... …をください
o kudasai 18, 37, 40

I'd like to ... …したいんですが
... sh(i)tain des(u) ga 36

I'll have ... …にします
... ni shimas(u) 37

I'm looking for ...
…を探しているんですが
... o sagashite irun des(u) ga 143

I've lost ...
…をなくしました
... o nak(u)shi mashita 153

ice アイス/氷 aisu/koori 38

ice cream アイスクリーム
ais(u) kuriimu 40, 160

ice cream parlour
アイスクリーム・パーラー
ais(u)kuriimu paaraa 35

icy 氷点下 hyootenka 122

identification 身分証明
mibu shoomee 136, 139

ill: I'm ill 気分がすぐれません
kibun ga sugure masen

illegal: is it illegal? 法律違反ですか
hooritsu ihan des(u) ka

imitation イミテーション
imiteeshon 134

immediately 今すぐ ima sugu 13

in front of ... ...の前 ... no mae 125

in the morning 朝 asa 140

in ... (object) ...の中 ... no naka 12

in ... (place) ...に ... ni 12

in ... (time) ...以内に ... inai ni 13

included 込み komi 23

included: is ... included? ...付きですか ... tsuki des(u) ka 98

incredible すてき suteki 101

indicate, to (driving) 指示を出す shiji o dasu

indigestion 消化不良 shooka furyoo

indoor pool 屋内プール okunai puuru 116

inexpensive 安い yasui 35

informal (dress) 普段着 fudangi

information 案内 an-nai 73, 97

Information (telephone) 番号案内 bangoo an-nai 127

information desk 案内所 an-nai gakari 73; **~ office** 案内所 an-nai jo 96

injection 注射 chuusha 168

injured, to be けがをする kega o suru 92, 162

innocent (legal) 無罪 muzai

insect 虫 mushi 25; **~ bite** 虫刺され mushi sasare 141; **~ repellent** 虫除け mushi yoke 141

inside 中 naka 12

insomnia 不眠症 fuminshoo

instant coffee インスタントコーヒー ins(u)tanto koohii 160

instead of ... ...の代わりに ... no kawari ni

instructions 説明書 setsumee sho 135

instructor コーチ coochi 115

insulin インシュリン inshurin

insurance 保険 hoken 86, 89, 93, 168

~ card (certificate) (car) 自動車保険証 jidoosha hoken shoo 93; **~ claim** 証の申請 hoken no shinsee 153; **~ company** 保険会社 hoken gaisha 93

interest (hobby) 趣味 shumi 121

interesting おもしろい omoshiroi 101

international money order 外国為替 gaikoku kawase 155

International Student Card 国際学生証 kok(u)sai gak(u)see shoo 29

Internet インターネット intaanetto 155

interpreter 通訳 tsuuyaku 93, 153

intersection 交差点 koosaten 95

introduce: may I introduce ... こちらは...さんです kochira wa ... wan des(u) 118

invitation 招待 shootai 124

iodine ヨードチンキ yoodochinki

Ireland アイルランド airurando 119

iron, to アイロン掛け airon kake 143

is it ...? ...ですか ... des(u) ka 17

is this ...? これは...ですか kore wa ... des(u) ka 145

is/are there ...? ...はありますか ... wa arimas(u) ka 17

island 島 shima 107

it is (it's ...) ...です ... des(u) 17, 221

Italian (cuisine) イタリア料理 itaria ryoori 35

itch: It itches かゆいです kayui des(u)

itemized bill 明細書 meesaisho 32

J **jacket** ジャケット/上着 jeketto/uwagi 144

jam ジャム jamu 159

jammed, to be 開かない akanai 25

January 一月 ichi-gatsu 219

Japan 日本 nihon 119

Japanese (language) 日本語 nihongo 11, 110, 126

Japanese noodle restaurant そば屋 soba ya 35

jazz ジャズ jazu 111

jeans ジーパン/ジーンズ jiipan/jiinzu 144

jellyfish くらげ kurage

jet lag: I'm jet lagged 時差ぼけしています jisaboke shite imas(u)

jet-ski ジェットスキー jetto s(u)kii 116

jeweler 宝石店 hooseki ten 131, 149
Jewish (people) ユダヤ人 yudaya jin
job: what's your job? お仕事は何ですか
o-shigoto wa nan des(u) ka
join, to 参加する sanka suru 115
join: may we join you ご一緒できます
か go-issho dekimas(u) ka 124
joint passport ジョイントパスポート
jointo pas(u)pooto 66
joke ジョーク jooku
journalist ジャーナリスト
jaanaris(u)to
judo 柔道 juudoo 114
jug (of water) 水差し mizusashi
July 七月 shichi-gatsu 219
jump leads ブースターコード
buus(u)taa koodo
jumper ジャンパー janpaa
junction (intersection) 交差点
koosaten
June 六月 roku-gatsu 219

K kaolin カオリン kaorin
karaoke カラオケ karaoke 111
karate 空手 karate 114
keep: keep the change!
お釣りはいりません
otsuri wa irimasen
kendo 剣道 kendoo 114
kerosene stove 小型コンロ
kogata konro 31
kerosine 灯油 tooyu
ketchup ケチャップ kechappu 38
kettle やかん yakan 29
key 鍵 kagi 27, 28, 88
key ring キーホルダー
kii horudaa 156
kiddie pool 子供用のプール
kodomo yoo no puuru 113
kimono 着物 kimono 156
kind (pleasant) 優しい yasashii
kind: what kind of ... どんな種類の…
don-na shurui no …
kiosk キオスク kios(u)ku
kiss, to キスする kisu suru
kitchen キッチン kitchin 29

knapsack ナップ
ザック
nappuzakku 31, 145
knickers ショーツ
shootsu
knife ナイフ naifu 39, 41,
148
knight (chess) ナイト naito
know: I don't know 分かりません
wakarimasen 23

L label ラベル raberu
lace レース reesu 145
lacquerware 漆器 shikki 156
ladder はしご hashigo
ladieswear 婦人服 fujin fuku 143
lake 湖 mizuumi 107
lamp ランプ ranpu 25, 29
land, to 到着する toochaku suru 70
language course 語学コース
gogaku koosu; **~ school** 語学学校
gogaku gakkoo
large 大きい ookii 69
larger もっと大きい motto ookii 134
last 最後 saigo 68, 75
last (with dates) 前の mae no 219
last name 姓 see 23
last train 終電 shuuden 80
last, to 続く tsuzuku
late 遅く osoku 125
late, to be (delayed) 遅れる
okureru 70
laundromat コインランドリー
koin randorii 131
laundry facilities 洗濯場 sentaku-ba 30;
~ service 洗濯サービス sentak(u)
saabisu 22
lavatory トイレ toire
lawyer 弁護士 bengoshi 152
laxative 通じ薬 tsuuji-yaku
lead, to (road) 通じる tsuujiru 94
leader (of group) リーダー riidaa
leak, to (roof/pipe) 漏れる moreru
learn, to (language/sport) 習う narau
leather 革 kawa 145
leave me alone! 構わないでください
kamawanaide kudasai 126

A-Z

leave, to *(depart to known destination)* 出発する shuppats(u) suru 32, 68, 81

leave, to *(go)* 行く iku 126

leave, to *(set off)* 出る deru 76, 78, 98

leave: I've left my bag バッグを忘れました baggu o wasure mash(i)ta

left, on the 左 hidari 76, 95, 159

left-luggage office 手荷物一時預り所 tenimotsu ichiji azukari jo 71, 73

legal: is it legal? 合法ですか goohoo des(u) ka

leggings スパッツ s(u)pattsu 144

lemon レモン remon 38

lemonade レモネード remoneedo

lend: could you lend me ...? …を貸してください … o kashite kudasai

length 長さ nagasa

lens レンズ renzu 151, 167

lens cap *(camera)* レンズのキャップ renzu no kyappu 151

lesbian club レスビアンクラブ resubian kurabu

lesson レッスン ressun

let, to: let me know! 知らせてください shirasete kudasai

letter 手紙 tegami 154

letterbox 郵便受け yuubin uke

level *(of ground)* 平らな tairana 31

library 図書館 toshokan

lie down, to 横になる yoko ni naru 164

life preserver [belt] 救命ベルト kyuumee beruto 81; **~boat** 救命ボート kyuumee booto 81; **~guard** 救助員 kyuujoin 116; **~jacket** 救命胴衣 kyuumee dooi

lift エレベーター erebeetaa 26, 132

lift *(ski)* リフト rifuto 117

lift pass *(ski)* リフト券 rifuto ken 117

light *(bicycle)* ライト raito 83

light *(color)* 薄い usui 134, 143

light *(electric)* 電気 denki 25

light *(vs dark)* 明るい akarui 14, 24

light *(vs heavy)* 軽い karui 14, 134

light bulb 電球 denkyuu 148

lighter *(cigarette)* ライター raitaa 150

like this *(similar to)* こんな kon-na

like, to 好き suki 101, 111, 121;
I ~ it 好きです suki des(u);
I don't ~ it 好きではありません suki dewa arimasen

like: I'd like ... …が欲しいんですが … ga hoshiin des(u) ga 133

limousine リムジン rimujin

line *(subway/metro)* 線 sen 80

linen 麻 asa 145

lipstick 口紅 kuchibeni

liqueur リキュール rikyuuru

liquor store 酒屋 saka-ya 131

liter リットル rittoru 87

little *(small)* 小さい chiisai

live, to 住む sumu 119

living room リビングルーム ribingu ruumu 29

lobby *(theater/hotel)* ロビー robii

local 地方 chihoo 37

local *(cuisine)* 郷土料理 kyoodo ryoori 35

lock 鍵 kagi 25

lock, to ロックする rokku suru 88

locked, to be 閉まる shimaru 26

long 長い nagai 14, 146

long hair ロングヘア rongu hea 152

long sleeves 長袖 nagasode 144

long way 遠く tooku 95

long-distance bus 長距離バス chookyori basu 78

long-sighted 遠視 enshi 167

look for, to 探す sagas(u) 18

look, to: I'm just looking 見ているだけです mite iru dake des(u)

looking for, to be 探している sagash(i)te iru 133

loose ゆるい yurui 146

lorry トラック torakku

lose, to なくす nakusu 28, 138, 153

188   *ENGLISH ➤ JAPANESE*

lose: I've lost … …がなくなりました
… ga nakunari mash(i)ta 71

lost property office お忘れ物承り所
o-wasure mono uketamawari jo 73

lost-and-found お忘れ物承り所 o-
wasure mono uketamawari jo 73

lost: I'm lost 道に迷いました
michi ni mayoi mash(i)ta 106

lots of fun とても楽しい
totemo tanoshii 101

louder (of voice) もっと大きな声
motto ookina koe 128

love: I love you あなたが好きです
anata ga suki des(u)

lovely 良い ii 122

low 少ない s(u)kunai 122

low beam ロービーム roo biimu 86

low-fat 低脂肪 tee shiboo

lower (berth) 下段 gedan 74

luck: good luck 幸運を祈ります
kooun o inori mas(u) 220

luggage 荷物 nimotsu 32, 67, 69, 71;
~ cart [trolley] カート kaato 71;
~ locker コインロッカー koin rokkaa
71, 73

lump (swelling) こぶ kobu 162

lunch 昼食/お昼 chuushoku/ohiru
98, 124

lung 肺 hai

M machine 機械 kikai 139;
~ washable 洗濯機で洗える
sentakki de araeru 145

madam 奥さま ok(u)sama

magazine 雑誌 zasshi 150

magnificent 立派 rippa 101

maid クリーナー kuriinaa 28

mail, to 郵送する yuusoo suru

mail 手紙 tegami 27; by ~ 手紙で
tegami de 22; ~box 郵便ポスト
yuubin pos(u)to 154

main road 大通り oodoori 95, 96

make an appointment, to 予約する
yoyaku suru 161

make-up メーキャップ meekyappu

male 男 otoko 152

mallet 木槌 kizuchi 31

man 男 otoko

manager (restaurant, hotel)
支配人 shihainin 25, 41

manager (shop) 店長
tenchoo 137

manicure マニキュア
manikyua 147

manual (car) マニュアル manyuaru

many たくさん tak(u)san 15

map 地図 chizu 94, 99, 106, 150

March 三月 san-gatsu 219

margarine マーガリン maagarin 160

married, to be 結婚する
kekkon suru 120

mascara マスカラ masukara

mask (diving) マスク mas(u)ku

mass ミサ misa 105

massage マッサージ massaaji 147

match 試合 shiai 114

matches マッチ matchi 31, 148, 150,

matinée マチネ machine 109

matt finish (photos) マット仕上げ
matto shiage

matter: it doesn't matter かまわないです
kamawanai des(u); what's the matter?
どうしましたか doo shimash(i)ta ka

mattress マットレス mattoresu

May 五月 go-gatsu 219

maybe もしかしたら
mosh(i)ka sh(i)tara

meal 食事 shokuji 23, 124

mean: what does this mean?
これは、何という意味ですか
kore wa nanto yuu imi des(u) ka 11

measure, to 測る hakaru 146

measurement 寸法 sunpoo

meat 肉 niku 41

medical certificate 診断書
shindan sho 168

medication {medicine} 薬
kusuri 141, 164

medium 中ぐらい chuu gurai 122

meet, to 待ち合わせる
machiawaseru 125

meeting place [point]
待ち合わせ場所
machiawase basho 12

member *(of club)* 会員
kaiin 112, 115
memorial *(war)*
(戦争) 記念碑
(sensoo) kinen hi 99
men *(toilets)* 男性用
dansee yoo
menswear 紳士服 shinshi fuku 143
mention: don't mention it
気にしないでください
ki ni shinai de kudasai 10
menu メニュー menyuu
message メッセージ messeeji 27, 155
metal 金属 kinzoku
metro 地下鉄 chikatetsu 80
metro station 地下鉄の駅
chikatetsu no eki 80, 96
microwave oven 電子レンジ
denshi renji
midday 正午 shoogo
migraine 偏頭痛 henzutsuu
milk 牛乳 gyuunyuu 159, 160
million 百万
hyaku-man 217
mind: do you mind? いいですか
ii des(u) ka 77, 126
mine 私の watashi no 16
mine: it's mine! それは私のです
sore wa watashi-no des(u)
mineral water ミネラルウォーター
mineraru wootaa
mini-bar ミニバー mini-baa 32
minimart コンビニ konbini 158, 159
minute 分 fun/pun 76
mirror 鏡 kagami
missing, to be *(lost)* いなくなる
inakunaru 152
mistake 間違い machigai 41
mistake: there's a mistake 違います
chigai mas(u) 32, 42
**misunderstanding: there's been a
misunderstanding** 誤解です
gokai des(u)
modern 新しい atarashii 14
moisturizer *(cream)* モイスチャライザー
mois(u)charaizaa
Monday 月曜日 getsu-yoobii 218

money お金/現金 o-kane/genkin
42, 136, 139, 153; ~ **order** 為替
kawase; **~-belt** マネーベルト
manee beruto
month 月 tsuki 219
more もっと motto 15
more: I'd like some more
もっとください
motto kudasai 39
morning, in the 朝 asa 222
mosque 回教寺院
kaikyoo jiin 105
mosquito 蚊 ka
mother 母 haha 120
motion sickness 乗物酔
norimono yoi 141
motorbike オートバイ
ootobai 83
motorboat モーターボート
mootaa booto 116
motorway 高速道路
koosoku dooro 88, 94
mountain 山 yama 107; **~ bike**
マウンテンバイク maunten baiku;
~ pass 山道 yama michi 107;
~ range 山脈 sanmyaku 107
moustache 口ひげ kuchi hige
mouth 口 kuchi 164
mouth ulcer 口内炎 koonaien
move, to *(disturb)* 動く ugoku 92
**move, to: I'd like to move to another
room** 部屋を替えてください
heya o kaete kudasai 25
movie 映画 eega 108, 110
movie theater 映画館
eega kan 96, 110
Mr. ... ...さん ... san
Mrs. ... ...さん ... san
much たくさん tak(u)san 15
mugged, to be 強盗にあう
gootoo ni au 152, 153
mugs マグカップ magukappu 148
multiplex cinema
マルチプレックスの映画館
maruchi purekqkusu no eega kan 110
mumps おたふくかぜ
otafuku kaze

museum 博物館 hakubutsukan 99

music 音楽 ongaku
111, 112, 121, 157

music store レコード屋
rekoodo-ya 131

musician ミュージシャン
myuujishan

Muslim (*n*) イスラム教徒
isuramu kyooto

mustard マスタード/からし
mas(u)taado/karashi 38

my 私の watashi no 16

myself: I'll do it myself
自分でやります
jibun de yarimas(u)

N name 名前 namae
22, 36, 93, 120

name: my name is …です
… des(u) 118

name: what's your name? お名前は
o-namae wa 118

napkin ナプキン nap(u)kin 39

nappies おむつ omutsu 142

narrow せまい semai 14

nationality 国籍 kok(u)seki 23

nature reserve 自然保護区域
shizen hogo kuiki 107

nausea 吐き気 hakike

near/nearby 近く chikaku 12, 21, 87

nearest いちばん近い
ichiban chikai 88, 130

necessary 必要な hitsuyoo na 89

neck 首筋 kubi suji 147

necklace ネックレス nekkuresu 149

need, to 要る iru 18

nephew 甥 oi

nerve 神経 shinkee

nervous system 神経系 shinkee kee

never mind 大丈夫です
daijoobu des(u) 10

new 新しい atarashii 14

newsagent キオスク kios(u)ku 131, 150

newspaper 新聞 shinbun 150

newsstand キオスク
kios(u)ku 131, 150

next 次 tsugi 68, 75, 78, 79, 80

next to …のとなり
… no tonari 12, 95

next week 来週
raishuu 219

nice すてき s(u)teki

niece 姪 mee

night 夜 yoru 222

nightclub ナイトクラブ
naito kurabu 112

no いいえ iie 10

no entry 立入禁止 tachi-iri kinshi 101

no flash (*photography*)
フラッシュお断り
furasshu okotowari 101

no one: there is no one 誰もいません
dare mo imasen 16

no overtaking 追越禁止
oikoshi kinshi 96

no passing 追越禁止 oikoshi kinshi 96

no photography 写真撮影禁止
shashin satsuee kinshi 101

no smoking 禁煙 kin-en 78

no way! いけません ikemasen 19

no: I have no … …がありません
… ga arimasen 41

noisy うるさい urusai 14, 24

non-alcoholic ノンアルコール
non arukooru

non-smoking (*adj*) 喫煙 kitsuen 36

non-smoking (*seat*) 禁煙席
kin-en seki 69

none: there is none 一つもありません
hitotsu mo arimasen 15, 16

nonsense! (*exclamation*) くだらない
kudaranai

noon 正午 shoogo 221

north 北 kita 95

North Korea 北朝鮮 kita-choosen 119

not bad 悪くない waruku na 19

not good: it's not good あまり、よく
ありません amari yoku arimasen 19

not yet まだ mada 13

note (*money*) お札 o-satsu 139

nothing else: there is nothing else
他には、何もありません hoka niwa
nani mo arimasen 15

notify, to 知らせる shiraseru 167

November 十一月 juu-ichi-gatsu 219

now 今 ima 13, 84

number 番号 bangoo 109, 138

number plate ナンバープレート nanbaa pureeto

nurse 看護婦 kangofu

nylon ナイロン nairon

O

o'clock …時 … ji 221

occasionally 時々 tokidoki

occupied: it's occupied 塞がっています fusagatte imas(u) 14

October 十月 juu-gatsu 219

odds (betting) 賭け率 kake ritsu 114

of course もちろん mochiron 19

off-licence 酒屋 saka-ya 131

off-peak (season) 閑散期 kansan ki

office オフィス ofisu

office (doctor's) 診療所 shinryoo jo 161

often ひんぱんに hinpan ni 13

oil オイル oiru/abura

okay オーケー ookee 10, 19

old (of people) 年寄り toshiryori 14

old (of things) 古い furui 14

old-fashioned 古い furui 14

olive oil オリーブオイル oriibu oiru

omelet オムレツ omuretsu

on … (day, date) …に … ni 13; **~ foot** 歩いて aruite 17, 95; **~ my own** ひとり hitori 120; **~ the hour** 毎時ちょうどに mai-ji choodo ni 76; **~ the left** 左に hidari ni 12; **~ the right** 右に migi ni 12; **~ the spot** ここで koko de 93

on/off switch スイッチ suitchi

once 一回 ikkai 218

one like that それみたいなもの sore mitaina mono 16

one-way 片道 katamichi 68, 74, 79

one-way street 一方通行 ippoo tsuukoo 96

open (bank) 営業中 eegyoo chuu 138

open (shop) 開館 kaikan 101

open, to (shop) 開く aku 100, 132, 140, 154

open, to (window) 開ける akeru 77, 164

open-air pool 屋外プール okugai puuru 116

open: is … open to the public? …に入れますか … ni haire mas(u) ka 100

open: it's open 開いています aite imas(u) 14

opening hours 開館時間 kaikan jikan 100

opera オペラ opera 108, 111

operation (medical) 手術 shujutsu

opposite 向かい mukai 12

optician 眼鏡店 megane ten 131, 167

or または matawa

orange (color) オレンジ色 orenji iro 143

orchestra オーケストラ ookes(u)tora 111

order, to 注文する chuumon suru 37, 41, 135

order, to (taxi) 呼ぶ yobu 32

ordering 注文 chuumon 37

organized hike ハイキングツアー haikingu tsuaa

ornaments 置物 okimono 156

others 他の hoka no 134

our(s) 私たちの watashi tachi no 16

out of stock 売り切れ urikire 135

outdoor 野外 yagai

outside 外 soto 12, 36

oval 楕円形の daenkee no 134

oven オーブン oobun

over here (near me) ここ koko 159

over there (not near either person) あそこ asoko 159

over there (near you) そこ soko 36

overcharge: I've been overcharged 余分に請求されました yobun ni seekyuu sare mash(i)ta

overdone 焼きすぎ yaki sugi 41

overheat 過熱 kanetsu

owe: how much do I owe?
いくらですか ikura des(u) ka
own: on my own 一人で hitori de 65
owner 持ち主 mochinushi

P p.m. 午後 gogo 101
pacifier おしゃぶり oshaburi
pack of cards トランプ一組
toranpu hito-kumi
pack, to 詰める tsumeru 69
package 小包 kozutsumi 155
packed lunch お弁当 o-bentoo 159
packet of cigarettes タバコ tabako 150
paddling pool 子供用のプール
kodomo yoo no puuru 113
padlock 南京錠 nankin joo
pail バケツ baketsu 157
pain, to be in 痛む itamu 167
painkillers 痛み止め itami dome 141
paint, to (picture) (絵を)描く (e o) kaku
painter 画家 gaka
painting 絵画 kaiga
pair of ..., a 一対の... ittsui no ... 218
pajamas パジャマ pajama
palpitations 動悸 dooki
panorama 展望/パノラマ
tenboo/panorama 107
pants (U.S.) ズボン zubon 144
panty hose パンスト pans(u)to 144
paper crafts 紙細工 kami zaiku 156
paper napkins 紙ナプキン kami
nap(u)kin 148
paraffin パラフィン parafin 31
paralysis 麻痺 mahi
parcel 小包 kozutsumi 155
package 小包 kozutsumi 155
pardon? すみません sumimasen 11
parents 両親 ryooshin 120
park 公園 kooen 96, 99, 107
parking lot 駐車場
chuusha joo 26, 87, 96
parking meter 料金メーター
ryookin meetaa 87
parliament building 国会議事堂
kokkai gijidoo 99

partner (husband/
wife) 配偶者 haiguusha
parts (components)
部品 buhin 89
party (social) パーティー
paatii 124
pass through, to 立ち寄る tachiyoru 66
pass, to 過ぎる sugiru 77
passport パスポート pas(u)pooto
23, 66, 69, 139, 153
passport number パスポート番号
pas(u)pooto bangoo 23
pastry shop ケーキ屋 keeki-ya 131
patch, to 継を当てる tsugi o ateru 137
patient (n) 患者 kanja
pavement 歩道 hodoo
pay 払う harau 67
pay a fine, to 罰金を払う
bakkin o harau 93
pay phone 公衆電話 kooshuu denwa
pay, to 払う harau 136, 158
paying 支払い shiharai 136
payment 支払い shiharai
peak 山頂 sanchoo 107
pearl 真珠 shinju 149, 156
pebbly (beach) 砂利浜 jari hama 116
pedestrian crossing 横断歩道
oodan hodoo 96
pedestrian zone 歩行者天国
hokoosha tengoku 96
pedicure ペディキュア pedikyua
pen ボールペン boorupen 150
penknife ペンナイフ pen naifu 31
people 人 hito 119
people carrier (minivan) ミニバン
mini ban
pepper コショウ koshoo 38
per day 一日/1日 ichi-nichi 30, 83, 86,
87, 115; ~ hour 1時間 ichi-jikan 87,
115, 155; ~ night 一泊 ippaku 21, 23;
~ week 1週間 isshuukan 83, 86
perhaps もしかしたら
mosh(i)ka sh(i)tara 19
period (historical) 年代 nendai 104
period (menstrual) 生理 seeri 167
period pains 生理痛 seeritsuu 167

perm, to パーマをかける paama o kakeru 147

petrol ガソリン gasorin 87, 88

petrol station ガソリンスタンド gasorin s(u)tando 87

pharmacy 薬局 yakkyoku 131, 140, 158

phone call 電話 denwa 152

phone, to 電話する denwa suru

phonecard テレホンカード terehon kaado 127, 155

photo 写真 shashin 151, 152

photo, to take a 写真を撮る shasin o toru

photo: passport-size photo パスポート写真 pas(u)pooto shashin 115

photocopier コピー機 kopii ki 155

photographer 写真家 shasinka

photography 写真撮影 shashin satsuee 151

photos, to take 写真を撮る shashin o toru 100

phrase 言葉 kotoba 11

pick up, to 受け取る uketoru 28, 109

pickup truck ピックアップ pikku appu

picnic ピクニック pikunikku

Pill (contraceptive) ピル piru 167

pillow 枕 makura 27

pillow case 枕カバー makura kabaa

pilot light 口火 kuchibi

pink ピンク pinku 143

pipe (smoking) パイプ paipu

pipe cleaners パイプクリーナー paipu kuriinaa

pipe tobacco 刻みタバコ kizami tabako

pitch, to (a tent) 張る haru

pizzeria ピザ・レストラン piza res(u)toran 35

place 場所 basho 23

place a bet, to 掛け金を払う kakekin o harau 114

place of birth 出生地 shosseechi 23

plain (n) 平野 heeya 107

plain (not patterned) 無地 muji

plan (map) 地図 chizu 96

plane (airplane) 飛行機 hikooki 68, 123

plans 予定 yotee 124

plant (n) 植物 shokubutsu

plastic bags ビニール袋 biniiru bukuro

plastic wrap ラップ rappu 148

plate 皿 sara 39, 148

platform ホーム hoomu 73, 76, 77

platinum プラチナ purachina 149

play (theater) 芝居 shibai 108

play group 託児所 takujisho 113

play, to する suru 121

play, to (music) 演奏する ensoo suru 111

playground 公園 kooen 113

playing field 運動場 undoojoo 96

playwright 作者 sak(u)sha 110

pleasant, nice 気持ち良い、すてき kimochi ii, s(u)teki 14

please (asking for a favour) お願いします onegai shimas(u) 10

please (offering a favour) どうぞ doozo 10

please (getting attention) お願いします onegai shimas(u) 37

plug プラグ puragu 148

plumber 配管工 haikan-koo

point of interest 観光名所 kankoo meesho 97

point to, to 指す sas(u) 11

poison 毒 doku

poisonous 有毒な yuudoku na

poker (cards) ポーカー pookaa

police 警察 keesatsu 92, 152; **~ report** 警察の証明書 keesatsu no shoomee sho 153; **~ station** 警察署 keesatsusho 96, 131; **~ sub-station** 交番 kooban 96, 131, 152

pollen count 花粉量 kafun ryoo 122

polyester ポリエステル poriesuteru

pond 池 ike 107

pop (music) ポップス poppusu 111

popcorn ポップコーン poppukoon 110

popular はやりの hayari no 157

popular, to be 人気がある
ninki ga aru 111

porcelain 磁器 jiki 156

port *(harbour)* 港 minato

porter 赤帽 akaboo 71

possible: as soon as possible
できるだけ速く
dekiru dake hayaku

post 手紙 tegami 27; **~box**
郵便ポスト yuubin pos(u)to 154;
~card 葉書 hagaki 154, 156; **~man**
郵便屋 yuubin-ya; **~ office** 郵便局
yuubin kyoku 96, 153, 154;

post, to 郵送する yuusoo suru

poste restante 局留め
kyoku dome 155

potato chips ポテトチップス poteto
chippusu 159, 160

potatoes ポテト poteto 38

pottery 陶器/焼き物/瀬戸物
tooki/yakimono/setomono 156

poultry 鶏肉 tori niku 158

pound *(Sterling)* ポンド
pondo 67, 138

power cut 停電 teeden

power points 電源 dengen 30

pram 乳母車 ubaguruma

pregnant 妊娠 ninshin 163

premium *(gas/petrol)* スーパー
suupaa 87

prescription 処方箋 shohoosen 141

present *(gift)* プレゼント purezento

press, to *(iron)* アイロンをかける
airon o kakeru 137

pretty かわいい kawaii

priest *(Buddhist)* お坊さん o-boo san;
(Catholic) 神父さん shinpu san;
(Protestant) 牧師さん bokushi san;
(Shinto) 神主さん kan-nushi san

prints *(n)* 版画 hanga 156

prison 刑務所 keemusho

probably 多分 tabun 19

produce store 食料品店
shokuryoohin ten 131

profession 職業 shokugyoo 23

program of events
催し物の案内 moyooshi
mono no an-nai 108

program プログラム
puroguramu 109

pronounce, to
発音する hatsuon suru

Protestant プロテスタント
purotes(u)tanto 105

pub パブ pabu

public bath お風呂 ofuro 26

public holiday 祝日
shukujitsu 220

pullover セーター seetaa 144

pump *(at gas/petrol station)*
ポンプ ponpu 87

puncture パンク panku 83, 88

puppet show 人形劇
ningyoo geki

pure cotton 綿100％
men hyak(u) paasento 145

purple 紫 murasaki 143

purse 財布 saifu 153

push-chair ベビーカー bebii kaa

put: where can I put ...?
...は、どこに置けばいいですか
... wa doko ni okeba ii des(u) ka

pyjamas パジャマ pajama

Q **quarter past ...**
...時十五分
... ji juu-go-fun 221

quarter to ... ...時十五分前
... ji juu-go-fun mae 221

quarter, a 四分の一
yon-bun no ichi 218

question 質問 shitsumon

queue, to 並ぶ narabu 112

quick 速い hayai 14

quickest: what's the quickest way?
(method) 一番速い方法は何ですか
ichiban hayai hoohoo wa nan
des(u) ka

quickly 速く hayaku 17

quiet 静か shizuka 14

quieter もっと静か
motto shizuka 24, 126

restroom 化粧室 keshoo shitsu 132

R

rabbi ラビ rabi

race (cars/horses)
レース reesu

racetrack [race course]
競馬場 keeba joo 114

racket (tennis, squash) ラケット
raketto 115

radio ラジオ rajio 25

railroad [railway] 鉄道 tetsudoo

rain 雨 ame 122

raincoat レーンコート reenkooto 144

raped, to be 強姦される
gookan sareru 152

rapids 急流 kyuuryuu 107

rare (steak) レア rea

rare (unusual) 珍しい mezurashii

rash 発疹 hasshin 162

razor カミソリ kamisori

razor blades カミソリの刃
kamisori no ha 142

reading 読書 dok(u)sho 121

ready, to be できる dekiru 137, 151

real (genuine) 本物 honmono 149

really? 本当ですか
hontoo des(u) ka 19

receipt レシート/領収書
reshiito/ryooshuusho
32, 89, 136, 137, 168

receipt (photo development) 引換券
hikikae ken 137

reception (desk) 受付 uketsuke

receptionist 受付係 uketsuke gakari

reclaim tag 荷物引換証
nimotsu hiikae shoo 71

recommend: can you recommend ...
...はありますか
... wa arimas(u) ka 97, 108

recommend, to 教える oshieru 21, 35

record shop レコード屋
rekoodo-ya 131

red 赤 aka 143

red wine 赤ワイン
aka wain 40

red-headed 赤毛
akage 152

reduction (discount) 割引
waribiki 24, 68

refreshments 軽食 keeshoku 78

refrigerator 冷蔵庫 reezooko 29

refund (n) 払い戻し harai modoshi 137

refuse bags ごみ袋 gomi bukuro 148

refuse tip ごみ捨て場 gomi sute ba

regards: give my regards to
...さんによろしく
... san ni yorosh(i)ku 220

region 地域 chiiki 106

registered mail 書留 kakitome 155

registration form 登録カード
toorok(u) kaado 23

registration number 車のナンバー
(kuruma no) nanbaa 23, 88, 93

regular (gas/petrol) レギュラー
regyuraa 87

religion 宗教 shuukyoo

remember: I don't remember
覚えていません oboete imasen

rent to 借りる
kariru 83, 86, 115, 116, 117

repair, to 修理する/直す
shuuri suru/naosu 89, 137, 168

repairs 修理 shuuri 89

repeat, to もう一度言う
moo ichido yuu 94, 128

repeat: please repeat that
もう一度、言ってください
moo ichido itte kudasai 11

replacement (n) 代わり kawari 167

replacement part 部品 buhin 137

required, to be 要る iru 112

reservation 予約 yoyaku 22, 68, 73, 112

reservation (restaurant) 予約
teeburu no yoyaku 36

reservations desk 予約窓口
yoyaku madoguchi 109

reserve, to 予約する yoyaku suru
21, 28, 36, 74, 81, 109

reserve: I'd like to reserve ...
...を予約したいんですが
... o yoyaku sh(i)tain des(u) ga 74

reserved seat 指定席 sh(i)tee seki 74

rest, to 休む yasumu

restaurant レストラン res(u)toran
35, 112

retired, to be 退職する
taishoku suru 121

return *(trip, ticket)* 往復
oofuku 68, 74, 79, 81

return, to *(surrender)* 返す kaesu 86

return, to *(travel)* 帰る kaeru 75

reverse the charges, to
コレクトコールをかける
korek(u)to kooru o kakeru 127

revolting まずい mazui 14

rheumatism リューマチ ryuumachi

rice ご飯 gohan 38

rice bowl 茶碗 chawan 148

rice wine 日本酒 nihonshu 156

right 正しい tadashii 14

right of way 優先権 yuusen ken 93

right, on the 右 migi 76, 95, 159

right: that's right そうです
soo des(u) 14

ring *(finger)* 指輪/リング
yubiwa/ringu 149

rip-off: it's a rip-off 高すぎます
taka sugimas(u) 101

river 川 kawa 107; **~ cruise**
遊覧船 yuuransen 81

road 道 michi 94, 95, **~ closed**
通行止め tsuukoo dome 96;
~ map 道路地図 dooro chizu 150

roasted ロースト roos(u)to

robbed, to be 強盗にあう
gootoo ni au 153

robbery 強盗 gootoo

rock music ロック rokku 111

roller blades ローラーブレード
rooraa bureedo

rolls *(bread)* ロールパン
rooru pan 160

romantic ロマンチック
romanchikku 101

roof *(house/car)* 屋根 yane

roof-rack ルーフラック ruufu rakku

room 部屋 heya 21

room service ルームサービス
ruumu saabisu 26

rope ロープ roopu

round *(circular)*
丸い marui 134;
(of golf) 1 ラウンド
ichi-raundo 115

round neck 丸首
maru-kubi 144

round-trip 往復 oofuku 68, 74, 79, 81

roundabout *(rare in Japan)*
ロータリー rootarii

route コース koosu 106

rubbish ゴミ gomi 28

rucksack リュック ryukku

rude, to be 侮辱する bujoku suru

run into, to *(crash)* ぶつかる
buts(u)karu 93

run out, to *(fuel)* 切れる kireru 88

running shoes スニーカー
s(u)niikaa 145

rush hour ラッシュアワー rasshu awaa

S safe *(lock-up)* 金庫 kinko 27;
(not dangerous) 大丈夫
daijoobu 116

safety 安全 anzen

safety pins 安全ピン anzen pin

salad サラダ sarada

sales rep 販売員 hanbai in; **~ tax**
消費税 shoohi zee 24; **~man**
セールスマン seerusuman 121

salt 塩 shio 38, 39

salty 塩辛い shio karai

same 同じ onaji 75, 143

same-day *(travel)* 日帰り higaeri 74

sand 砂 suna

sandals サンダル sandaru 145

sandwich サンドイッチ sandoitchi 40

sandy beach 砂浜 suna hama 116

sanitary napkins [towels]
生理用ナプキン
seeri yoo nap(u)kin 142

satelite TV 衛星放送付テレビ
eesee hoosoo tsuki terebi 22

satin サテン saten

Saturday 土曜日 do-yoobi 218

saucepan 鍋 nabe 29

sauna サウナ sauna 26
sausages ソーセージ sooseeji 160
say: how do you say ...?
…は何といいますか
… wa nan to iimas(u) ka
scarf スカーフ s(u)kaafu 144, 156
scenic route 眺めの良いコース
nagame no ii koosu 106
scheduled flight 定期便 teeki bin
school 学校 gakkoo 96
school path 通学路 tsuugaku ro 96
scissors はさみ hasami 148
scooter スクーター s(u)kuutaa 83
scouring pad 研磨たわし
kenma tawashi
screwdriver ドライバー doraibaa 148
sea 海 umi 107
seafront 海岸通り kaigan doori
seasick: I feel seasick 船酔いしました
funayoi shimash(i)ta
season 季節 kisetsu 219
season ticket 定期券 teeki ken
seat 席 seki 74, 77, 108, 109
second 二番 ni-ban 218; ~ **class**
普通車 futsuu-sha 74; ~**hand**
中古 chuuko
secretary 秘書 hisho
security 警備 keebi 139
security check セキュリティチェック
sekyuritii chekku 9
sedative 鎮静剤 chinseezai
see, to 見る miru 18, 24, 93, 98
see you soon! じゃあ、また
jaa mata
self-employed 自営業 jieegyoo 121
self-service セルフサービス
serufu saabisu 87, 133
sell, to 売る uru 135
send, to (mail)
送る okuru 154, 155, 157
senior citizen 高齢者
kooreesha 74, 100
separately 別々に betsubetsu ni 42
September 九月 ku-gatsu 219
service (religious) 礼拝式
reehai-shiki 105

service: is service included?
サービス料込みですか
saabisu ryoo komi des(u) ka 42
serviette ナプキン nap(u)kin 39
sesame oil ゴマ油 goma abura
set menu セットメニュー/定食
setto menyuu/teeshoku 37
sex (act) セックス sekkusu
shady 日陰 hikage 31
shallow 浅い asai
shampoo シャンプー shanpuu 142
shampoo and set シャンプーとセット
shanpuu to setto 147
shape 形 katachi 134
share, to (room) いっしょに使う
issho ni tsukau
sharp (object) 刃物
hamono 69
shaving brush ひげそり用ブラシ
higesori yoo burashi; ~ **cream**
シェービングクリーム sheebingu
kuriimu
she 彼女 kanojo
sheath (contraceptive) コンドーム
kondoomu
sheets (bedding) シーツ shiitsu 28
Shinto shrine 神社 jinja 96, 99, 105
ship 船 fune 81
shirt (men's) ワイシャツ waishatsu 144
shock (electric) 感電 kanden
shoe laces 靴ひも kutsu himo;
~ **polish** 靴墨 kutsu zumi; ~ **repair**
靴の修理 kutsu no shuuri; ~ **store**
靴屋 kutsu-ya 131
shoes 靴 kutsu 145
shop assistant 店員 ten-in
shopping area 商店街 shootengai 99;
~ **basket** 買い物かご kaimono kago
158; ~ **cart** カート kaato 158;
~ **centre** ショッピングセンター
shoppingu sentaa 130; ~ **mall**
ショッピングセンター shoppingu
sentaa 130; ~ **street** 商店街
shooten gai 96; ~ **trolley** カート
kaato 158
shopping, to go 買い物に行く
kaimono ni iku

shore (sea/lake) 岸 kishi

short (height) 低い hikui 14; (length) 短い mijikai 14, 146; **~ hair** ショートヘア shooto hea 152; **~sighted** 近眼 kingan 167; **~ sleeves** 半袖 hansode 144

shorts (boys' and mens') 半ズボン han zubon 144

shorts (girls' and ladies') ショートパンツ shooto pantsu 144

shovel シャベル shaberu 157

show ショー shoo 112

show, to 見せる miseru 133, 134

show: can you show me? 教えてください oshiete kudasai 106

shower シャワー shawaa 21, 26, 30

shut, to 閉まる shimaru 132

shut: it's shut 閉っています shimatte imas(u) 14

sick: I'm going to be sick 吐き気がします hakike ga shimas(u)

side order 付け合わせ tsuke awase 38; **~ street** 横道 yoko michi 95; **~walk** 歩道 hodoo

sights 名所 meesho

sightseeing tour 観光ツアー kankoo tsuaa 97

sightseeing, to go 観光に行く kankoo ni iku

sign 標識 hyoosh(i)ki 93, 95

sign, to 署名する/サインする shomee suru/sain suru 139

signature 署名/サイン shomee/sain 23

signpost 標識 hyooshiki

silk 絹 kinu

silver 銀 gin 149

silver-plate 銀メッキ gin mekki 149

singer 歌手 kashu 157

single (room) シングル shinguru 21, 81

single (trip, ticket) 片道 katamichi 68, 74, 79

single (unmarried) 独身 dok(u)shin 120

sink 流し nagashi 25

sister (older) 姉 ane 120

sister (younger) 妹 imooto 120

sisters (plural) 姉妹 shimai 120

sit down, please お座りください o-suwari kudasai

sit, to 座る suwaru 36, 77, 126

size サイズ saizu 146

skates スケート靴 s(u)keeto gutsu 117

skating rink スケートリンク s(u)keeto rinku

ski(s) スキー s(u)kii 117; **~ boots** スキー靴 s(u)kii gutsu 117; **~ poles** ストック s(u)tokku 117; **~school** スキースクール s(u)kii s(u)kuuru 117

skiing スキー s(u)kii 117

skin-diving equipment ダイビング用具 daibingu yoogu 116

skirt スカート s(u)kaato 144

sleep, to 眠る nemuru 167

sleeper 寝台車 shindai-sha 74

sleeping bag 寝袋/スリーピングバッグ nebukuro/suriipingu-baggu 31

sleeping car 寝台車 shindai-sha 74, 77

sleeping pill 睡眠薬 suimin-yaku

sleeve 袖 sode 144

slip (undergarment) スリップ surippu

slippers スリッパ surippa 145

slow 遅い osoi 14

slow down! ゆっくり yukkuri

slow, to be (clock) 遅れる okureru 222

slowly ゆっくり yukkuri 11, 17, 94, 128

SLR (single lens reflex) camera 一眼レフカメラ ichigan refu kamera 151

small 小さい chiisai 14, 24, 117, 134

small change 小銭 kozeni 138

smaller もっと小さい motto chiisai 134, 136

smell: there's a bad smell いやな臭いがします iya na nioi ga shimas(u)

smoke, to 煙草を吸う tabako o suu 126

smoking (seat) 喫煙席 kitsuen seki 36, 69

snack bar スナックバー
sunakku baa 73

snacks スナック sunakku

sneakers スニーカー
suniikaa

snorkel スノーケル
sunookeru

snow 雪 yuki 117, 122

soaking solution (contact lenses)
コンタクトレンズのクリーナー
kontakuto renzu no kuriinaa

soap 石鹸 sekken 142

soccer サッカー sakkaa 114

socket ソケット soketto

socks 靴下/ソックス
kutsush(i)ta/sokk(u)su 144

soft drink ソフトドリンク
sof(u)to dorinku 110, 160

sold out 売切れ urikire 109

sole (shoes) 靴底 kutsu zoko

solist ソリスト soris(u)to 111

something 何か nanika 16

sometimes 時々 tokidoki 13

somewhlere どこかで
dokoka de 108

son 息子 mus(u)ko 120, 162

soon もうすぐ moosugu 13

soon: as soon as possible
できるだけ早く
dekirudake hayaku 161

sore throat 喉の痛み
nodo no itami 141

sore throat, to have a のどが痛む
nodo ga itamu 163

sore: it's sore 痛みます itami mas(u)

sorry! ごめんなさい gomen nasai 10

sort (type) 種類 shurui 134

soul music ソウル souru 111

soup 石鹸 sekken 27

soup dish スープ皿 suupu zara 148

sour 酸っぱい suppai 41

south 南 minami 95

South Africa 南アフリカ
minami afurika

South African (n) 南アフリカ人
minami afurika jin

South Korea 韓国 kankoku 119

souvenir お土産 o-miyage 98, 156

souvenir guide ガイドブック
gaido bukku 156

souvenir store お土産屋
omiyage-ya 131

soya sauce 醤油 shooyu 38

space (room) 場所 basho 30

spade シャベル shaberu 157

spare (extra) 予備 yobi

speak, to 話す hanas(u) 128

speak, to: can I speak to …
…をお願いします
… o onegai shimas(u) 18

speak: do you speak English?
英語ができますか
eego ga dekimas(u) ka 11

speak: does anyone here speak English?
英語ができる人はいますか
eego ga dekiru hito wa imas(u) ka 67

speak: I'd like to speak to the manager
支配人を呼んでください
shihainin o yonde kudasai 41

special delivery 速達 sok(u)tatsu 155

special requirements 特別な注文
tokubetsu na chuumon 39

specialist 専門医 senmon-i 164

spectacles 眼鏡 megane

speed, to スピード違反する
s(u)piido ihan 93

spicy 芳しい koobashii

sponge スポンジ s(u)ponji 148

spoon スプーン s(u)puun 39, 41, 148

sport スポーツ s(u)pootsu 114, 121

sporting goods store スポーツ用品店
supootsu yoohin ten 131

sports club スポーツクラブ
s(u)pootsu kurabu 115

sports ground 運動場 undoojoo 96

sprained 捻挫 nenza 164

spring 春 haru 219

square 四角い shikakui 134

stadium スタジアム s(u)tajiamu 96

stain しみ shimi

stainless steel ステンレス
s(u)tenresu 149

stairs 階段 kaidan 132

stall (theater) ストール s(u)tooru 109

stamp (postage) 切手 kitte 150, 154

stand in line, to (queue) 並ぶ
narabu 112

standby ticket キャンセル待ちの
チケット kyanseru machi no chiketto 98

start, to 出発する shuppats(u) suru 98

start, to (car) スタートする
s(u)taato suru 88

statement: to make a statement
陳述する chinjuts(u) suru 93

station 駅 eki 96

stationer's 文房具屋 bunboogu-ya

statue 銅像 doozoo 99

stay, to (accommodation) 泊まる
tomaru 123, 139

steak house ステーキハウス
s(u)teeki hausu 35

sterilizing solution 消毒液
shoodoku eki 142

still: I'm still waiting
まだ待っています mada matte imas(u)

stockings ストッキング
s(u)tokkingu 144

stolen, to be 盗まれる
nusumareru 71, 152, 153

stomach 胃 i 141

stomach ache, to have a
お腹が痛む o-naka ga itamu 163

stools (faeces) 大便 daiben 164

stop 商店 shooten 130

stop (bus/streetcar) 停留所 teeryuujo 79

stop (road sign) 止まれ tomare 96

stop at ...., to ....に止まる
... ni tomaru 78

stop, to 止まる tomaru 77, 98

stopcock ストップコック
s(u)toppu kokku 28

store 商店 shooten 130

store guide 店内の案内
ten-nai no an-nai 132

stormy 雷 kaminari 122

stove コンロ konro 28

straight ahead まっすぐ massugu 95

strained muscle, to have a
筋を違える suji o chigaeru 162

strange 変 hen 101

straw (drinking) ストロー s(u)toroo

strawberry ストロベリー
s(u)toroberii 40

stream 小川 ogawa 107

streetcar 市電 shiden 79

strong (potent) 強力な
kyooryoku na

student 学生 gak(u)see 74, 100, 121

study to 勉強する benkyoo suru 121

style 様式 yooshiki 104

subtitles 字幕 jimaku 110

subway 地下鉄 chikatetsu 80, 96

subway station 地下鉄の駅
chikatetsu no eki 80

sugar 砂糖 satoo 38, 39

suggest: can you suggest ...?
...はありますか
... wa arimas(u) ka 123

suit スーツ suutsu 144

summer 夏 natsu 219

sumo 相撲 sumoo 114

sun block 日焼け止めクリーム
hiyake dome kuriimu 142

sunbathe, to 日光浴をする
nikkooyoku o suru

sunburn 日焼け hiyake 141

Sunday 日曜日 nichi-yoobi 218

sunglasses サングラス sangurasu

sunshade パラソル parasoru 116

sunstroke 日射病 nisshabyoo 163

suntan lotion サンタン・ローション
santan rooshon 142

super (gas/petrol) スーパー suupaa 87

superb 素晴らしい subarashii 101

supermarket スーパー suupaa 131, 158

supplement 割増料金 warimashi
ryookin 68, 69

sure: are you sure? 確かですか
tashika des(u) ka

surfboard サーフボード
saafuboodo 116

surgery (doctor's) 診療所
shinryoo jo 161

surname 名字 myooji

sushi restaurant 寿司屋 sushi ya 35

sweatshirt トレーナー toreenaa 144

sweet (taste) 甘い amai

sweets キャンデー kyandee 150

swim, to 泳ぐ oyogu 116

swimming 水泳 suiee
114; **~ pool** プール
puuru 22, 26, 116;
~ trunks 海水パンツ
kaisui pantsu 144;

swimsuit 水着 mizugi 144

switch スイッチ suitchi 25

swollen, to be 腫れる hareru

symptoms 症状 shoojoo 163

synagogue ユダヤ教会
yudaya kyookai 105

synthetic 合成繊維 goosee sen-i 145

T T-shirt T シャツ
tii shatsu 144, 156

table (place) 席 seki 112

table (restaurant) テーブル teeburu 36

tablet (medication) 錠 joo 140

take out [away] (n) テークアウト
teekuauto 40

take out, to (extract) 抜く nuku 168

take photographs, to 写真を撮る
shashin o toru 98

take, to (carry, transport) 運ぶ
hakob(u) 71

take, to (medicine) 飲む nomu 140, 141

take, to (time) かかる kakaru 78

take, to: I'll take it (of hotel room) 泊まり
ます tomari mas(u) 24; (of a purchase)
それにします sore ni shimas(u) 135

talcum powder タルカムパウダー
tarukamu paudaa

talk, to 話す hanasu

tall 高い takai 14

tampons タンポン tanpon 142

tan 日焼け hiyake

tap 蛇口 jaguchi 25

taxi タクシー tak(u)shii 70, 71, 84

taxi rank [stand] タクシーのりば
tak(u)shii noriba 84, 96

tea 紅茶 koocha 40

tea bags ティーバッグ tii baggu 160

teacher 教師 kyooshi 121

team チーム chiimu 114

teat (for baby) 乳首 chikubi

telegrams 電報 denpoo 155

telephone 電話 denwa 22, 32, 92;
~ booth 電話ボックス denwa
bokkusu 127; **~ directory** 電話帳
denwa choo 127; **~ number** 電話番号
denwa bangoo 127

telephone calls, to make
電話をかける denwa o kakeru 32

television テレビ terebi 25

tell, to: tell me 教えてください
oshiete kudasai 79

temperature 熱 netsu 164

temporarily 応急の ookyuu no 89, 168

ten thousand (standard unit for counting
money) 一万 ichi-man 217

tennis テニス tenisu 114

tennis court テニスコート
tenisu kooto 115

tent テント tento 30, 31; **~ pegs**
ペッグ peggu 31; **~ pole** ポール
pooru 31

terminus ターミナル taaminaru 78

terrace テラス terasu 109

terrible ひどい hidoi 19

terrific たいへん結構
taihen kekkoo 19, 101

tetanus 破傷風 hashoofuu 164

thank you (very much)
（どうも）ありがとう
(doomo) arigatoo 10, 126

that one (not near either person)
あれ are 134, 159

that one (near you) それ sore 16

that's all それで全部です sore de
zenbu des(u) 133

that's enough もう十分です
moo juubun des(u) 19

that's true もっともです
mottomo des(u) 19

theater 劇場 gekijoo 96, 99, 110, 111

theft 盗難 toonan 153

their(s) 彼らの karera no 16

theme park テーマパーク teema paaku

then (time) その時 skono toki 13

there そこ／そちら soko/sochira 12, 17

there is ... …があります
… ga arimas(u) 17

ENGLISH ➤ JAPANESE

thermometer (clinical) 体温計 taionkee

thermos flask 魔法瓶 mahoo bin

these これ kore 134, 159

thick (size) 厚い atsui

thief 泥棒 doroboo

thigh 腿 momo

thin 薄い usui

think of, to: what do you think of ..? …
はどう思いますか
… wa doo omoi mas(u) ka 119

think, to 考える kangaeru 135

think: I think there's a mistake
違っているようです
chigatte iru yoo des(u) 42

third 三番 san-ban 218

third party insurance
第三者賠償責任保険
dai-san-sha baishoo sekinin hoken

third, a 三分の一 san-bun no ichi 218

thirsty: I am thirsty のどが渇きました
nodo ga kawaki mash(i)ta

this one (near me) これ kore
16, 134, 159

those (not near either person)
あれ are 134, 159

thousand 千 sen 217

three times 三回 san-kai 218

thrombosis 血栓症 kessenshoo

Thursday 木曜日 moku-yoobi 218

ticket チケット/切符/ chiketto/kippu
68, 69, 75, 77, 79, 81, 108, 109, 114, 153

ticket gate 改札口 kaisatsu guchi 73

ticket office きっぷうりば
kippu uriba 73, 79

ticket vending machine
券売機 kenbaiki 73, 79

tie ネクタイ nek(u)tai 144

tight (vs loose) きつい kitsui 146

tights パンスト pans(u)to 144

time, on 時間通り jikan doori 76

time: can you tell me the time?
何時ですか nan-ji des(u) ka 221

time: free time 自由時間 jiyuu jikan 98

time: what time? 何時 nan-ji 76

timetable 時刻表 jikoku hyoo 75

tin opener 缶切り kankiri 148

tip チップ chippu 42, 71

tire (n) タイヤ
taiya 83

tired: I'm tired
疲れました tsukare
mash(i)ta

tissues ティッシュペーパー
tisshu peepaa 142

to ... (place) …へ … e 12

tobacco 刻みタバコ kizami tabako 150

tobacconist タバコ屋 tabako-ya
130, 150

today 今日 kyoo 89, 124, 161, 219

together 一緒に issho ni 42

toilet トイレ toire 25, 26, 29, 98, 113

toilet paper トイレットペーパー
toiretto peepaa 25, 29, 142

toiletries 化粧品 keshoohin 142

tomorrow 明日 ash(i)ta 84, 89, 124,
126, 161, 219

tonight 今晩 konban 110, 124

tonight, for 今晩の konban no 108

tonsillitis 扁桃炎 hentoo-en

too ... …すぎる sugiru 17, 93, 146

too much: it's too much (quantity)
多すぎます oo sugimas(u) 15

too: too expensive 高すぎる
taka sugiru 135

toothbrush 歯ブラシ ha-burashi

tooth 歯 ha 168; **~ache** 歯痛 ha-ita;
~paste 歯磨き粉 hamigaki ko 142

top 上 ue 147

torch 懐中電灯
kaichuu dentoo 31

torn (muscle) 裂傷 resshoo 164

torn: this is torn 破けています
yabukete imas(u)

tough (of food) 固い katai 41

tour ツアー tsuaa 97, 98, 101; **~ guide**
ツアーコンダクター tsuaa
kondak(u)taa 27; **~ operator** ツアー
オペレーター tsuaa opereetaa 26

tourist 観光客 kankoo kyaku

tourist office 観光案内所
kankoo an-nai jo 97

tow truck 牽引車 ken-in-sha 88

towards ... …の方へ … no hoo e 12

towel タオル taoru

town 町 machi 94
town center 中心地 chuushin-chi 21
town hall 市役所 shiyak(u)sho 99
toy おもちゃ omocha 157
toy store おもちゃ屋 omocha-ya 131
traditional 伝統的な dentooteki na 35
traditional Japanese hotel 旅館 ryokan 123
traffic 交通 kootsuu; ~ jam 交通渋滞 kootsuu juutai; ~ violation [offence] 交通違反 kootsuu ihan
trail ハイキング haikingu 106
trailer キャンピングカー kyanpingukaa 30, 81
train 列車 ressha 75, 76, 77, 123; ~ station 駅 eki 73; ~ times 列車の時刻 ressha no jikoku 75
training shoes スニーカー s(u)niikaa 145
tram 市電 shiden 78, 79
transfer 連絡会社線 renraku kaisha sen 80
transit トランジット toranjitto
translate, to 訳す yakus(u) 11
translation 翻訳 hon-yaku
translator 翻訳者 hon-yaku sha
trash ゴミ gomi 28
trash cans ゴミ箱 gomi bako 30
travel agency 旅行代理店 ryokoo dairiten 131; ~ sickness 乗物酔 norimono yoi 141
traveler's check(s) [cheque(s)] トラベラーズチェック toraberaazu chekku 136, 138
tray トレー toree
tree 木 ki 106
trim (hair) トリム torimu 147
trolley カート kaato 158
trousers ズボン zubon 144
trouser press ズボンプレッサー zubon puressaa
truck トラック torakku
true: that's not true それは違います sore wa chigai mas(u)
try on, to 試着する shichaku suru 146

Tuesday 火曜日 ka-yoobi 218
tunnel トンネル ton-neru
turn down, to (volume, heat) 下げる sageru
turn off, to 消す kesu 25
turn on, to 付ける tsukeru 25
turn up, to (volume, heat) 上げる ageru
turn, to (change direction) 曲がる magaru 95
TV テレビ terebi 22
tweezers ピンセット pinsetto
twice 二回 ni-kai 218
twin bed ツインベッド tsuin beddo 21
twist: I've twisted my ankle 足首を捻挫しました ashikubi o nenza shimash(i)ta
two-door car 2ドア車 tsuu-doa sha 86
type: what type? どんな don-na 112
tyre タイヤ taiya 83

U ugly みにくい minikui 14, 101
ulcer 潰瘍 kaiyoo
umbrella パラソル parasoru 116
uncle 伯父 oji 120
unconscious, to be 意識がない ish(i)ki ga nai 92, 162
under 下 shita
underdone (adj) 生焼け nama yake 41
underground 地下鉄 chikatetsu 80
underpants パンツ/ブリーフ pantsu/buriifu 144
underpass 地下道 chikadoo 96
understand, to 分かる wakaru 11
understand: do you understand? 分かりますか wakari mas(u) ka 11
understand: I don't understand 分かりません wakari masen 11, 67
undress, to 服を脱ぐ fuku o nugu 164
uneven (ground) でこぼこ dekoboko 31
uniform 制服 seefuku
United Kingdom [U.K.] イギリス igirisu
United States [U.S.] アメリカ amerika 119

unlimited mileage 距離制限無し
 kyori seegen nashi
unlock, to 鍵を開ける kagi o akeru
unpleasant 気持ち悪い
 kimochi warui 14
unscrew, to ネジを外す neji o hazusu
until ... (time) ...まで ... made 222
up to ... (place) ...まで ... made 12
upper berth 上段 joodan 74
upstairs 上 ue 12
urgent 至急 sh(i)kyuu 161
urine 尿 nyoo 164
U.S.A. アメリカ合衆国
 amerika gasshuu koku
use, to 使う tsukau 139
use: it's for my personal use
 私が使います
 watashi ga tsukai mas(u) 67

V neck Vネック bui-nekku 144
vacancy: do you have any
vacancies? 部屋はありますか
 heya wa arimas(u) ka 21
vacant: it's vacant 空いています
 aite imas(u) 14
vacation 観光/ホリデー
 kankoo/horidee 66, 123
vaccinated against, to be
 予防注射を受ける
 yoboo chuusha o ukeru 164
vaginal infection 膣炎 chitsu-en 167
valid 有効 yuukoo 75, 136
valley 谷間 tanima 107
valuable 貴重な kichoona
value 値段 nedan 155
valve ストップコック
 s(u)toppu kokku 28
vanilla (flavor) バニラ banira 40
VAT 消費税 shoohi zee 24
vegetarian ベジタリアン
 bejitarian 35, 39
vehicle registration document
 自動車登録証
 jidoosha toorok(u) shoo 93
ventilator 換気扇 kankisen
very とても totemo 17

very good
 たいへん結構
 taihen kekkoo 19
video game テレビ
 ゲーム terebi geemu;
 ~ **recorder** ビデオカメラ
 bideo kamera; **~cassette**
 ビデオテープ bideo teepu 157
view:... with a view of the sea
 海が見える... umi ga mieru ...
viewpoint 展望台 tenboo dai 99, 107
village 村 mura 107
vinaigrette フレンチドレッシング
 furenchi doresshingu 38
visa ビザ biza
visit, to 見舞う mimau 167
visiting hours 開館時間
 kaikan jikan 101
vitamin tablets ビタミン剤
 bitamin zai 141
volleyball バレーボール
 bareebooru 114
voltage 電圧 den-atsu
vomit, to もどす modos(u) 163

W wait, to 待つ matsu
 36, 41, 76, 89, 140
wait! 待ってください
 matte kudasai 98
waiting room 待合室 machiai shitsu 73
wake, to 起こす okos(u) 70
wake-up call モーニングコール
 mooningu kooru
walking boots 登山靴 tozan gutsu 145
walking route ハイキングコース
 haikingu koosu 106
walking gear ハイキング用具
 haikingu yoogu
wallet 財布 saifu 42, 153
want, to 欲しい
 hoshii 135
ward (hospital) 病室 byooshitsu 167
warm 暖かい atatakai 14
warm something up, to 温める
 atatameru 159
washbasin 洗面台 senmen dai

A-Z

washing machine 洗濯機
sentakki 29; **~ powder**
洗剤 senzai 148;
~-up liquid 中性洗剤
tyuusee senzai 148

wasp すずめバチ suzume
bachi

watch 腕時計 ude dokee 149, 153

watch TV, to テレビを見る
terebi o miru

water 水 mizu 87; **~ bottle** 水筒
suitoo; **~ heater** 湯沸かし
yuwakashi 28; **~skis** 水上スキー
suijoo s(u)kii 116; **~fall** 滝 taki 107;
~proof 防水 boosui; **~proof jacket**
アノラック anorakku 145

wave 波 nami

waxing ワックス wakkusu 147

way: I've lost my way
道に迷いました
michi ni mayoi mash(i)ta 94

way: on the way 途中 tochuu 83

we 私たち watashi tachi

wear, to 着る kiru 152

weather 天気 tenki 122

weather forecast 天気予報
tenki yohoo 122

wedding 結婚式 kekkon shiki

wedding ring 結婚指輪 kekkon yubiwa

Wednesday 水曜日 sui-yoobi 218

week 週 shuu 23, 97, 219

weekend rate 週末料金
shuumatsu ryookin 86

weekend, on [at] the 週末に
shuumatsu ni 219

well-done *(of food)* ウェルダン
werudan

Welsh *(adj)* ウェールズの
weeruzu no

Welsh *(language)* ウェールズ語
weeruzu go

Welsh *(people)* ウェールズ人
weeruzu jin

west 西 nishi 95

wetsuit ウェットスーツ wetto suutsu

what do you do? *(job)*
何をしていますか
nani o sh(i)te imas(u) ka 121

what kind of …?
どんな…/何の…
don-na …/nan no … 37, 106

what time? 何時 nan-ji 68, 78, 81

wheelchair 車いす kuruma isu

when? いつ itsu 13

where are you from? どちらからですか
dochira kara des(u) ka 119

where is the …? …はどこですか
… wa doko des(u) ka 99

where? どこ doko 12

which? どちら dochira 16

whist *(cards)* ホイスト hoisuto

white 白 shiro 143

white wine 白ワイン shiro wain 40

who? 誰 dare 16

whole まるごと marugoto 140

whole: the whole day 一日中
iti-nichi juu

whose? 誰の dareno 16

why? なぜ naze 15

wide 広い hiroi 14

wife 家内 kanai 120, 162

wildlife 野生の生物 yasee no seebutsu

windbreaker ウインドブレーカー
uindobureekaa 145

window 窓 mado 25, 77

window (shop) ウインドー
uindoo 134, 149

window seat 窓際の席
madogiwa no seki 69, 74

windscreen ワイドスクリーン
waido s(u)kuriin

windy, to be 風が強い
kaze ga tsuyoi 122

wine ワイン wain 40, 156, 160

wine list ワインリスト
wain ris(u)to 37

winter 冬 fuyu 219

with … …と… … to 17

withdraw, to *(money)* 引き出す
hikidas(u) 139

within … *(time)* …以内 … inai 13

without … …無しで … nash(i) de 17

witness 証人 shoonin 93
wood 林 hayashi 107
woodblock prints 木版 mok(u)han 156
wool ウール uuru 145
Worcestershire sauce ソース soosu 38
work for, to 勤める tsutomeru 121
work, to (operate) 使う tsukau 28
work: it doesn't work
壊れています
kowarete imas(u) 25 137
worse もっと悪い motto warui 14
worst 一番悪い itiban warui
write down, to 紙に書く
kami ni kaku 136
writing paper 便箋 binsen 150
wrong 違う chigau 14, 136
**wrong number: you have the wrong
number** 番号をお間違えです
bangoo o o-machigae des(u) 128
wrong: there's something wrong with ...
...がおかしいんですが
... ga okashiin des(u) ga 137

X Y Z
x-ray レントゲン rentogen 164
yacht ヨット yotto
year 年 toshi 219
yellow 黄色 kiiro 143
yen 円 en 67, 138
yes はい hai 10
yesterday 昨日 kinoo 219
yoghurt ヨーグルト yooguruto
you (sing & pl) あなた anata
young 若い wakai 14
your(s) (sing & pl) あなたの
anata no 16
youth hostel ユースホステル
yuusu hos(u)teru 29, 123
zebra crossing 横断歩道 oodan hodoo
zero ゼロ zero
zip(per) ファスナー fasunaa
zoo 動物園 doobutsuen 113

Glossary
Japanese-English

This Japanese-English Glossary covers all the areas where you may need to decode written Japanese: hotels, public buildings, restaurants, stores, ticket offices, airports, and stations. The Japanese is written is large type to help you identify the character(s) from the signs you see around you.

General 一般的標示

左	hidari	LEFT
右	migi	RIGHT
入口	iriguchi	ENTRANCE
出口	deguchi	EXIT
トイレ/お手洗	toire/o-tearai	TOILETS
男性	dansee	MEN (TOILETS)
女性	josee	WOMEN (TOILETS)
禁煙	kin-en	NO SMOKING
危険	kiken	DANGER
立入禁止	tachiiri kinshi	NO ENTRY
引く/押す	hiku/osu	PULL/PUSH

General 一般的標示

遺失物取扱所	ishitu butsu toriatsukai jo	LOST PROPERTY
水泳禁止	suiee kinshi	NO SWIMMING
飲料水	inryoosui	DRINKING WATER
関係者以外 立入禁止	kankeesha igai tachiiri kinshi	PRIVATE
地下道	chikadoo	UNDERPASS [SUBWAY]
足元注意	ashimoto chuui	MIND THE STEP
ペンキ塗り立て	penki nuritate	WET PAINT
頭上注意	zujoo chuui	MIND YOUR HEAD
グリーン車	guriin sha	FIRST CLASS

Road Signs 道路標識

止まれ	tomare	STOP
徐行	jokoo	SLOW
右によれ	migi ni yore	KEEP RIGHT
左によれ	hidari ni yore	KEEP LEFT
車線減少	shasen genshoo	LANES NARROW
一方通行	ippoo tsuukoo	ONE WAY
追越し禁止	oikoshi kinshi	NO PASSING
駐車禁止	chuusha kinshi	NO PARKING
高速道路	koosoku dooro	HIGHWAY [MOTORWAY]
料金	ryookin	TOLL
信号	shingoo	TRAFFIC LIGHTS
交差点	koosaten*	JUNCTION
インターチェンジ	intaa chenji^	INTERCHANGE

on ordinary roads
^ on highways [motorways]

案内	an-nai	INFORMATION
1番ホーム	ichi-ban hoomu	PLATFORM 1
1番ゲート	ichi-ban geeto	GATE 1
免税	menzee	DUTY FREE
課税	kazee	DUTIABLE
入国管理	nyuukoku kanri	IMMIGRATION
到着	toochaku	ARRIVALS
出発	shuppatsu	DEPARTURES
コインロッカー	koin rokkaa	LUGGAGE LOCKERS
荷物引渡場	nimotsu hikiwatashi joo	LUGGAGE RECLAIM
手荷物カート	tenimotsu kaato	CARTS [TROLLIES]
バス/鉄道	bas(u)/tetsudoo	BUS/TRAIN
レンタカー	rentakaa	CAR RENTAL
地下鉄	chikatetsu	SUBWAY [METRO]

Hotel/Restaurant
ホテル/レストラン

案内	an-nai	INFORMATION
フロント	furonto	RECEPTION
予約	yoyaku	RESERVED
非常口	hijooguchi	EMERGENCY/FIRE EXIT
湯	yu	HOT (WATER)
冷	ree	COLD (WATER)
関係者以外立入禁止	kankeesha igai tachiiri kinshi	STAFF ONLY
クロークルーム	kurooku roomu	CLOAKROOM
庭	niwa	GARDEN
テラス	terasu	TERRACE
バー	baa	BAR

Shops 店

営業中	eegyoo chuu	OPEN
閉店	heeten	CLOSED
昼食	chuushoku	LUNCH
売場	uriba	DEPARTMENT
階	kai	FLOOR
地下	chika	BASEMENT
エレベーター	erebeetaa	ELEVATOR/LIFT
エスカレーター	esukareetaa	ESCALATOR
会計	kaikee	CASHIER
大売り出し/セール	oo uridashi/seeru	SALE

Sightseeing 観光

入場無料	nyuujoo muryoo	FREE ADMISSION
大人	otona	ADULTS
子供/小人	kodomo	CHILDREN
割引 (学生/高齢者)	waribiki (gak(u)see/kooreesha)	CONCESSIONS (students/s. citizens)
お土産	o-miyage	SOUVENIRS
軽食	keeshoku	REFRESHMENTS
手を触れない でください	te o furenai de kudasai	DO NOT TOUCH
撮影禁止	satsuee kinshi	NO PHOTOGRAPHY
静粛に	seeshuku ni	SILENCE
立入禁止	tachiiri kinshi	NO ACCESS

Public Buildings 公共施設

病院	byooin	HOSPITAL
医者	isha	DOCTOR
歯医者	ha-isha	DENTIST
警察	keesatsu	POLICE
銀行	ginko	BANK
郵便局	yuubin kyoku	POST OFFICE
プール	puuru	SWIMMING POOL
市役所	shiyak(u)sho	TOWN HALL
タクシー乗場	tak(u)shii noriba	TAXI STAND [RANK]
博物館	hakubutsukan	MUSEUM

Reference

Numbers	217	**Public holidays**	220
Days	218	**Time**	221
Months/Dates	219	**Map**	223
Greetings	220	**Quick reference**	224

GRAMMAR

In Japanese, there are general numbers (listed opposite) used for talking about sums of money, telephone numbers, etc., and there is a system for combining a number with an object-specific counter. This system groups objects into types according to shape and size. Thus there are specific ways of counting flat objects, machines, animals, people, etc. Luckily the *counter system* only applies to numbers from 1 – 10. After 10 the general number is used. When you are not sure of the correct counter, you can always try using the general numbers (**ichi**, **ni**, **san**, etc.) or better, the "all-purpose" counters listed below.

"All-purpose" counters (numbers 1 – 10)

These counters are strictly used to count "unclassifiable" objects (objects where shape or size are difficult to determine) but can be used as "all-purpose" counters. When you don't know the specific counter use:

1	**hitotsu**	2	**futatsu**
3	**mittsu**	4	**yottsu**
5	**itsutsu**	6	**muttsu**
7	**nanatsu**	8	**yattsu**
9	**kokonotsu**	10	**too**

If you don't know the counter for a bottle, use the "all-purpose" system, for example:

I'd like two bottles of beer.
Biiru o <u>futatsu</u>, kudasai.
("all-purpose" counter)

I'd like two bottles of beer.
Biiru o <u>ni-hon</u>, kudasai.
(counter for long, thin objects)

Note that the counter usually follows the word is qualifies.

Other counters

Flat objects (*stamps, paper, etc.*)		People		Long, thin objects (*pen, bottle, umbrella, etc.*)	
ichimai	1	**hitori**	1	**ippon**	1
nimai	2	**futari**	2	**nihon**	2
sanmai	3	**sannin**	3	**sanbon**	3
yonmai	4	**yonin**	4	**yonhon**	4
gomai	5	**gonin**	5	**gohon**	5

Numbers 数

In Japan will see numbers written both in English and Japanese numerals. Use of the latter tends to be confined to traditional shops and restaurants.

0	零/ゼロ	*ree/zero*	26	二十六	*ni-juu-roku*
1	一	*ichi*	27	二十七	*ni-juu-shichi/ ni-juu-nana*
2	二	*ni*			
3	三	*san*	28	二十八	*ni-juu-hachi*
4	四	*shi/yon*	29	二十九	*ni-juu-kyuu/ ni-juu-ku*
5	五	*go*			
6	六	*roku*	30	三十	*san-juu*
7	七	*shichi/nana*	31	三十一	*san-juu-ichi*
8	八	*hachi*	32	三十二	*san-juu-ni*
9	九	*kyuu/ku*	40	四十	*yon-juu/ shi-juu*
10	十	*juu*			
11	十一	*juu-ichi*	50	五十	*go-juu*
12	十二	*juu-ni*	60	六十	*roku-juu*
13	十三	*juu-san*	70	七十	*nana-juu/ shichi-juu*
14	十四	*juu-shi/juu-yon*			
15	十五	*juu-go*	80	八十	*hachi-juu*
16	十六	*juu-roku*	90	九十	*kyuu-juu*
17	十七	*juu-shichi/ juu-nana*	100	百	*hyaku*
			101	百一	*hyaku ichi*
18	十八	*juu-hachi*	102	百二	*hyaku-ni*
19	十九	*juu-kyuu/ juu-ku*	103	百三	*hyaku-san*
			200	二百	*ni-hyaku*
20	二十	*ni-juu*	500	五百	*go-hyaku*
21	二十一	*ni-juu-ichi*	1,000	千	*sen*
22	二十二	*ni-juu-ni*	10,000	一万	*ichi-man*
23	二十三	*ni-juu-san*	35,750	三万五千七百五十	*san-man go-sen nana-hyaku go-juu*
24	二十四	*ni-juu-shi/ ni-juu-yon*			
25	二十五	*ni-juu-go*	1,000,000	百万	*hyaku-man*

Numerical expressions 数の表現

first	一番	*ichi-ban*
second	二番	*ni-ban*
third	三番	*san-ban*
fourth	四番	*yon-ban*
fifth	五番	*go-ban*
once	一回	*ikkai*
twice	二回	*ni-kai*
three times	三回	*san-kai*
a half	半分	*hanbun*
half an hour	三十分	*sanjuppun*
half a tank	タンクの半分 *tanku no hanbun*	
a quarter	四分の一	*yon-bun no ichi*
a third	三分の一	*san-bun no ichi*
a pair of ...	一対の...	*ittsui no ...*
a dozen ...	一ダースの...	*ichi-daasu no ...*
1998	一九九八年 *sen kyuu-hyaku kyuu-juu hachi nen*	
2001	二〇〇一年	*ni-sen ichi nen*
the 1990s	一九九〇年代 *sen kyuu-hyaku kyuu-juu nen dai*	

Days 曜日

Monday	月曜日	*getsu-yoobi*
Tuesday	火曜日	*ka-yoobi*
Wednesday	水曜日	*sui-yoobi*
Thursday	木曜日	*moku-yoobi*
Friday	金曜日	*kin-yoobi*
Saturday	土曜日	*do-yoobi*
Sunday	日曜日	*nichi-yoobi*

Months 月

January	一月 *ichi-gatsu*
February	二月 *ni-gatsu*
March	三月 *san-gatsu*
April	四月 *shi-gatsu*
May	五月 *go-gatsu*
June	六月 *roku-gatsu*
July	七月 *shichi-gatsu*
August	八月 *hachi-gatsu*
September	九月 *ku-gatsu*
October	十月 *juu-gatsu*
November	十一月 *juu-ichi-gatsu*
December	十二月 *juu-ni-gatsu*

Dates 日付

It's ...	...です。 *... des(u)*
July 10	七月十日 *shichi-gatsu tooka*
Tuesday, March 1	三月一日、火曜日 *san-gatsu tsuitachi, ka-yoobi*
yesterday	昨日 *kinoo*
today	今日 *kyoo*
tomorrow	明日 *ash(i)ta*
this .../last ...	今度の.../前の... *kondo no .../mae no ,,,*
next week	来週 *raishuu*
every month/year	毎月/年 *mai tsuki/toshi*
on [at] the weekend	週末に *shuumats(u) ni*

Seasons 季節

spring	春 *haru*
summer	夏 *natsu*
fall [autumn]	秋 *aki*
winter	冬 *fuyu*
in spring	春に *haru ni*
during the summer	夏の間 *natsu no aida*

Greetings あいさつ

Happy birthday!	お誕生日おめでとう。	*o-tanjoobi omedetoo*
Merry Christmas!	メリークリスマス。	*merii kurisumasu*
Happy New Year!	明けましておめでとうございます。	*akemash(i)te omedetoo gozaimas(u)*
Best wishes!	よろしくお願いします。	*yorosh(i)ku onegai shimas(u)*
Congratulations!	おめでとう。	*omedetoo*
Good luck!/All the best!	幸運を祈ります。/頑張って。	*kooun o inori mas(u)/ganbatte*
Have a good trip!	気をつけて。	*ki o tsukete*
Give my regards to ...	...さんによろしく。	*... san ni yorosh(i)ku*

Public holidays 祝日

January 1	*ganjitsu/gantan*	New Year's Day
January 14	*seejin no hi*	Adult's Day
February 11	*kenkoku kinen no hi*	National Foundation Day
March 21*	*shunbun no hi*	Vernal Equinox Day
April 29	*midori no hi*	Greenery Day
May 3	*kenpoo kinen bi*	Constitution Day
May 5	*kodomo no hi*	Children's Day
September 15	*keeroo no hi*	Respect for the Aged Day
September 23*	*shuubun no hi*	Autumnal Equinox Day
October 10	*taiiku no hi*	Health–Sports Day
November 3	*bunka no hi*	Culture Day
November 23	*kinroo kansha no hi*	Labor Thanksgiving Day
December 23	*ten-noo tanjoobi*	Emperor's Birthday

* These dates are lunar and change year by year.

Japanese shops and stores are mostly open on national holidays. When a holiday falls on a Sunday, the Monday is counted as a holiday.

If you intend to be in Japan during New Year, "Golden Week" (April 29 – May 5 and adjacent weekends), or the school holidays (March/April and July/August), make your reservations well in advance, as hotels will be full and public transportation more packed than ever.

Time 時間

In ordinary conversation time is expressed as shown above. For airline and train timetables, however, the 24-hour clock is used.

Japan is nine hours ahead of GMT all year round. Japan does not change its clocks to reflect winter and summer time.

Excuse me, can you tell me the time?	すみません。今、何時ですか。	sumimasen, ima nan-ji des(u) ka
It's …	…です。	… des(u)
five past one	一時五分	ichi-ji go-fun
ten past two	二時十分	ni-ji juppun
a quarter past three	三時十五分	san-ji juu-go-fun
twenty past four	四時二十分	yo-ji ni-juppun
twenty-five past five	五時二十五分	go-ji ni-juu-go-fun
half past six	六時半	roku-ji han
twenty-five to seven	七時二十五分前	shichi ji ni-juu-go-fun mae
twenty to eight	八時二十分前	hachi-ji ni-juppun mae
a quarter to nine	九時十五分前	ku-ji juu-go-fun mae
ten to ten	十時十分前	juu-ji juppun mae
five to eleven	十一時五分前	juu-ichi-ji go-fun mae
twelve o'clock (noon)	十二時（正午）	juu-ni-ji (shoogo)

at dawn	夜明けに *yoake ni*
in the morning	朝 *asa*
during the day	日中 *nitchuu*
before lunch	昼食前 *chuushok(u) mae*
after lunch	昼食後 *chuushok(u) go*
in the afternoon	午後 *gogo*
in the evening	夕方 *yuugata*
at night	夜 *yoru*

I'll be ready in five minutes.
5分で用意ができます。
go-fun de yooi ga deki mas(u)

He'll be back in a quarter of an hour.
15分後に戻ります。
juugo-fun go ni modori mas(u)

She arrived half an hour ago.
30分前に着きました。
sanjuppun mae ni tsuki mash(i)ta

The train leaves at …
列車は…時に出ます。
ressha wa … ji ni demas(u)

| 13:04 | 13時4分 *juusan-ji yon-pun* |
| 00:40 | 0時40分 *ree-ji yonjippun* |

The train is 10 minutes late/early.
列車は10分遅れ/早めです。
ressha wa juppun okure/ hayame des(u)

It's 5 minutes fast/slow.
5分進んで/遅れています。
go-fun susunde/okurete imas(u)

from 9:00 to 5:00
9時から5時まで
ku-ji kara go-ji made

between 8:00 and 2:00
8時から2時の間
hachi-ji kara ni-ji no aida

I'll be leaving by …
…までには出ます。
… made niwa demas(u)

Will you be back before …?
…までには戻りますか。
… made niwa modori mas(u) ka

We'll be here until …
…まで、ここにいます。
… made kokoni imas(u)